Mysticism and Language

MYSTICISM AND LANGUAGE

Edited by
STEVEN T. KATZ

New York   Oxford
OXFORD UNIVERSITY PRESS
1992

Oxford University Press

Oxford New York Toronto
Delhi Bombay Calcutta Madras Karachi
Kuala Lumpur Singapore Hong Kong Tokyo
Nairobi Dar es Salaam Cape Town
Melbourne Auckland

and associated companies in
Berlin Ibadan

Copyright © 1992 by Oxford University Press, Inc.

Published by Oxford University Press, Inc.
200 Madison Avenue, New York, New York 10016

Oxford is a registered trademark of Oxford University Press

All rights reserved. No part of this publication may be reproduced,
stored in a retrieval system, or transmitted, in any form or by any means,
electronic, mechanical, photocopying, recording or otherwise,
without the prior permission of the publisher.

Library of Congress Cataloging-in-Publication Data
Mysticism and language / edited by Steven T. Katz.
p. cm. Includes bibliographical references.
ISBN 0-19-505455-5
1. Mysticism. 2. Language and languages — Religious aspects.
I. Katz, Steven T., 1944–
BL625.M885 1992 291.4′22′014—dc20 91-31701

2 4 6 8 9 7 5 3 1
Printed in the United States of America
on acid-free paper

Editor's Introduction

One of the recurring, fundamental issues in the study of mysticism is the status of language. Or put more exactly, the question is regularly raised whether language can appropriately apply to the objects/subjects of mystical concern and to mystical experience. Most often the mystics themselves and those who study them answer no and adopt, at least nominally, some form of the ineffability thesis; that is, they argue that ultimate objects/subjects and ecstatic moments transcend linguistic description. So common, in fact, is this position in the primary and secondary literature that it is often presented as an unassailable truth, an unquestionable premise, of any and all study of mystical sources. Yet our libraries are full of texts that purport to help others in the pursuit of such putatively ineffable experiences and that, in some oblique sense at least, describe mystical occurrences after they have transpired. Moreover, the place and purpose of mystical experience within the larger structure of religious traditions is unambiguously described in theoretical and doctrinal works of all sorts. Texts ranging from the autobiographical and poetic to the dogmatic and theological do not tell us everything about mystical experiences, but they do tell us a good deal. And they certainly reveal far more than a simplistic reading of claims of ineffability would suggest.

Something more than is usually assumed and asserted is at work here. The relationship of mysticism to language is more variegated and complex than once believed. Yet it is no easy matter to define this relationship—to bring into the open the subterranean principles and unspoken premises of mystical discourse. The very difficulty of comprehending how language interacts with—and even penetrates—the mystical experience makes this an appropriate, indeed required, subject for further study. Building on the revisionist methodological, epistemological, historical, and philosophical foundations set out in two prior volumes, *Mysticism and Philosophical Analysis*, edited by Steven T. Katz (New York, 1978), and *Mysticism and Religious Traditions*, also edited by Steven T. Katz (New York, 1983), this collection of original essays seeks to explore some of the primal issues raised by the linguistic dimension of mysticism. No one approach has been accepted by all contributors, but all have accepted the premise that, rather than a priori assumptions about what must be the case, fresh, methodologically sophisticated, technically competent work, growing out of intimate familiarity with the world's mystical traditions, is required. Moreover, as was the case with the 1978 and 1983 volumes, all the contributors to this collection offer their work for public scrutiny and scholarly discussion—there is no wish to install new dogmas in place of the old.

As I ready this collection for publication, it is a great pleasure to thank those who have helped make it a reality. First, I would like to thank Raihana Zaman and Phyllis Emdee, of the Department of Near Eastern Studies at Cornell University, who have helped with a variety of secretarial tasks. Second, a great debt is owed to Cynthia Read, my editor at Oxford University Press. As always, her extraordinary patience, deep concern, and sound advice have made my life much easier and the book much better than it would have been otherwise. Third, I want to publicly thank all the contributors for their participation. Without exception, they have made my job relatively painless. Finally, and of a different order, I would like to publicly express my loving gratitude to my children, Shira, Tamar, and Yehuda, and to my wife, Rebecca, who together make it all possible.

S.T.K.

Contents

1. Mystical Speech and Mystical Meaning, 3
   Steven T. Katz

2. Reification of Language in Jewish Mysticism, 42
   Moshe Idel

3. Literal and Nonliteral in Reports of Mystical Experience, 80
   William P. Alston

4. What Would Buddhaghosa Have Made of *The Cloud of Unknowing*? 103
   Ninian Smart

5. Mystic Analogizing and the "Peculiarly Mystical," 123
   Stephen H. Phillips

6. Mysticism and Ineffability: Some Issues of Logic and Language, 143
   Bimal Krishna Matilal

7. Fair and Unfair Language Games in Chan/Zen, 158
   Bernard Faure

8. Mystical Language and the Teaching Context in the Early Lexicons of Sufism, 181
   Carl W. Ernst

9. The Language of Love in Christian and Jewish Mysticism, 202
   Bernard McGinn

10. Bonaventure's Mysticism of Language, 236
    Ewert H. Cousins

    Contributors, 259

Mysticism and Language

1

Mystical Speech and Mystical Meaning

STEVEN T. KATZ

> When you say, "words are of no account," you negate your own assertion through your words. If words are of no account, why do we hear you say that words are of no account? After all, you are saying this in words.
>
> RUMI, *Fihi mā fihi*

The Problem

"Mystics do not say what they mean and do not mean what they say." This is the near universal wisdom on the subject of the relationship that is said to exist between mystical experience and the language used to report it. Trapped by the unclosable abyss between experience and utterance, the adept uses a language he or she knows to be necessarily inferior, hopelessly inadequate to the descriptive task at hand. Such futilely employed language is most often the familiar tongue of a particular religious tradition and specific sociohistorical environment, but this is merely an unavoidable contingency. The mystic knows that all language, including the sacred, dogmatic, ritual language of his or her religious community, is too impoverished to perform the descriptive role assigned it and that, in any case, the true unity of Being transcends both linguistic expression and the very particularity that language necessarily entails. "If I have spoken of it," Meister Eckhart warns, "I have not spoken, for it is ineffable."[1] So the inherited wisdom, both first person and scholarly secondhand, of the study of mysticism.

But is this all there is to say on such an essential matter? Are we to take the canonical position as self-authenticating? Or, alternatively, does the close study of mystical language, of mystical literary sources in their various forms, reveal a more complex and very different picture of the way things are, sincere claims to the contrary notwithstanding? That is, do mystics use language in ways that belie the superficial claims, the naive architectonic disjunction, that dominate the history, as well as the contemporary study, of this subject?[2]

Of Texts and Experience

Before entering into our detailed philosophical and hermeneutical analysis, we remind readers of four facts that require recognition.

1. The main legacy we have of the great mystics is their *writings* and related *linguistic* creations.[3] We have no access to their special experience independently of these texts. What we call the great historical mystical traditions of the world are in fact a series of documents of differing sorts. No one has any privileged access here to the original mystics' experience outside its textual incorporation. And it is these documents that are the data for all analytic decipherment and scholarly reconstructions.

2. These literary remains, in their variegated forms, necessarily and inescapably include "interpretive" structures. Neither mystics nor we, their readers, can overcome this fact. What we have are the already encoded experiences now reported—this and this alone is what is available for study. Whatever the epistemological complexities that intrude on, that constitute, the act of mystical knowing or awareness—that is, whatever the interpenetration of prior "conditioning," inherited and willed intentionality, and the experience had,[4]—what we have in the mystical source per se is the entangled and nonreductive product of this extraordinary epistemic process.

3. It must be recognized that mystical literature is composed from differing perspectives and in different ways: (a) first-person reports; (b) the mystic's own interpretation of his or her experience; and (c) the "interpretation" of such reported experience by mem-

bers of one's own religious community or again by members of other religious traditions. All these situations can be more or less highly ramified.

4. Mystical literature comes in many forms, and the modality chosen as the means of communication in any instance is not incidental or tangential to its content. These diverse forms include biography, biblical exegesis, aphorisms, theoretical and theosophical treatises, poems, prayers, polemics, dogmatics, and didactic compositions.[5] All these genres enrich and complicate the decoding of mystical reports. In this essay, I shall not concentrate on the decipherment of these literary-theological forms, but the significance of the complexity of the literary corpus that composes the world's mystical traditions should be understood.

Language and Contextualization

One further preliminary observation, to be described here only schematically, must also be made at this juncture. It is my view, argued in detail elsewhere, that mystical reports do not merely indicate the postexperiential description of an unreportable experience in the language closest at hand. Rather, the experiences themselves are inescapably shaped by prior linguistic influences such that the lived experience conforms to a preexistent pattern that has been learned, then intended, and then actualized in the experiential reality of the mystic.[6]

Although this reading has been the subject of much scholarly discussion[7] since I first argued it,[8] I have not yet been dissuaded of its correctness. Therefore, this *contextual* model will be presumed in the present essay.[9] And, against this larger revisionist background, the main objective of this paper will be to attempt to enrich our understanding of the many roles and functions that language plays in mystical traditions.

Language as Transformational

It is customary, and not unreasonably so, to think of language as descriptive in character. The word "book" refers to a "book," and the sentence "The book is on the table" refers to the factual, ontological circumstance of a book being on a table. In this referential and semantic model, the language of absolutes, such as God and Brahman, must likewise refer to the Absolute (known by its different "names"), and it is just this grammatical possibility that negative and apophatic theologies deny. Indeed, by refusing to accept that any predicates can be correctly ascribed to the Absolute (called by whatever "name"), this premise of denial gives rise to the consensus that language and the Absolute remain always asymmetrical and incongruous: "Yáto váco nívartante óprāpya mánasā sahá" ("[The Absolute is that] from which all words return—having failed to reach it with the mind") declares the *Taittirīyopanishad* 2.4. But even if one accepts this argument, which I do not, such denotative and referential meaning is not the only sense that mystical (and other) language can have. Much classical mystical language and many mystical linguistic forms have other purposes, an essential one being the transformation of consciousness.

The clearest and best-known example of this occurs in Zen *kōans*. In posing the *kōan*, the master is *not* attempting to pass information of a doctrinal or dogmatic sort to his student—although what is taught by the master and what is learned by the student does carry such content in an extended or a translated sense. Rather, the master is seeking to revolutionize the student's consciousness, particularly in the context of meditation—when consciousness is particularly sensitive—such that it breaks free of and transcends the regulative categories of knowing and thereby is opened up to new forms of awareness that are conducive to, and permit, *satori*. Here language performs an essential mystical task, but it is not a *descriptive* task. Meditation on the "nonsensical" *kōan*, defined by paradox or absurdity, "the sound of one hand clapping," is the *linguistic* means whereby language corrects itself; that is, it corrects the errors of propositional and descriptive language that lead the mind to false ontic commitments, particularly in the Buddhist context in terms of selfhood, the substantiality of things, and the existence of a (or the) One. By denying, logically and necessarily, any logical, and hence transcendental, analysis, by repudiating regular and regulative forms of epistemic construction and deconstruction, the *kōan* undermines the absoluteness of the ordinary, the force of the syllogism, the requirements of the law of the excluded middle, the metaphysical and epistemological claims of an ontology of substance, and pushes the disciple toward the deeper, highly counterintuitive, truth of "not-self" and *nirvāṇa*, or, in Nāgārjuna's language, *sūnyatā* (Emptiness). It is to be emphasized that it is language, if in highly unusual, even contested, forms—for example, paradox, "category mistakes," and the like—that induces this positive aberration of consciousness and the creation of the new possibility of *samyegdrsti* (right view), *samkalpa* (right thought), and *prajña* (wisdom), thereby opening up the route to a proper understanding of the truth of *anātman* (the doctrine of "no-self") and hence to *nirvāṇa* (or better, "being nirvanized"; *nirvāṇa* is not, at least in early Buddhism, a place). It is the ability of language to induce "breakthroughs" of consciousness by being employed "nonsensically," literally non-sense-ically, that is fundamental to the traversal of the mystical path, to the movement from consciousness A to consciousness B.

Hakuin, the great Zen master, taught:

> By pursuing a single *kōan* he [the Zen disciple] comes to a point where his mind is as if dead and his will as if extinguished. This state is like a wide void over a deep chasm and no hold remains for hand or foot. All thoughts vanish and in his bosom burns hot anxiety. But then suddenly it occurs that with the *kōan* both body and mind break. This is the instant when the hands are released over the abyss. In this sudden upsurge it is as if one drinks water and knows for oneself heat and cold. Great joy wells up. This is called rebirth (in the Pure Land). This is termed seeing into one's own nature . . .[10]

It is, as we see here, the *linguistic* device of the *kōan* that allows us to discern that "the state of all-knowledge itself cannot be taken hold of, because it cannot be seized through a sign."[11]

Such linguistic ploys exist in many places throughout the world, usually connected with the conscious construction of paradoxes whose necessary violation of the laws of logic are intended to shock, even shatter, the standard epistemic security of "disciples," thereby allowing them to move to new and higher forms of insight/knowledge. That is, mystics in certain circumstances know that they are uttering nonsensical propositions, but in so doing they intend, among other things, to force the hearers of such propositions to consider who they are—to locate themselves vis-à-vis normal versus transcendental "reality." The object of such exercises is existential rather than propositional (though this practice involves propositional claims that are inherent in the respective metaphysical systems of which such linguistic practices are a part). The many philosophical efforts to reduce the well-formed contradictions and delicious paradoxes that bound in the world's mystical literature—in Plotinus, in Pseudo-Dionysius, in the *Tao te Ching*, in the Victorines, in Eckhart, in Nāgārjuna, in the Upanishadic tradition, in Shankara, in Hakuin and the entire Zen tradition—to only *apparent* contradictions and paradoxes is largely, if not altogether, misconceived for just this reason. The transmutational effect of *kōans* and other nonsensical genres would be lost if there were an answer to "What is the sound of one hand clapping?" within the regulative linguistic and conceptual categories of the world of *nāma-rūpa*, the ordinary realm of things and words.

In that the mechanisms of knowing *necessarily* impinge on, even create, the substantive knowledge gained in mystical experience no less than in the more mundane epistemological contexts, language is a, if not the, key issue in re-forming those structures required for obtaining mystical awareness. Language creates, when used by the mystical adept—the guru in the training of his disciple, or the *mekubbal* or Sufi in their meditative practices—the operative process through which the essential epistemic channels that permit mystical forms of knowing and being are made accessible.[12] An indispensable part of this process is the recognition that language is multiform, that it is more than a series of nouns, more than a series of ostensive definitions, more than a correspondence theory of truth (à la Carl Hempel's "snow is white").[13] One recalls here the Buddhist philosopher Asaṅga's criticism in his *Mahāyānasaṃgraha* of *manojalpa* (mumblings of the mind), the term he pejoratively applies to the insidious practice of naming things and therefore reifying them in improper ways. What language as employed here seeks to accomplish is to effect a transformation of awareness, thus enabling us to understand/experience that which presently transcends our understanding/experience. In this sense, such special employment of language moves us from consciousness A (ordinary awareness) to consciousness B (mystical awareness).

Buddhist tradition provides another surprising example of this transformatory power of language in the austere, complex, doctrinal, *abhidharma* text. Although the Buddhist equivalent to, say, Aquinas's *Summa*, this text is, as Robert Gimello has noted,

> as much prescriptive as it is descriptive, that it is said not only to reflect reality but also to shape one's experience thereof. Deliberate and extended exposure to the rigorously depersonalized discourse of *abhidharma* (which is but an extreme example of the relative impersonality of most canonical Buddhist discourse) conditions the mind to relax its hold upon deep-seated notions of selfhood. It obstructs the kind of reinforcement that conventional language can give to such false concepts. Thus, when the more advanced disciplines of meditation are undertaken, the mind of the canonically informed practitioner is all the more receptive to their granulating, deconstructive effects and is led to have corroborating experiences precisely of the selflessness, the linguistic expression of which is the style of the texts he has studied.[14]

The nature of the *abhidharma* discourse is so structured as to mirror the "no-self" doctrine such that study of the one directly encourages the production, the lived reality, of the other. There is an *affective* parallelism and interconnection between words and states of consciousness, as compared with, and in contravention of, the more usual word–thing relationship. The psychometaphysics of meditation, though not overtly linguistic, is, in this instance, at a minimum, facilitated by the mutational power of very artfully constructed linguistic–literary forms.

On at least some venerable readings,[15] the *Catuskoti* of Nāgārjuna has a similar deconstructive purpose. His famous tetralemma:

> *sarvaṃ tathyaṃ na vā tathyaṃ tathyaṃ*
> *cātathyam et'a ca /*
> *naivātathyaṃ naiva tathyam etad*
> *buddhānuśāsanam //*

> Everything is such as it is, not such as it is, both such as it is and not such as it is, and neither such as it is nor such as it is not. That is the Buddha's teaching. (*Mūlamadhyamakakārikā* 18.8)[16]

is not asserting propositions but is clearing away, in the language of the *Prasannapada*, "obstructions" to that understanding that is a prerequisite to authentic—salvific (in the Buddhist sense)—awareness.[17] On this reading the language of the tetralemma is seen as destroying the most pernicious psychological and ontological assumption about words: the reification of words into things that engender those false desires that block the attainment of *nirvāṇa*. *Śūnyatā*, though the obverse of words, is its obverse dialectically[18] — words, in their destructive function, lead to the transcendence of words *but only through using words*. In that words, as employed in the *Catuṣkoṭi*, annihilate thought, they extirpate desire — but words are, at a minimum, functionally salient for the true knowledge (*paramār-thasatya*) that is metakarmic.

In Indian tradition, mantras have much the same function. As Frits Staal has recognized:

> The case of mantras is particularly instructive in this regard. In Indian religions, mantras are now mainly regarded as aids or means to meditation or concentration. There are other similar aids, e.g., *yantras* (diagrams) which are objects of contemplation, representations or images of deities which are objects of worship, etc. In Vedic times, the Vedic mantras came to be regarded as effective when properly recited at the proper time and place during the elaborate ritual — not when interpreted or provided with a meaning, a more transient, academic and individualistic pastime. The person who adopted that view in its most radical form was an ancient ritualist, Kautsa, whose thesis was that "the mantras are meaningless" (*amarthakā mantrāh*). Renou has drawn attention to the fact that one of the phonetic and phonological treatises attached to the *Atharvaveda* is attributed to the same Kautsa (L. Renou, *La destin du Véda dans l'Inde*, Paris, 1960, p. 68). Now treatises on phonetics and phonology traditionally exclude meaning by definition. The *Atharvaveda*, moreover, is largely a repository of magical practices. It is not surprising, therefore, that those ritualists who treated the mantras as charms were hardly in a position to regard them at the same time as linguistically meaningful utterances.[19]

Mantras are not propositions, ostensive indicators, or referential signs. They operate under a cosmic law of sympathetic magic that includes the very structure of reality. *Om* does not "say" something, does not "tell" something, but it *does* something. The mantra is theurgic, allowing for, and interpreted within, the alternative structural forms of Hinduism and Buddhism. It *causes*, necessarily and without further activity, desirable changes both in and for the one who recites the mantra, as well as in the "nature of things" to which the mantra is directed. To understand this fact, this performance, is not to understand a proposition *about* the mantra—a proposition of the form: "the content of the mantra is . . ."—but to recognize a causal law operative in the metaphysical realm as certain and given as the law of gravity in the physical realm. And this awesome activity is triggered by the inherently remarkable linguistic act of reciting the sacred syllable.

It is for this reason that in later times

> mantras are used as instruments that may bring about almost anything. At the same time they assume sounds and shapes so different from anything found in natural Indian languages that their literal meaninglessness is apparent. This tendency culminates in Tantrism, where we meet with such mantras as OṂ A OṂ ĀḤ HŪṂ PHAṬ SVĀ (D. L. Snellgrove, *The Hevajra Tantra*, Oxford, 1950, vol. 1, p. 50). Their only precursors in the Vedic period were the so-called *stobhas* of the *Sāmaveda*, whose function was partly melodic, though they were also used to conceal the real meaning (e.g., HĀ BU HĀ BU HĀ BU HĀ Ū HĀ Ū HĀ Ū / KĀ HVĀ HVĀ HVĀ HVĀ HVĀ KĀ HVĀ HVĀ HVĀ HVĀ HVĀ KĀ HVĀ HVĀ HVĀ HVĀ HVĀ, etc.: hear Levy and Staal [*The Four Vedas* (record album)] 1968). Though it would be correct to say that the Tantric mantras are literally meaningless, it is of course always possible to provide them with symbolic interpretations. The *Māndukyopaniṣad*, and other Upaniṣads, had already done this for the sound constituents of the famous mantra OM. . . . The main function of such mantras, however, has nothing to do with the expressive function of a natural language. They are instruments bringing about a change in mental state, and are used, for example, as aids in meditation. To insist that mantras are irrationalistic is therefore to miss the point. And what holds for mantras holds for many other religious statements. The therapeutic value of such statements does not support irrationalism.[20]

The repetition of *OM* has, according to Sankara and others, four elements: the letters *A*, *U*, and *M*, and the final synthesis, the sound *OM*. And these four elements correspond to four states of consciousness, the fourth of which—homologous to the unitive mystical syllable *OM*—

> is held to be that which is cognitive neither outwardly nor inwardly, nor the two together, nor is undifferentiated cognition, nor knowing, nor unknowing; which is invisible, ineffable, intangible, indefinable, inconceivable, nor designable, whose essence is the experience of its own Self, which is beyond diversity, which is tranquil [*sántam*], benign [*śivam*], without a second [*advaitam*]. This is Atman, the Self, which is to be realized.[21]

This is to see that language—here the great mantra—helps create the transmogrifying conditions of that purified consciousness that allows one to become immediately aware of the existential truth that Atman is Brahman in one's own life. The mantra overcomes the illusion of the permanence or ultimacy of *saṁsāra*. In a Buddhist context—in the Shingon School, for example—the mantra is the enabling device that experientially confirms the truths of *śūnyatā* (Emptiness) and *anātman* (no-self). The distortions of egotism are shattered by the power of the mantra. From the *paramārthasatya*, the vantage of the higher truth induced by the mantra, we see the essential falsity of *svabhāva*, of selfhood, and are able to experience *svabhāva śūnyatā*, the emptiness of self. "It is because of *śūnyatā*," Nāgārjuna explains, "that all things and events can be established. Without *śūnyatā* nothing can be established."[22]

This revised perspective is, in fact, the perspective of the *Bodhisattva*, even of the Buddha. The mantra facilitates the *adhisthana*, the enfolding power, of the Buddha that facilitates that fundamental alteration whereby the I comes to recognize the Buddha-hood within.

The *Amitabha* practice here interfuses with this form of understanding. Based on the Buddha's teaching to Ananda—"Remember this sermon and rehearse it to the assembly. . . . By this sermon I mean the name *Amitabha*"—certain Mahayana schools, particularly the Sukhavati and Jodo schools of "Pure-Land" Buddhism,[23] began a devotional and meditative technique centering on the repetition of the Buddha's name. Such meditativelike repetition, tied to doctrines taught in the specific *Sukhavati* (Pure-Land) texts, unmade the believer and gave rise to the possibility of nirvanization.

Although the subject of intense criticism in certain Buddhist circles—by Nichiren and his school, for example—no form of Buddhist devotion ever reached the popularity, especially in Japan, of *Amita* devotion and piety.

The elemental practice of *dhikr* ("recollection" of the Divine Names) also has this function, among many others, in Sufi doctrine and reality. Rooted by tradition in the Koranic injunction of *Sura* 17:110, the adept, much as the Hindu initiate repeating his mantra, recites the Divine Name(s) of Allāh, or the central doctrinal formula *lā ilāha illā* Allāh, in order to transpose himself into a state of ecstasy. Although the names of Allāh have many functions[24] and meanings in Sufism, and in Islam more generally, in this context the purpose of *dhikr* is not to impart propositional knowledge, as occurs, for example, in certain of the extended theosophical reflections of Ibn Arabi, but to spiritualize the reciter. "He who remembers God permanently is the true companion of God."[25] Constant recitation, later involving various acts of purification and common meditative techniques such as those of controlled breathing, had the power to alter one's spiritual condition—not to make one wiser with the wisdom of worldly knowing but *different*, different in one's most essential nature. "The faithful engaged in *dhikr*, is like a green tree in the midst of dried-up trees."[26]

In kabbalistic practice one finds similar techniques. Making oneself an appropriate subject for mystical ascent is one of the many functions language serves. This type of personal transformation through the recitation of various forms of Divine Names already appears, if in an inchoate way, in *Merkavah* and *Hekhalot* sources of the Talmudic and early medieval eras.[27] Its full development, however, is found in the high Middle Ages after 1200, being particularly notable in the ecstatic Kabbalah of Abraham Abulafia,[28] whence it found its way into the mainstream of kabbalistic practice, especially sixteenth-century Lurianic[29] circles, which, in turn, became "normative" for all post-1600 Kabbalah. Rabbi Isaac Ibn Latif, writing in the mid-thirteenth century, speaks of the mystical elevation of consciousness this way: "[Mystical comprehension comes] by means of the Name which is completely and utterly hidden."[30] Abulafia goes still further and, correlating various techniques of deconstructing and permutating the Divine Names— based on earlier techniques of *gematria* and the like—views these purely linguistic rearrangements as corresponding to the desired reconstruction of mystical knowing: "In the thoughts of your mind combine [the Divine Names] and be purified."[31] Such formalized and formulaic acts of linguistic combination and reorganization prepare one for the exalted states of transcendental wisdom and experience:

> And begin to combine small letters with great ones, to reverse them and to permutate them rapidly, until your heart shall be warmed through their combinations and rejoice in their movements and in what you bring about through their permutations; and when you feel thusly that your heart is already greatly heated through the combinations . . . then you are ready to receive the emanated influx.[32]

These doctrines found a warm reception in Safed and appear to have been taught by the great sixteenth-century triumvirate of Yosef Karo, Moses Cordovero, and, most importantly, Isaac Luria, and to have been an essential part of the mystical devotions of Luria's disciples, especially Hayyim Vital. In his *Ma'amar Hitbodedut* (the famous and controversial fourth chapter of the *Sha'arei Qedushah*, first published in Constantinople in 1734 without this fourth chapter), Vital gives a striking illustration of the theme through his technique of reciting *Mishnayot* (sections of the early rabbinic legal corpus known as the *Mishnah* redacted circa 200 C.E. by Rabbi Judah the Prince in the Land of Israel). After setting out stringent preliminary acts of preparation and purification, he instructs the adept:

> Seclude yourself in a lonely house, as mentioned above; wrap yourself in a prayer-shawl, and sit and close your eyes, divesting yourself of the material world as if your soul had left your body, and was ascending to heaven. Following this abstraction [from matter], recite whichever single *mishnah* that you wish, many times in uninterrupted succession. Concentrate your mind upon attaching your soul to that of the *tanna'* [sage] mentioned in the *mishnah*. And this is what you should concentrate your mind upon: That your mouth is an instrument which articulates the letters of the text of this *mishnah*. And that the voice that you produce from the mouth's organ consists of the sparks of your inner soul which emerge and recite this particular *mishnah*. The soul becomes a throne so that in it there may be invested the soul

of this *tanna'*, the author of the *mishnah*, and so that his soul will be invested in your own. When you become exhausted from reciting the text of the *mishnah*—if you are worthy of it—it is possible that the soul of this *tanna'* will abide in your mouth, and he (the *tanna'*, i.e., his soul) will become invested within your mouth while you are reciting the *mishnah*. And then while you are still reading the *mishnah* he will speak with your mouth and offer you a salutation of peace. Everything that you then think of asking him he will answer you. He will speak with your mouth and your ears will hear his words. It is not you yourself speaking, but he is the one who speaks. This is the meaning of: "The spirit of the Lord speaks by me and His word is upon my tongue." (II Sam. 23:2)[33]

That Vital's suggestion here is in no way idiosyncratic is seen from the comparable practice of Yosef Karo, who also, if in different fashion, recited *Mishnayot* in order to gain access to his heavenly *maggid* (angelic guide).[34]

Christian mysticism has a much less well-developed tradition of such linguistically induced techniques. This is due largely to the very different status of scripture and the strong apophatic influence drawn from Neoplatonism in Christian spirituality. Yet while lacking a tradition of anything like the Zen *kōans*, in the "Jesus prayer" and other motifs, such techniques are to be found in segments of the Christian world as well. That is to say, in all the major mystical traditions, recognizing their real and undeniable phenomenological diversity, language as a psychospiritual means of radical reorientation and purification is present. And its presence points to the inherent linguistic element in spirituality: language is integral to mystical practice. This is not to exaggerate this fact or, yet, to attack the central issue of ineffability, but it is to begin to widen our parameters, to broaden our understanding, as to how language relates to mystical experience.

On Alphabets and Lexicons

An elemental premise of the dominant theory regarding the insufficient fit between language and transcendental experience is that language is a human convention. As such it is earth-bound, ill-suited to objects/subjects of ultimate concern. But this repercussive thesis is not universally accepted. Many of the world's most significant religious and mystical traditions begin with the belief that their language is sacred—the very language of God or Being—and as such possesses an ontic status altogether different from merely immanent/conventional languages, making it capable of expressing transcendental *realia* in various ways, with a particular competence. This claim, among others, is made by kabbalists on behalf of Hebrew, Sufis on behalf of Arabic, and Hindus on behalf of Sanskrit. In each case, the mystic of the said tradition sees him- or herself as possessing, in language, both the vehicle of divine/transcendental expression and one of the very sources of divine creativity. As such, the employment of linguistic forms in these languages, particularly as embodied in sacred texts, is not subject to the same restrictions as are imposed by the utilization of conventional semiotic systems. Knowledge of the Tetragrammaton, for example, and its appropriateness vis-à-vis the Divine is not the same as either the correspondence between the word "chair" and a chair, or even that between the English word "God" and the Divine. For the Tetragrammation is the Absolute's *self*-identification, possessing powers, by virtue of this ontic ground, this metaphysical source and connectedness, that other linguistic ascriptions lack. For the kabbalist, therefore, meditation and manipulation of the four-lettered Name is a theurgic, meditative, and transformative act made possible by the *necessary* link between it and its transcendental source/Object.

Consider here, as paradigmatic, the theurgical and contemplative manipulation of letters found in the *Sefer Yetzira*. In this most important of all early Jewish mystical texts (after the Bible), the metaphysical fecundity of language is seen with special clarity. The letters of the Hebrew alphabet, out of which words are composed, are the fundamental building blocks of creation. The letters have ontic capacity and can be—indeed, have been—employed by God to create the world and everything within it. In this reading, the creation accounts wherein "God speaks" are taken with extreme, if original, literalness. The process of creation resides in the manipulation of the alphabetical ciphers.

1. By means of thirty-two wonderful paths of wisdom, YH, YHVH of Hosts, ELOHIM of Israel, Living ELOHIM, and Eter-

nal King, EL SHADDAI, Merciful and Gracious, High and Uplifted, Who inhabits Eternity, exalted and holy is His Name, engraved. And He created His universe by three principles: by border and letter and number.[35]

Specifically as regards the letters of the Hebrew alphabet:

> 2. Twenty-two letters are the foundation: He engraved them, He hewed them out, He combined them, He weighed them, and He set them at opposites, and He formed through them everything that is formed and everything that is destined to be formed.[36]

And these twenty-two letters then can be permutated and combined in a variety of ways:

> 4. Twenty-two letters are the foundation: He set them in a wheel, like a kind of wall, with two hundred and thirty-one gates. And the wheel rotates forward and backward. And the sign of the thing is:
> there is no goodness above pleasure ('NG) and
> there is no evil below pain (NG').

> 5. How did He combine them, weigh them and
> set them at opposites?
> Aleph with all of them, and all of them with
> Aleph,
> Bet with all of them, and all of them with
> Bet.
> It rotates in turn, and thus they are in two
> hundred and thirty-one gates.
> And everything that is formed and everything
> that is spoken goes out from one term.[37]

All that is is the consequence of this linguistic activity.

Although uniquely an aspect of God's own mysterious creativity in the first instance, He benevolently shares with mankind this world-consequential power, this capacity for and use of language, as a gift of grace. Like the God in whose image we are created, human beings can learn to replicate—so the high purpose, at least in part of the *Sefer Yetzira*—the dynamic processes of creation. It is for this reason that the text of *Sefer Yetzira* ends by praising Abraham as a magical creative presence:

7. When Abraham our father, may he rest in
peace, came: he
> looked, and
> saw, and
> understood, and
> explored, and
> engraved [through the Hebrew alphabet],

and
> hewed out [through the Hebrew alphabet],

and
> succeeded at Creation as it is said,

"And the bodies[38]
> they had made in Haran." [Genesis 12:5][39]

These intriguing notions are variously recycled in later Kabbalah, most popularly in traditions concerning the creation of a *golem*,[40] a Frankenstein-like creature energized by the power of the Divine Name, as well as in more recondite speculations on the Tetragrammaton and related Divine Names,[41] in aspects of the theosophical doctrine of the *Zohar* and the many traditions deriving therefrom,[42] and in the anachronistic teaching of Abraham Abulafia,[43] among many apposite loci. Let one suggestive, if difficult, medieval teaching on this stand for many. Rabbi Reuven Zarfati taught:

> Know that the epitome of human perfection is that one knows the secret of the Angel of the Countenance by means of letter combination. Then he will know the seventy languages. Do not think that they are, literally, languages, for if you believe this, you foolishly believe in error. Indeed, the true faith is that you attain the perception of the Angel of the Countenance, whose name is identical with the Name of his Master.[44]

Ultimate wisdom, *Chachmah*, resides in the secret processes of the permutations and combinations of the letters of the Hebrew alphabet. This is the source of real cosmogonic and cosmological power.

Kabbalah is, of course, not alone in offering up these types of alphabetical speculations. Pythagoreans[45] as well as Muslims and individual Christian mystics engaged in these sorts of explorations, sharing the presupposition that language is not merely utilitarian, conventional, or instrumental in character. In Sufism, for example, Arabic words and roots connected to the ninety-nine names of

Allāh, particularly the supreme name Allāh itself, were manipulated in much the same way as the Hebrew names of God were by kabbalists in order to construct prayers and incantations for various contemplative and practical (e.g., healing) purposes. As part of *al-asmā al ḥusnā*, the theology of the Divine Names, Sufis have employed these names in order to empower their spiritual movement heavenward and to affect the world below. The "teaching of the names" is the opening by which the Sufi gains an insight into the essence, the "name," of things that in turn reflects some manifestation of the Divine Names; that is, all names, all knowledge, derive from the transcendental attributes of Allāh. Implicating an emanationist metaphysics, drawn, as in the Zoharic schema, from Neoplatonic sources, the Names reveal the nature of things, that secret supernal nature that the Sufi seeks to excavate and utilize in order to annihilate (*fanā*) his physical limitations, thereby making possible transcendental communion involving a complex set of technical Sufi notions such as *baqā* (subsistence in Allāh) and *ittihad* (unification with Allāh). Abû Hurayrah, in the name of the Prophet, records: "There are 99 names that are Allāh's alone. Whomever learns, understands and enumerates them enters Paradise and achieves eternal salvation."[46]

A related, extended corollary of these linguistic characteristics of Sufism—usually imaged as radically apophatic—is the important and intriguing creation of specialized, technical lexicons by Sufis organized in order to assist the mystical adept in his or her spiritual progress. Qushayrī describes the significance of his mystical lexicon as "increasing understanding for those who discuss, or facilitating for the people of this art the comprehension of their meanings without restriction."[47] Sufis have a common vocabulary that has a *shared* meaning: "This group [Sufis] employs words on matters they share, through which they intend to reveal their meanings to themselves, and to summarize and conceal from those who oppose them in the path." Language, special language, read in particular ways, following agreed-upon rules, including the authority of religious masters communicated secretly to their disciples, conveys a precise and didactic meaning: "By the commentary on these words we wish to facilitate the understanding among the wayfarers of these paths and the followers of their example who wish to comprehend their meanings."[48] Such language—assumed a priori to be meaningful and possessing a meaning that can be shared — may be intended only for initiates, only for those qualified to participate in the esoteric dialogue. But this must not be confused with ineffability, with the more usual claim that language is inappropriate to such concerns, for these "insiders" speak to one another in an intelligible common language, however constrained its circulation, and convey information of some sort by so doing. As such, this language had meaning, and its meaning is properly associated with, and revelatory of, the secrets of the *tariqah*. These lexical terms are, in Rūzbihān's phrase, "vessels for secrets."[49] And their origin is the Divine Will, the mind of Allāh, and therefore they convey meanings that are sure, final, absolute — and shareable.

There is much more to be said on these salient language-linked features of mystical systems. But for our present purposes, let this brief comment on alphabets and lexicons point toward a more comprehensive recognition that the great mystical traditions have both found rich and subtle ways of conveying primal aspects of their truth in language and recognize that language, in certain forms, most often connected to the Divine's own self-disclosure in the transhistorical authoritative revelations of scripture, is integral to and inseparable from these very truths.

Language as Power

Language as *power* is one of the elemental employments of language in mystical traditions. Contrary to aggressively asserted, oft-championed apophatic claims, most mystical streams are keenly sensitive to the energizing ontic possibilities that (certain) language, employed with spiritual integrity and in normatively efficacious manner, is said to possess. This understanding manifests itself in, for example, the manipulation of alphabetical signs in the world's mystical teachings in order to achieve contemplative and cosmic ends. Here, however, I would like to consider this idea in several of its additional manifestations, beginning with the conception that language directly aids in mystical ascents to other worlds and realms of being.

In this context, words have locomotive power. They transport the spiritual self from the world below in the world above. Perhaps the clearest expression of such a doctrine, an unambiguous representative expression of such compelling force, even of such experience,[50] is found in the *Hekhalot* and *Merkavah* texts of the rabbinic era (i.e., texts of the first six centuries of the common era).[51] In these documents, words serving as magical names, formulations, and "seals" make it possible for the adept to ascend to a hierarchically arranged heaven where, with their aid, he is able to continue his upward journey until he comes to the Seventh Heaven, in which he encounters the Almighty (*kivyachol*, as if one could say this) seated on His celestial throne[52] (see Isaiah 6:11 for the origin of this description). *Hekhalot Rabbati*, for example, is, in one extended sense, an elaborate, practical answer to Rabbi Ishmael's opening query, "What songs does someone recite who wishes to catch a glimpse of the Chariot?"[53] And again in the text of *Ma'aseh Merkavah*, Rabbi Akiba, in answer to Rabbi Ishmael's question, "How is it possible to . . . see what RWZNYM Adonai God of Israel does?" reveals a specific prayer to be recited. The efficacy of this now-revealed liturgical formulation is vouchsafed by Rabbi Akiba, who confidently reports: "As soon as I prayed this prayer I [ascended] saw [in the world above] 640 thousand myriads of angels (of service) of glory who stand opposite the throne of glory and I saw the knot of the tefillin of GRWYY Adonai God of Israel . . ."[54] In this perilous ascent, moreover, correct mystical prayer is absolutely required at each heaven to pass from the first through to the seventh. As Rabbi Akiba is careful to explain:

> He said to me: When I ascended to the first palace,
> a prayer "and I saw from the first palace" I prayed and I saw from the palace
> [to] of the first firmament up to the palace of the seventh firmament
> and as soon as I ascended to the seventh palace I recited (the names
> of) two angels and
> I gazed at above the Seraphim and these are them STR UGLYWN.

And as soon as I recited their names,
they came and grabbed me and they said
to me:
Human, do not be afraid.⁵⁵

In a variant of this, Rabbi Ishmael teaches those who would ascend to employ magical seals

> 1. R. Ishmael said: When you come and stand at the gate of the first palace, take two seals, one in each hand—[the seals] of Tootrusea-YHVH, Lord of Israel, and of Surya, the Angel of the Presence. Show the seal of Tootrusea-YHVH, Lord of Israel, to those who stand on the right, and [the seal] of Surya to those on the left. Then, Bahbiel—the angel who is in charge of the gate of the first palace, is appointed over the palace [itself], and who stands on the right—and Tofheil—the angel who stands to the left of the threshold—you [the initiate], give you peace, and send you forth with radiance [*mashlimin u-mazhirin alekha*] to Tagriel, the angel who is in charge of the gate of the second palace and who stands to the right of its threshold, and to Matpiel, who stands with him to the left of its threshold.⁵⁶

Without the proper magical recitations or markers, the danger of ascent is enormous, as Rabbi Ishmael makes clear in the *Hekhalot Rabbati*:

> 6. Now, the guards of the sixth palace make a practice of killing those who "go and do not go down to the Merkabah without permission." They hover over them, strike them, and burn them. Others are set in their place and others in their place [and the same thing happens]. The mentality [of those who are killed] is that they are not afraid nor do they question: "Why are we being burned?" [The mentality of the guards is that they do not ask:] "What profit do we have that we kill those who go and do not go down to the Merkabah without permission?" Nevertheless, such is the mentality of the guards of the sixth palace.⁵⁷

Language here is dynamic and prophylactic; it facilitates the heavenly journey and provides needed protection from the potentially annihilatory powers encountered on the way.

> R. Ishmael said: (With) seven seals I
> sealed myself when
> PDQRS angel of the Countenance

descended.
Blessed are you Adonai who created
heaven and earth
by your wisdom and your understanding.
Your name lives forever
>YP SYSYP >YLWSS KYSY TNYY.
(The) name of your servant >WRYM SSTYY
is on my feet.
>BG BGG is on my heart.
/>RYM TYP> is on my right arm./
LYBYY >RWM TYP> is on my left arm.
>BYT TLBG >RYYN DWY>L is on my neck.
>P >K QYTR ŠM >HD (one) YDYD
(friend) YD YH
to guard my soul.
RYR GWG GDWL (great) TP YP HP THWR
(pure)
HHWS
HHY HH HH HZ KRWT (I recited?) <WLM
(eternal)
Let you be blessed, lord of wisdom
because all the might is yours, it is.
Blessed are you Adonai, lord of might,
high and exalted, great in rule.[58]

Even the angelic realm responds to language properly employed, revealing thereby the ontological parallelism between speech and being.[59]

The theme of ascent likewise plays a central role in Sufism.[60] Related essentially to Muhammed's *mi'rāj*, the Sufi seeks to replicate the Prophet's heavenly journey[61] through prayer and meditation. Although Muhammed's *mi'rāj* lacks the linguistic and magical elements of *Hekhalot* and *Merkavah* ascents (the only residue of this earlier tradition being Muhammed's examination by the angel Isma'il, which Muhammed passes successfully),[62] the disciple wishing to make a similar ascent uses words, especially prayer, after Muhammed's own teaching on prayer, to facilitate his transport. It is not at all surprising that Sufis from the time of Bāyezid Bistamī employed the language of the *mi'rāj* as the primal linguistic resource from which to draw the vocabulary for their own transcendental experiences.[63] Even in Ibn Arabi, prayer transposes the self, if not spatially, then, to use Henry Corbin's term, "imaginatively"; that is, prayer *causes* man to "ascend" to a novel spiritual level in which his vision of the Real is wholly transmuted.

Dhikr, the recollection of Allāh's names, or some related formula (e.g., *la ilāha illā Allah*), plays a complementary role in Sufism as well. Most of the main handbooks of Sufi teaching emphasize this activity as a key to mystical ascension. Najmuddīn Kubrā (Abū 'l-Jannāb Ahmad), in his well-known *Faivā'ih al jamāl wa fawātih al jalāl*,[64] for example, includes such linguistic performances as among the required ritual activities of the Sufi Ten-Fold Path. *Dhikr* causes man to be present to Allāh and Allāh to man; on hearing Allāh's name(s), the soul is transported. And it is this meaning that many Sufis give to the Koranic passage "I am the prayer companion of whoever remembers [read *dhikr*] me; and when my servant seeks Me, he finds Me."[65] The repetition of Koranic verses and the recitation of religious poems are also known to have caused the exalted states sought by the *sālik*.

Mantras, *kōans*, mystical alphabets and lexicons, ascent texts, prayers, the repetition of scripture, the recitation of religious poetry, and still other linguistic acts embody a primal, radiant, metaphysical energy. They incorporate and encapsulate a dynamic power, the dynamic power, that enlivens the entire cosmic order. By deciphering their meaning, by utilizing their potential, the mystical personality is *empowered* to alter its own nature and fate, and thereby effect the historical and metahistorical order of things.

Language as Information: The Doctrine of Neoplatonic Emanation Taken as a Paradigm

In addition to the transformative, magical, and theurgical tasks language regulatively performs in the world's mystical traditions, language, in a variant of William James's attribution of a noetic quality to mystical states, operates informatively. It is used to describe, however this term is qualified—and it is, of course, regularly so qualified—that "knowledge" that is gained in the mystical moment. This use of language, constantly undervalued by analysts of mysticism, presents us with particular and fascinating intellectual puzzles. I would like to examine some of these by focusing on the use of language in Neoplatonic theories of emanation, in particular on kabbalistic variants of this tradition. My purpose is to show that, contrary to their own sincere declamations regarding ineffability, the structural logic of such theories necessarily *tells us* more than proponents of apophasis recognize. *And this fact should be taken as paradigmatic of mystical systems universally*; despite their avowal of *neti neti*, the reality is otherwise. That is, mystics reveal, however unintentionally, more of the "truth" they have come to know in language than their overt negations of meaning and content would suggest.

Several forms of language usage are to be noted in this connection. The first is the "inadvertent" nature of mystical descriptions of the Ultimate—represented, for example, by Philo's emanationist theory, which claims that the Divine is "unnameable and ineffable."[66] In making this argument, Philo draws on Pythagorean ideas of the One as the transcendent *Nous*, on Platonic doctrines of the One adumbrated in the *Parmenides*, and on the Middle Academy's distinction between *hyparxis* (unqualified being) and *poiotês* (qualified being) to substantiate his claims. Moreover, in depicting the Absolute and His primordial activity in bringing that which is into being, Philo contradicts his negative theology as often as is necessary to his exegesis. Among the small but telling cluster of attributes that the Philonic Diety ultimately possesses we find:

1. Being per se as compared with Being *per accidens*. We might even say "necessary *Being*," though such a gloss bears Anselmian and Scholastic associations that could confuse the issue. Philo asserts: "God alone has true being" (*Quod Deterius Potiori Insidiari Soleat*, 44, 160).
2. Being is One. Philo means not only numerically one, but simple and unified and, arguably, indivisible.[67]
3. Being is the First Principle (*De Vita Contemplativa*, 2; *Quaestiones et Solutiones in Exodum* II:68).
4. Being is immaterial. This becomes a "content" claim, though it originates in apophatic assertions wherein God is said repeatedly to be beyond space, time, and the Aristotelian categories (*Quod Deus Sit Immutabilis* II; *Quis Rerum Divinarum Heres*, 187).
5. Being is "unchangeable" (*Legum Allegoria* II, 9, 33, 24).[68]

6. Being is *Mind*, absolute or universal Intelligence. The Forms are God's thoughts (*De Opificio Mundi*, 17-19); their "place" is the logos of God (*De Opificio Mundi*, 20; *De Cherubim*, 49).[69]
7. The Forms are the cosmic blueprint. They become actualized through the Divine Will rather than necessity, as emphasized by Plato (with some ambiguity in the *Timaeus*) and Aristotle, and then Plotinus and his pagan disciples.
8. God's freedom of action is connected to the deeply held premise that "it is the property [*idion*] of God to act" (*De Cherubim*, 24, 77). Impelled by the biblical account, Philo insists: "It is impious and false to conceive of God in a state of complete inactivity. We ought . . . to be astounded at His powers as maker and Father" (*De Opificio Mundi* 2, 7).[70]
9. Moreover, as "Maker and Father," God acts "benevolently" (*Legum Allegoria* III, 68) and out of His "goodness" (*Legum Allegoria* I, 15; *De Abrahamo*, 268).

This much, then, is clear regarding Philo's account: the principle of ineffability that he asserts and defends is certainly elastic. Unless one wishes to crush Philo in a logical vise, it must be taken nonliterally.

Beyond this, the exegesis of Philo's large corpus reveals something still more philosophically fecund: his God, however "ineffable," is rooted conceptually in a matrix that is both Greek and Jewish. Philo is at his most Philonic in his valiant struggle to do justice to both traditions and in his effort to show their ultimate harmony and congruence. His "apophatic" readings are highly colored, fundamentally shaped, by the inherited problematics of middle Platonism as they had developed in the Hellenistic age—in particular, by the problems of eidetic causation and participation. Yet, simultaneously, Philo's *Weltanschauung* demands the centrality of the Torah, although, conversely, the sinaitic revelation must conform to the truths discerned by the immortal Plato. Thus there is no disjunction between the God of the philosophers and the God of Abraham, Isaac, and Jacob. The Philonic One, to use the Platonic/Plotinian terminology, must be understood as a response to specific ontological problems, Greek and Hebraic. The notions of Being, Will, and Necessity that Philo wrestles with come to him with a history and a rich penumbra of meanings. So it was not "being" or "necessary being" in some neutral sense that Philo predicated of the God of Isreal, but "Being" understood in a well-defined, channelized, philosophical tradition oriented by distinctive conceptions, say of limit and form. His rendering of God as a subject is consciously and critically shaped by his effort to adjudicate between the Aristotelian principle of necessity and the biblical insistence on Divine Freedom.

If Philo's corpus reveals the "inadvertent" utilization of substantive concepts, consider now a related, but separate, employment of informed philosophical opinion, carrying a vast amount of conceptual content, despite assertions as to ineffability, among Philo's Jewish Neoplatonic heirs beginning with Isaac Israeli[71] and Solomon Ibn Gabirol. These Jewish Neoplatonists wrestled repeatedly with one issue that was absolutely central to various forms of Neoplatonic emanationist thought: Does the One have a Will? Despite the claimed embargo on content that the ineffability thesis entails, Solomon Ibn Gabirol, in his *Mekor Ḥayyim* (pt. II, sec. 17-20), not only argues for an emanationist theory but feels able to maintain the volitional imperative of Hebraic thought. That is, he attributes the creation of form to the Divine Will (so defending the God of Israel) and the creation of matter to God's essence—that is, necessity (so trying to reconcile the biblical God with the metaphysical imperatives of Greek philosophy). Given Gabirol's close affinity to the mainstream of pagan Neoplatonism, his positing of a Divine Will as a necessary feature of the architectonic principles of creation is striking.[72] Like the Ikhwân al-Safâ, the Muslim Sincere Brethren (tenth century),[73] Gabirol rejects the Plotinian doctrine of "spontaneous necessity"[74] and the versions of this teaching widely circulated, for example, in the *Theology of Aristotle* and its Arabic clones, and opts instead for the reality of the Divine Will at the origin of the emanative process. Even in its Latin translation, the *Mekor Ḥayyim* makes abundantly clear that "the creation of things by the Creator, the going out of the forms from the prime source, is from the will [*voluntate*]."[75] One has only to compare this description with Plotinus's treatment of the same stage in the creative process to appreciate its biblical resonances.[76] Plotinus writes: "There is in everything the act of the essence and the act of going out from the essence: the first act is the thing itself in its realized identity, the second act is an *inevitably* following outgo from the first, an emanation distinct from the thing itself."[77] I am not dissuaded from seeing here a sharp disjunction between Gabirol and Plotinus, despite John Rist's nondeterministic reading on the latter, which seems to me anachronistic.[78]

It is illuminating to trace these two "traditions": the Judaic Neoplatonic deriving from Philo through Isaac Israeli and down to Gabirol and beyond, and the Plotinian, a stage further, among the post-*Bahir* kabbalists. Those influenced more heavily by the tradition stemming from Plotinus, Proclus, and Pseudo-Dionysius argued not only for the absolute transcendence and ineffability of the *Eyn Sof*, but also for its impersonality. Others, like Philo, were more sensitive to the scriptural imperatives affecting the doctrine of the One. They sought to "personalize" the One, referring to *ha-Eyn Sof*, the Infinite, rather than to just *Eyn Sof*, that which is "Endless" or "Boundless." Both formulations appear in the *Zohar*, but it certainly seems to favor the Philonic view, at least with regard to the question of God's freedom to create. This volitional position was later taken up by Moses Cordovero (sixteenth century) in his *Commentary* on the *Zohar* and by Isaac Luria (sixteenth century) in his remarkable teaching that the first movement of creation was made possible by God's willed self-contraction (*zimzum*).[79] The supernal reality that the *Zohar* calls the *Attika Kadisha* (Holy Ancient One) indeed is more than pure negation possessing Will. The exact relation of *Eyn Sof* or *ha-Eyn Sof* to the *Attika Kadisha* is the subject of widespread debate, but there is no question that the *Tikkunei Zohar* specifically and clearly teaches that the two are identical: "It is called *Eyn Sof* internally and *Keter Elyon* externally."[80] Yet even as these assertions are being debated, all the kabbalists agree that nothing can be known or said about *Eyn Sof*.

Given this specifically Jewish Neoplatonic tradition, revealed, for example, in this debate over the nature and mechanics of creation, we can make two generalizations: (1) "God," or the "One," or the "Absolute," is not only a name, an arbitrary verbal sign, a cipher, but also and necessarily in all meaningful contexts, a "disguised description." (2) Even the One about whom one can only offer negations, who transcends all predicates, is a definite individual: the "disguised descriptions" establish a meaning-giving context that shapes the content of their descriptiveness. For example, in

Philo, in the Plotinian tradition,[81] in the Spanish Jewish Neoplatonists, and in the *mekubbalim* (masters of the Kabbalah), there is agreement that the negation of all attributes is not an indication of negativity per se, of nothingness or meaninglessness. Nor is it an indication that at the center of being there is only randomness and chaos. Rather, in contradistinction to a negative reading of negation, all these sources concur that the One is intrinsically *Good*, as both Plato (*Republic* VI. 509C) and scripture teach. Moreover, this *Good* is *the* creative origin and designing *telos* of all that is. All comes from the One/Good, and all returns to the One/Good.

We have gone very far in this putatively apophatic tradition beyond apophasis.

Then, too, in deconstructing the unexpected uses of language in Jewish Neoplatonism, we must consider the highly complex issues relating to what I shall call the logic of emanation. Here I mean to point toward the logical, ontological, and linguistic implications of the process of emanation and the relationship of the One to the realities that flow from It: given the definition of emanation, there is a particular and informative reciprocity between the One and the many. For example, Philo can point to the outcome of Divine action—creation—as affording some inferential awareness of Him. Likening the Platonic forms to biblical "causes"—that is, to Divine Action—he argues, glossing Moses' prayer in Exodus, that "He himself alone is incomprehensible—but He may come to be apprehended and known by the powers that follow and attend Him." Although Philo immediately adds the qualification that "these make evident not His essence but His existence,"[82] his remark is especially provocative, given the related, even entailed, ontological implications of an emanationist metaphysics: that the cause and effect are, in some primal and definitive sense, the same, of one shared being.

Plotinus tells us, despite all his negations, that the central concept of ontic participation unfolds against the background of the emanationist principle: "The One is all things and no one of them; the source of all things is not all things; and yet it is all things in a transcendental sense, all things, so to speak, having run back to it; or more correctly, not all as yet are within it, they will be."[83] Thus "the One, remains intact . . . since the entities produced in its likeness . . . owe their existence to no other. . . . Just as there is, primarily or secondarily, some form or idea from the monad in each of the successive numbers—the later still participating, though unequally, in the unit—so the series of Beings following upon The First bear, each, some form or idea derived from that source."[84] Accordingly, if I understand Plotinus correctly, things incorporate and hence reflect and reveal that from which they derive. Therefore, by indirection, insofar as we speak of "things" we are describing or naming something of the One. Plotinian emanation implicates the One cataphatically as a consequence of its ontological choreography.

Similarly, Rabbi Azriel of Gerona, in explaining the emanated status of the *Sefirot* in relation to *Eyn Sof*, writes:

> I have already informed you that *Eyn-Sof* is perfect . . . that the agent which is (initially) brought forth from Him must also be perfect. Thus the dynamic of emanation is fittingly the beginning of all creation, for the potency of emanation is the essence of all things.

Extending this exegesis, he affirms:

> The One is the foundation of the many and in the many no power is innovated—only in Him . . . although this first is the dynamic order of the other . . . the metaphor for this is the fire, the flame, the sparks . . . they are all of one essence.[85]

The emanation of the *Sefirot* is a process within the Godhead, not a descent into space-time, but Rabbi Azriel's description does lead us to ask what it is we may potentially come to know, to say, of the *Eyn Sof*. Given that "that potency of emanation is the essence of all things" and that the *Sefirot* (by definition) "are all one essence" with the One (*Eyn Sof*), does it not follow that our unquestioned ability to know the *Sefirot* entails that we can, in some sense, know the *Eyn Sof*? As Gershom Scholem writes, "The hidden God in the aspect of the *Eyn Sof* and the God manifested in the emanation of the *Eyn Sof* are one and the same viewed from two different angles."[86] Analogously, among later kabbalists, whatever the hermeneutical and metaphysical ambiguities, there emerges a kabbalistic consensus that the emanative process continues downward and is responsible for the sublunary and material worlds. So these lower realms also participate in and reflect the *Sefirot* from which they emerge, although at a remove, they are continuous with the *Eyn Sof*. Even in the *'alma de-peruda*, the world of separation, when things are seen mystically, "everything is revealed as One."[87] At a far lower level, therefore, we can learn about the *Eyn Sof* (through the mediation of the *Sefirot*) by way of the things in our world; by knowing and naming these, we know and name the *Eyn Sof*, obliquely but authentically. Moses de Leon, the author of the *Zohar*, notes in his *Sefer Ha-Rimmon*:

> Everything is linked with everything else down to the lowest ring of the chain, and the true essence of God is above as well as below, in the heavens and on the earth, and nothing exists outside of him. . . . Meditate on these things and you will understand that God's essence is linked and connected with all worlds, and that all forms of existence are linked and connected with each other, but derived from His existence and essence.[88]

Correspondingly, the inherent dialectic of return to the Source, seeking felicity by reversing the ontic process of differentiation and procession that is central to both Kabbalah and philosophical Jewish Neoplatonism, is rooted in the metaphysical unity of all things from above to below. The elemental doctrines of *nizozot* (sparks), *bittul ha-yesh* (annihilation), *hithpashtuth* (egression), and *histalkuth* (regression) are connected with and to be deciphered by reference to the primordial participation of all that is in the *Eyn Sof* through the "mediation" of the *Sefirot*, which are manifestations of the Godhead itself. That is to say, the theory of regress, the inversion of the metaphysics of emanation, like emanation itself, raises many profound questions. For it casts new light, perhaps some would say shadows, over the status of the *Eyn Sof*'s transcendence of all conceptual and linguistic forms.

The regressive accessibility of the One allows the possibility of *devekut*,[89] or union beyond intellection or language, of which the kabbalists and philosophers speak. The recommendation and the hope that seek this end are predicated on the assumption that ultimately there is commonality, a shared ontic nature, that will become apparent and dominant once ordinary restraints have dropped away in the ascent, or return, of the soul to its source. In the Neoplatonic expression of Rabbi Ezra: "Everything issues from the first cause and everything returns to the first cause." Given the possibility of *devekut* and of the return of the *Sefirot* to *Ayin*,[90] can we say that we know nothing and can say nothing of *Eyn Sof*?

The emanationist model presumes a hierarchial descent from the *Eyn Sof*, and correspondingly relates "degrees of being" to one's place in the hierarchy: the "higher" and closer to the *Eyn Sof*, the more "spiritual"; the "lower" and farther from the *Eyn Sof*, the more "material." This scheme is inescapably conceptual and linguistic. It depends for its cogency on an order of beings, "beyond which," though somehow related, is the One. The egress of meta-Being/*Eyn-Sof* to Being/*Sefirot* — that is, the emanation of *'Olam ha-azilut*, down to the emanation of material beings in the *'Olam ha-'asiyyah*, our terrestrial world, and the regress from *'Olam ha-'asiyyah* to the Sefirotic realm and then to *Ayin* — is thus a process that is, in a real sense, cataphatic. The Neoplatonic mystic, the advocate of emanation, appears to know more, far more, of the *X* of *X*s than would at first seem possible given the systematic negations of Neoplatonic epistemology.

This sort of descriptive performance, this, if only implied, content conveyance, these substantive entailments of the logic of emanation, should be taken as an example of the complexity of mystical reports and their scholarly analysis. Related types of decipherment could be, should be, carried out with regard, for example, to the Buddhist doctrine of *śūnyatā* and the sophisticated Advaitan metaphysical claims regarding *Brahman*. Nāgārjuna's *Madhyamaka-Kārikās* and Sankara's *Brahmasūtrabhāsya*, to take two of many examples, would provide wonderful, classical texts for just such rigorous analysis, as would the biblical commentaries of Meister Eckhart and the remarkable *Al-Futūhāt al makkiyya* of Ibn Arabī. All would show that the mystical use of even radical apophatic language is not the simplistic rejection of language that it is usually thought of as being.

Conclusion

Although this essay has touched only schematically on a number of subjects relevant to a full exploration of the relationship of mysticism to language, it has the virtue of indicating that this relationship involves surprising richness and complexity. Whatever else the world's mystics do with language, they do not, as a rule, merely negate it. Pressed to the outer limits of the "sayable" by the transcendental objects/subjects of their concern, yet often assisted by the resources of positive revelation and/or the content of their (and others') "noetic" experience (including states of consciousness reached through various forms of meditation) and, as a rule, urgently desirous of sharing these extraordinary truths and experiences, they utilize language to convey meaning(s) and content(s) in a variety of amazingly imaginative ways. It is, indeed, their *success* at just this sort of substantive communication that allows us to speak of, to learn of, and to participate in mystical traditions at all. This fact does not yet explain or resolve the still more recalcitrant logical problems generated by claims of ineffability and the like, but it indicates that resolution must be sought in ways more informed by what mystics actually say about the meaning of language, and its relationship to mystical experience and *realia*, than has hitherto been the case.

Notes

1. James Clark, ed., *Meister Eckhart: An Introduction to the Study of His Works with an Anthology of His Sermons* (New York, 1975), p. 83.

2. Parenthetically, it is to be noted that the common denial of *written* expression by many great religious and mystical figures should not be equated with the rejection of language per se, as is usually the case. What is rejected in such cases is written forms of expression because such forms are said to lack the organic vitality of oral communication; words as speech communicate the "truth," while words in their print form do not. It is told of the Ba'al Shem Tov (who founded Hasidism in the mideighteenth century) that during his lifetime a book of his teachings appeared without authorization. That night the Besht dreamed that he saw the devil carrying this book. The next day, he asked his followers about it, and when he was given the book in question he said, "There is not a single word of my teaching in this volume." This sort of incident can be found in many religious and mystical traditions worldwide. In addition, there is a related but different concern expressed clearly, for example, in the Talmudic-rabbinic tradition that esoteric doctrines—called in this context

maaseh bereshit (the secrets of creation) and *maaseh merkavah* (the secrets of the chariot, referring to Ezekial's vision, and more generally taken to indicate metaphysical and transcendental "secrets") — should not be put into print lest they fall into the wrong hands. This problem finds expression, for example, in Maimonides's *Guide for the Perplexed*; the controversy over the printing of the *Zohar* and Lurianic works in the sixteenth century, parts of which remain unprinted for this reason; and the introduction to the *Tanya* by the Hasidic leader Shneur Zalman of Liadi in the early nineteenth century. Again, this sort of inhibition is found in non-Jewish traditions as well.

3. Here I refer to their ideas and writings and not, of course, to the religious communities and traditions they may have generated.

4. For more on this issue, I refer readers to my essay, "Language, Epistemology, and Mysticism," in Steven T. Katz, ed., *Mysticism and Philosophical Analysis* (New York, 1978), pp. 22-74.

5. For further details on these forms of mystical literature, see Carl Keller, "Mystical Literature," in Katz, ed., *Mysticism and Philosophical Analysis*, pp. 75-100.

6. The full theoretical formulation of this contextual approach to mystical materials has been set out in some detail in my prior studies, "Language, Epistemology, and Mysticism," and "The 'Conservative' Character of Mystical Experience," in Steven T. Katz, ed., *Mysticism and Religious Traditions* (New York, 1983), pp. 3-60.

7. See, for example, Robert Foreman, ed., *Problem of Pure Consciousness* (New York, 1990), the recent collection of essays essentially devoted to responding to my work; Michael Bagger, "Critical Notice: Ecumenicalism and Perennialism Revisited," review of *Problem of Pure Consciousness*, edited by Robert Foreman, *Religious Studies* 27 (1991): 399-412; the somewhat confused essay by Donald Evans, "Can Philosophers Limit What Mystics Can Do? A Critique of Steven Katz," *Religious Studies* 25 (1989): 53-60; J. William Forgie, "Hyper-Kantianism in Recent Discussions of Mystical Experience," *Religious Studies* 21 (1985): 205-18; and Jerry Gill, "Mysticism and Mediation," *Faith and Philosophy* 1 (1984): 111-21. Aspects of my work have also been analyzed by William Wainwright, *Mysticism: A Study of Its Nature, Cognitive Value and Moral Implications* (Madison, Wis., 1981), pp. 19-22; and Wayne Proudfoot, *Religious Experience* (Berkeley, 1985), pp. 122-28.

8. Katz, "Language, Epistemology, and Mysticism."

9. I have been, of late, referred to as a "constructivist," but given the meaning attached to this designation by my critics, I reject this term, preferring to describe my approach as "contextualist." The most extensive use of the term "Katzian Constructivism" will be found in Foreman, ed., *Problem of Pure Consciousness*.

10. Hans Waldenfels, *Absolute Nothingness: Foundations for Buddhist-Christian Dialogue* (New York, 1980), p. 68.

11. *The Perfection of Wisdom in Eight Thousand Lines, and Its Verse Summary*, trans. E. Conze (London, 1968), p. 85. This is an English translation of the Mahayana treatise called the *Aṣṭasāhasrikā Prajñāpāramitā*.

12. This is to be understood as one way of coming to mystical knowledge or experience; that is, the knower actively seeks to alter his consciousness in order to facilitate the desired nonordinary experience. This approach is neither universal nor is it to be taken as the only approach found in the mystical traditions of the world. It is complemented (not contradicted) by an alternative position that views mystical experience as an act of God or the transcendent that requires no prior or technical preparation, and that explains the specialness of such experience by reference to the specialness of the *object* of such experience—for example, Allāh or Brahman.

13. See Carl Hempel's fuller discussion of his correspondence theory of truth in *Aspects of Scientific Explanation* (New York, 1965).

14. Robert Gimello, "Mysticism in Its Contexts," in Katz, ed., *Mysticism and Religious Traditions*, p. 75.

15. See the reading of R. H. Robinson, *Early Mādhyamika in India and China* (Madison, Wis., 1967), pp. 56-59, and Frits Staal, *Exploring Mysticism* (Harmondsworth, 1975), pp. 44-51. See also Alex Wayman, "Who Understands the Four Alternatives of the Buddhist Texts?" *Philosophy East and West* 27 (1977): 3-21.

16. Quoted in Staal, *Exploring Mysticism*, p. 44.

17. Further discussion of the logic of the *Catuskoti* can be found in V. K. Bharadwaja, "Rationality, Argumentation and Embarrassment: A Study of Four Logical Alternatives (Catuskoti) in Buddhist Logic," *Philosophy East and West* 34 (1984): 303-19; F. J. Hoffman, "Rationality in Early Buddhist Fourfold Logic," *Journal of Indian Philosophy* 10 (1982): 309-37; P. T. Raju, "The Principle of Four-Cornered Negation in Indian Philosophy," *Review of Metaphysics* 7 (1953-54): 694-713; R. D. Gunaratne, "The Logical Form of Catuskoti: A New Solution," *Philosophy East and West* 30 (1960): 211-39; and R. Pandeya, "The Logic of *Catuskoti* and Indescribability," in R. Pandeya, ed., *Indian Studies in Philosophy* (Delhi, 1977), pp. 89-103.

18. Note the analysis of K. Bhattacharya, "The Dialectical Method of Nāgārjuna," *Journal of Indian Philosophy* 1 (1971): 217-61. I recall with pleasure my conversations with Professor Bhattacharya in India in 1977 and 1978. Although we disagreed on just about everything, he helped me understand the profundity of the Indian spiritual tradition.

19. Staal, *Exploring Mysticism*, p. 35.

20. Staal, *Exploring Mysticism*, pp. 35-36.

21. Mircea Eliade, *Yoga, Immortality and Freedom* (Princeton, N.J., 1958), pp. 123-24. Eliade here quotes Heinrich Zimmer (with slight modifications), *Philosophies of India*, ed. Joseph Campbell (Princeton, N.J., 1951), p. 375. I have followed Zimmer's original translation of the last sentence rather than Eliade's, whose translation I otherwise employ.

22. *Madhyamika-Kārikās*, chap. 24, stanza 14.

23. This practice would, of course, later spread throughout much of the Buddhist world.

24. For example, they are employed in various magical practices. Such usage is described in Annamarie Schimmel, *Mystical Dimension of Islam* (Chapel Hill, N.C., 1975), pp. 177-78.

25. Rūbihān Baqli, "Sharh-l-shathiyāt," in *Les Paradoxes des soûfis*, ed. Henri Corbin (Tehran and Paris, 1966), sec. 638.

26. Abū Hāmid al-Ghazzali, *Ihyā' 'ulum ad-din*, vol. 1, p. 265, quoted in Annamarie Schimmel, *As Through a Veil: Mystical Poetry in Islam* (New York, 1982), p. 142.

27. This early rabbinic material is analyzed in Gershom Scholem, *Jewish Gnosticism, Merkabah Mysticism and Talmudic Tradition* (New York, 1965); Ithamar Grunewald, *Apocalyptic and Merkabah Mysticism* (Leiden, 1980); David Halperin, *The Merkabah in Rabbinic Literature* (New Haven, Conn., 1980); and, most recently, Naomi Janowitz, *The Poetics of Ascent: Theories of Language in a Rabbinic Ascent Text* (Albany, N.Y., 1989).

28. Explored in detail in two volumes by Moshe Idel, *The Mystical Experience in Abraham Abulafia* (Albany, N.Y., 1988), and *Language, Torah, and Hermeneutics in Abraham Abulafia* (Albany, N.Y., 1989).

29. For more on Lurianic Kabbalah, see Gershom Scholem, *Major Trends in Jewish Mysticism* (New York, 1954), chap. 7, and the relevant sections of Scholem, *Kabbalah* (New York, 1974).

30. Isaac Ibn Latif, *Ginzê ha-Melek*, chap. 41, in Adolph Jellinek, *Kokve Yizḥaq* 34 (1867), p. 16. I quote it from Idel, *Mystical Experience in Abraham Abulafia*, p. 18.

31. *Sitrê Torah*, fol. 157b., quoted in Idel, *Mystical Experience in Abraham Abulafia*, p. 26.

32. Abraham Abulafia, *Ḥayyê ha-'Olam ha-Ba*, Ms. Oxford 1582, fol. 52a, quoted in Idel, *Mystical Experience in Abraham Abulafia*, p. 39. See also the advice of Rabbi Judah al-Botini, *Sullam ha-'Alujah* (late fifteenth to early sixteenth century), chapters 8 to 10 of which were published by Gershom Scholem in *Kirjath Sefer* 22 (1945): 162-71, which gives detailed and extended examples of how these permutations are to be conducted. An English translation of this material, with helpful commentary, is avail-

able in David Blumenthal, ed., *Understanding Jewish Mysticism* (New York, 1982), vol. 2, pp. 42-79.

33. Quoted in Lawrence Fine's interesting essay, "Recitation of *Mishnah* as a Vehicle for Mystical Inspiration: A Contemplative Technique Taught by Hayyim Vital," *Revue des etudes juives* 141 (January-June 1982): 183-99.

34. For more on Karo's practice, see R. J. Z. Werblowsky, *Joseph Karo, Lawyer and Mystic* (Philadelphia, 1977).

35. *Sefer Yetzira*, chap. 1, *Mishnah* 1, quoted in Blumenthal, ed., *Understanding Jewish Mysticism*, vol. 1, p. 15.

36. *Sefer Yetzira*, chap. 2, *Mishnah* 2.

37. *Sefer Yetzira*, chap. 2, *Misnayot* 4 and 5.

38. Some commentators read this as indicating that Abraham made the first *golem*. More commonly, however, this is understood to refer to Abraham's ability to bring others to a correct understanding of God.

39. *Sefer Yetzira*, chap. 6, *Mishnah* 7. It has become the generally accepted view among traditional students of *Sefer Yetzira* that Abraham was the author of this text. See Saadya Gaon, *Commentary on Sefer Yetzira*, trans Y. Karpah (Jerusalem, 1972), p. 13, and Judah Halevi, *Ha-Kuzari*, 4, 25.

40. On the rich tradition of the *golem*, see the catalog from the exhibition held at the Jewish Museum in New York City: *Golem! Danger, Deliverance and Art* (New York, 1988). The catalog includes a full bibliography.

41. Speculations related to the Tetragrammaton are discussed in L. Blau, *Das altjüdische Zauberwesen* (Leipzig, 1898); W. Bacher, "Shem ha-Meforash," *Jewish Encyclopedia* (New York, 1905), vol. 11, cols. 262-64; Samuel Cohon, "The Names of God: A Study in Rabbinic Theology," *Hebrew Union College Annual* 27 (1951): 579-604; Jarl Fossum, *The Name of God and the Angel of the Lord* (Tübingen, 1985); and Gershom Scholem, "The Name of God and the Linguistic Theory of the Kabbala," *Diogenes* 79 (1972): 59-80, and *Diogenes* 80 (1972): 164-94.

42. Zoharic theosophy is analyzed, in connection with these linguistic aspects, in Gershom Scholem, *On the Kabbalah and Its Symbolism* (New York, 1969), and *Major Trends in Jewish Mysticism*.

43. Abulafia's work is now available, thanks primarily to the pioneering studies of Moshe Idel. See note 28.

44. Quoted in Idel, *Language, Torah, and Hermeneutics in Abraham Abulafia*, p. 10.

45. An excellent introduction to Pythagorean thought is provided in W. K. C. Guthrie, *A History of Greek Philosophy*, vol. 1: *The Earlier Presocratics and the Pythagoreans* (Cambridge, 1971). Further sources can

be found in the bibliography of Kenneth S. Guthrie, *The Pythagorean Sourcebook and Library* (Grand Rapids, Mich., 1987), pp. 335-53.

46. Abû Hurayrah, *The Most Beautiful Names*, comp. Tosun Bayrak al-Jerrahi al-Halveti (Putney, Vt., 1985), p. 3.

47. The vocabulary of the Torah plays a similar lexicographic role, providing a comparable *corpus symbolicum*, for kabbalists.

48. Abū al-Qāsim 'Abd al-Karīm al-Qushayrī, *al-Risālah al-Qushayruyyah*, translated by Carl W. Ernst (chapter 8, this volume).

49. Rūzbihān, *Masrab al arivāh, wa huwa Mashhūr bi-Hazār u Yak Maqām*, ed. Naẓif Muḥarram Khwājah (Istanbul, 1973), p. 544, called to my notice by Carl Ernst in chapter 8 of this volume.

50. How much real experience and how much doctrine these rabbinic texts represent is an open scholarly question. I, for one, do not question an authentic experiential component.

51. These texts have now been carefully edited by Peter Schaefer, *Synopse zur Hekhalot-Literatur* (Tübingen, 1981).

52. The subject of the most exalted states connected especially with the Song of Songs and the *Shiür Komah* texts. For more details, see Scholem, *Jewish Gnosticism, Merkabah Mysticism and Talmudic Tradition*.

53. Schaefer, ed., *Synopse zur Hekhalot-Literatur*, p. 40.

54. Quoted in Janowitz, *Poetics of Ascent*, pp. 33, 35.

55. Quoted in Janowitz, *Poetics of Ascent*, p. 64. For more on this notion of protecting the body from harm by use of magical seals, see the material cited by Elliott Wolfson, "Circumcision and the Divine Name: A Study in the Transmission of Esoteric Doctrine," *Jewish Quarterly Review* 78 (1987): 83, n. 14.

56. Quoted in David Blumenthal, ed., *Understanding Jewish Mysticism* (New York, 1978), vol. 1, p. 66.

57. Quoted in Blumenthal, ed., *Understanding Jewish Mysticism*, vol. 1, pp. 67-68.

58. Quoted in Janowitz, *Poetics of Ascent*, p. 48.

59. Gruenwald's contention that "Merkabah mysticism is neither a magical nor a theurgic experience" is clearly in need of moderation (*Apocalyptic and Merkabah Mysticism*, p. 109).

60. According to Morton Smith, the magical and theurgical power of language in these *Hekhalot* and *Merkavah* texts has parallels in other ancient magical and gnostic traditions, including Greek mithra texts ("Observations on Hekhalot Rabbati," in Alexander Altmann, ed., *Biblical and Other Studies* [Cambridge, Mass., 1963], pp. 142-60). Although this has recently been questioned by Janowitz (*Poetics of Ascent*, p. 7), and recognizing that some of Smith's arguments are not convincing, there still remains a residue of interesting analogical truth to his claim.

61. Also composed of seven heavens (*Koran* 67:3 and 78:12).

62. None of the classic accounts of this ascent mention Muhammed's employment of secret names or seals. For details, see Ibn Ishāq, *Sirat rasūl Allah* (Göttingen, 1859-1860); Al-Bukhari, *Kitāb ǧāmi 'as-sahih*, ed. L. Krehl and W. Juynboll (Leiden, 1862-1908), vol. 3, pp. 271-73; and Abū Dja'Far Al Tabarī, *Tafsir* (New York, 1903 [microfilm]), vol. 15, pp. 10-13 (on Sura 17:1 and subsequent).

63. For more details, see Schimmel, *Mystical Dimensions of Islam*, p. 219.

64. Najmuddīn Kubrā, *Faivā'ih al jamāl wa fawātih al jalāl*, ed. Fritz Meier (Wiesbaden, 1957). See also Kubrā, *Risāla fi faḍilat aṣ-ṣalāt*, which deals with ritual prayer.

65. See, for example, Abu Muhammed Sahl al-Tustarī, *Tafsir* (Cairo, 1908), p. 26.

66. Philo, *De Somniis* I, 11, p. 67. See also *De Mutatione Nominum*, p. 2, 11; *Legum Allegoria* III, p. 206; *De Posteritate Caini* 16, p. 168. The works of Philo are quoted from the Loeb Classical Library edition, ed. F. H. Colson and G. H. Whittaker (Cambridge, Mass., 1929-1962).

67. The theme is constantly invoked by later Jewish Neoplatonists. See, for example, Solomon Ibn Gabirol, "The Royal Crown" (*Keter Malkhut*), sec. 2, ed. I. A. Zeidman (Jerusalem, 1950); the most fluent English translation is Bernard Lewis, *The Kingly Crown* (London, 1961). See also Bahya Ibn Paquda, *Ḥovot Ha-Levavot*, chaps. 8, 9; the original Arabic version of this work, *Kitab al-Hidaya ila Faraid al-Qulub*, was edited by A. S. Yahuda (Leiden, 1912), and the best English translation is Manahem Mansoor, *The Book of the Direction to the Duties of the Heart* (London, 1973). Augustine, another classical Neoplatonist caught in the same theological tension as Philo, says of God: *est per essentiam suam* ("He exists by His own essence"). See Augustine, *Comments on Psalms*, 134:4, and *City of God*, 8.6, 12.2.

68. See also *De Cherubim*, p. 19, and *Quaestiones et Solutiones in Genesin* I, p. 93.

69. See Augustine's use of this notion in his *Book of Eighty Three Questions*, question 46, 1-2, in J. P. Migne, ed., *Patrologia Latina* (Paris, 1844-64), vol. 33, pp. 29-31.

70. I am indebted to Harry Wolfson, *Philo* (Cambridge, Mass., 1947), vol. 1, pp. 131-35. Philo appears to argue in this passage that God produces the *logos* eternally and that His creative activity is continuous and eternal. Yet this continuity of the creative process is not the result of some blind necessity in the One/God.

71. For a discussion of this important issue in Isaac Israeli's speculations, see Alexander Altmann, "Creation, Emanation and Natural Causality," in Alexander Altmann and S. M. Stern, eds., *Isaac Israeli: A Neo-Platonist Philosopher of the Early Tenth Century* (Oxford, 1958), and

Harry A. Wolfson's reply to Altmann's reading of Israeli: "The Meaning of *Ex nihilo* in Isaac Israeli," *Jewish Quarterly Review* 50 (1959): 1–12 (reprinted in I. Twersky, ed., *Studies in the History of Philosophy and Religion* [Cambridge, Mass., 1973], vol. 1, pp. 222–23). See also Altmann, "Isaac Israeli's 'Chapter on the Elements' (Ms Mantua)," *Journal of Jewish Studies* 7 (1956): 31–57. In "Creation and Emanation in Isaac Israeli: A Reappraisal" (*Essays in Jewish Intellectual History* [Hanover, N.H., 1981]), Altmann maintains his position. Also relevant here is S. M. Stern, "Ibn Hasday's Neoplatonist: A Neoplatonic Treatise and Its Influence on Isaac Israeli and the Longer Version of the Theology of Aristotle," *Oriens* 13–14 (1961): 58–120.

72. See Judah Halevi's critique of the Neoplatonic and Aristotelian position in *Kuzari* II, sec. 6.

73. *Rasâ'il Ikhwân al-Sufâ'* (Beirut, 1957), vol. 1, p. 338; but see also the ambiguous analysis in vol. 3, p. 518.

74. I use this locution in light of A. H. Armstrong's reminder: "Though this production or giving out is necessary in the sense that it cannot be conceived as not happening, or as happening otherwise, it is also entirely spontaneous: there is no room for any binding or constraint, internal or external, in the thought of Plotinus about the One. The One is not bound by necessity; it establishes it. Its production is simply the overflow of its superabundant life, the consequence of its unbounded perfection" (*Cambridge History of Later Greek and Early Medieval Philosophy* [Cambridge, 1967], p. 241).

75. Solomon Ibn Gabirol, *Fons Vitae*, pt. V, sec. 41, in Altmann, "Creation and Emanation in Isaac Israeli," p. 33, n. 25.

76. For further comment on the theme of voluntarism in Gabirol, see Julius Guttmann, *Philosophies of Judaism* (New York, 1964), pp. 116–17, and the sources cited by Guttmann in his important footnote on this issue (pp. 485–87, n. 65).

77. Plotinus, *Enneads* bk. V, tractate 4.2, quoted in Altmann, "Creation and Emanation in Isaac Israeli," p. 24; cf. V.3.12.40; V.1.6; V.3.16.

78. John Rist, *Plotinus: The Road to Reality* (Cambridge, 1967), p. 27. Rist proposes that VI.8.19 is meant to "deter the reader from supposing there is any necessary production of the hypostases." Even recognizing the nuances introduced by Armstrong, I find Rist's position extreme, not allowing sufficient weight to Plotinus's "inevitability."

79. Details of Luria's immensely influential teachings can be found in Scholem, *Major Trends in Jewish Mysticism*, pp. 244–86.

80. *Tikkunei Zohar*, end of *Tikkun* 22.

81. See, for example, Proclus, *Elements of Theology*, prop. 7.

82. Philo, *De Posteritate Caini* 48, p. 169.

83. Plotinus, *Enneads*, bk. V, tractate 2.1, trans. Stephen McKenna (London, 1917-1930).

84. Plotinus, *Enneads*, bk. V, tractate 5.5.

85. Azriel of Gerona, *Perush Eser Sefirot*, "Explanation of the Ten Sefirot," found as a prolegomenon to Meir Ibn Gabbai, *Sefer Derekh Emunah* (Warsaw, 1850), pp. 3-9.

86. Scholem, *Kabbalah*, p. 98.

87. *Zohar* I, 241a.

88. Moses de Leon, *Sefer Ha-Rimmon*, quoted in Scholem, *Major Trends in Jewish Mysticism*, pp. 223, 402, n. 4. This work has been critically edited by Elliot Wolfson (Ph.D diss., Brandeis University, 1986).

89. For more on the concept of *devekut*, see Scholem, *Major Trends in Jewish Mysticism*, and Gershom Scholem, "Devekuth," in *The Messianic Idea in Judaism* (New York, 1972), pp. 203-36. For additional material of importance and a disagreement with Scholem's view, consult Isaiah Tishby, *Mishnat Ha-Zohar* (in Hebrew) (Jerusalem, 1961), vol. 2, pp. 301-6 — now available in an excellent English translation: *The Wisdom of the Zohar*, ed. David Goldstein (Oxford, 1989), vol. 3, pp. 994-98 — and Moshe Idel and Bernard McGinn, eds., *Mystical Union and Monotheistic Faith, an Ecumenical Dialogue* (New York, 1989).

90. Another kabbalistic term for the *Eyn Sof* that literally means "Nothingness," though, as noted above, this Nothingness carries a positive metaphysical status. A fuller discussion of the notion of *Ayin* can be found in Daniel Matt, "Ayin: The Concept of Nothingness in Jewish Mysticism," in Foreman, ed., *Problem of Pure Consciousness*, pp. 121-59.

2

Reification of Language in Jewish Mysticism

MOSHE IDEL

At the beginning of the nineteenth century, Rabbi Moses Eliaqim Beriah, the son of the famous Maggid of Kuznitz, started his commentary on the Pentateuch as follows:

> *Bereshit Bara* ect.[1] It is said in the *Tiqqunim*:[2] [the word] *Bereshit* [is composed of] *Beit Rosh* [House Head] and it seems that this may be explained on the basis of the verse "The stone rejected by the builders, is the selfsame stone that was the cornerstone."[3] It is because it is written in *Sefer Yeẓirah* [*Book of Creation*] that the letters are called stones and the words are called houses.[4] And the person who approaches the [study of] Torah and prayer,[5] ought to build a house, which is the combinations of letters, filled by illumination and perfection [and] to prepare a Tabernacle[6] for God, Blessed be He, to dwell there in those words of the prayer. This is the meaning [of the verse] "The stone rejected by the builders," namely the letters, whom the builders, that are the persons who pray, despise them; "This selfsame stone will become a cornerstone."[7] Those letters that were at the beginning of the creation, God, Blessed be He and His name, . . . He created by them heaven and earth and all their hosts. This is the meaning of the cornerstone, namely [it is] the beginning of the creation of the world, at the moment God turned to this world in order to create it. And the [main] purpose is to reach this level, by his cleaving to the supernal worlds, and thereby he is worthy to

pronounce [his] speech before God in a perfect way and full of illumination. This is the intention of the *Tiqqunim* by positing the combination of letters *House Head*, namely to make a house to the Head that is God, Blessed be He and His name, [so] that He may dwell in the words and the speeches of his Torah and his prayer.[8]

In creation and in ritual, the Hebrew language was considered by Jewish mystics as playing a role much more important than the common communicative one that language regularly plays. It was the main instrument of the creation of the world, and it is the vessel that is prepared by man to contain the divine light that is attracted therein in order to experience an act of union or communion. In both cases, the letters do not serve, in any way, as a channel of transmitting meaning; too powerful an instrument, the letters are conceived of as creative elements that enable different types of communication, averbal ones, that accomplish much more than merely conveying certain trivial information. Letters are regarded as stones, as full-fledged entities, as components intended to build up an edifice of words to serve as a temple for God and a place of encountering Him for the mystic. After the Temple was destroyed, it was prayer that replaced the sacrifices; according to some important conceptions of Jewish mysticism, Jews constantly rebuild the Temple by their daily prayer and study of the Torah, when performed properly.[9] As God was able to create a world by means of letters, man is supposed to rebuild the Temple in his ritual usage of language.[10] Initially intended to be performed in the Temple, the ritual is now conceived by Jewish mystics as a means to supply a surrogate for it, in order to reestablish the link with the divine. The "masonic" aspects of the divine and the human activity reveal a hidden and mighty dimension of the Hebrew letters that underlies their mystical conceptions. The letters are understood to constitute a mesocosmos that enables operations that can bridge the gap between the human—or the material—and the divine.[11]

The sermon of Rabbi Moses Eliaqim is far from exceptional; in my opinion, it is a concise and dense presentation of the common eighteenth-century Hasidic understanding of language, cultivated by this important segment of mystical Judaism. In the following pages, I shall survey the basic understandings of language that culminated in the Hasidic mystical attitude toward language. Mystical interpretations of language are functions of the major mystical interests of the comprehensive system that generate them. Jewish mysticism offers a series of different conceptions of language that correspond to the mystical foci that dominated its various trends. I propose to distinguish between four basic views of language:

1. Language was regarded as instrumental in the process of the creation of the world and as a natural component of reality. This emphasis on the constitutive nature of language is widespread in all forms of Jewish mysticism.
2. Language and its elements reflect, according to another important kabbalistic view, the divine structure by way of symbolism and by virtue of an organic link between the symbol and the object it symbolizes. Consequently, the mystic is able to affect the divine structure by the proper use of language. This approach is characteristic of the theosophical–theurgical Kabbalah, as represented in the *Zohar* and Lurianic Kabbalah. Although this view is dominant in these bodies of literature, traces are to be found also in eighteenth-century Hasidic mysticism.
3. Language, especially its discrete components, is considered to be a technique to attain a mystical experience. This instrumental concept of language is characteristic of those types of Jewish mysticism that focused on ecstatic experiences as an important religious ideal, such as the medieval ecstatic Kabbalah and late Polish Hasidism.
4. Finally, language is considered to be a means by which one can attract or capture the divine in the lower world. This "talismatic" conception has obvious affinities with some aspects of medieval Arabic magic, which entered Kabbalah in fourteenth-century Spain, became important in Cordoverean Kabbalah in Safed, and played a paramount role in Hasidic mysticism.

An obvious common denominator of views 1, 2, and 4 is the assumption that a unique plane exists where language plays a role different from the conventional one it usually plays in ordinary communication. Beyond its informative function, a certain degree of independent reality of language is surmised, this extraordinary level of existence serving variegated purposes. In other words, language is ontologized as a preliminary assumption that it can fulfill the purposes posited by the different types of Jewish mysticism. Implicitly, and sometimes explicitly, the ontologized or "reified" conception of language appears also in view 3—overtly in the Hasidic type[12]—and eventually also in ecstatic Kabbalah,[13] as will soon become clear. Therefore, we may regard Jewish mysticism as viewing language as a reality in itself, generally fraught with divine features, bridging the gap between the corporeal—or the human—plane and the divine plane. We shall first survey these four views and afterward address some related issues.

Letters: The Constitutive Elements of Creation

The biblical conception of creation is commonly described as the *fiat* concept; the major instrument of this alleged biblical view is, according to the *fiat* manner of creation, the divine speech, which calls into being those entities whose names were pronounced *in illo tempore*. A reading of Genesis, however, complicates this simplistic description. The first act of creation is mentioned before any speech of God is related; after the mentioning of creation, it is not self-evident whether each particular speech innovates the particular thing it is related to *ex nihilo* or causes a distinction in the chaotic mass, organizing the particular entity according to the specific structure intended by the divine. It seems that, much more than creating, speech functions in the biblical account of creation as an organizing factor, imposing division and orderliness on chaos.[14]

The Talmudic–Midrashic literature offers several different ways of understanding the biblical account. One of them, possibly influenced by Platonic thought, portrays God as consulting Torah as an architectonic model and creating the world according to its pattern. The universe of language, as it was preestablished in the sacrosanct structure of the canon, is the blueprint of the material cosmos. The peculiar arrangement of the linguistic material in the Torah is apparently regarded as compulsory for God Himself. He merely enacts, on another plane and using other material, the content of a preexistent Torah. I would like to emphasize the fact that, according to this view, creation is an act of imposing the inner structure of the Torah on an undefined material. What seems to be absent from this description is the conception that letters are the raw material out of which the world is going to be created. Its hylic material is not specified, and its "form," to speak in Aristotelian terms, is the language as embodied in the Torah. Interestingly, this presentation of the creation did not specify whether the contemplation of the Torah by God was accompanied by a pronunciation of its content as part of creation. This way of describing the creative process envisions Torah as the paradigm and is especially important for understanding the paramount centrality of Torah in Judaism, more specifically its commandments, whose performance is regarded as safeguarding the existence of heaven and earth.[15]

Another version of creation connected to language is expressed, tangentially, in a well-known statement, of utmost importance for our further discussion, according to which Bezalel created the Tabernacle using his knowledge of the way heaven and earth were created by the combination of letters.[16] According to this interpretation of the Talmudic statement, Bezalel was cognizant of this peculiar method of creation—the technique of combination of letters, rather than letters used as raw material—as implied in the interpretation proposed by Scholem.[17] Depicted as the paragon of Jewish artisans, Bezalel was described as uniquely wise, being in the shadow of God. His knowledge of the divine device, based on linguistic technique, enabled him to create the Tabernacle, which is considered second only to the creation of God. The exceptional wisdom of the builder of the Temple, Solomon, is well known; however, even he is not described as being in possession of the combinatory practice that served God. It is important to remark that in this description of creation, it is not clear whether God or Bezalel pronounced the peculiar combination of letters that was involved in the creational process.

The third Midrashic theory regarding linguistic creation depicts God as using divine names. According to one version, He used the letters that form His name in order to create heaven and other letters in order to create earth.[18] Again, it would be unreasonable to assume that these letters entered into the physical constitution of the creation; they are, apparently, the creative forces that served God, rather than the basic elements of the universe. Also, in this description the pronunciation of the divine name is not implied.

The next important theory of linguistic creation, seemingly the most influential one, argues that the actual pronunciation of the creational words, mentioned in Genesis 1, explains the account of creation.[19] God is sometimes referred to as "He who spoke and the world came to being." The authors of this view identify in Genesis 1 ten creative words, designated as *ma'amarot*. Interesting mystical speculations stemming from this assumption were to emerge later in a long series of Jewish mystical sources.[20]

However, the crucial formulation of the linguistic creation that served as the cornerstone of medieval linguistic mysticism in Judaism is to be found in a short treatise that is not part of the classical Talmudic–Midrashic literature. It is *Sefer Yeẓirah* (*Book of Creation*), which contributed the theory that the letters of the Hebrew alphabet entered the process of creation not only as creative forces but also as the elements of its material structure.[21] Language, according to this theory, was considered not only the archetype of the world but also its stuff. Another cardinal topic that occurs only in this version of linguistic creation is the description of the formation of the letters of the alphabets from the second *Sefirah*, the pneuma, out of which God has carved the alphabet. After the completion of the twenty-two letters, God combined them in all possible permutations of two letters, as part of the creational process. There is no mention of the Torah as the archetype, nor are the divine names crucial for the understanding of the process of creation in the *Book of Creation*. It is noteworthy that this theory, which focuses on letters and their combinations rather than on the Torah and the divine names, occurs in a work that was composed outside the literary genres characteristic of the Halakic–Midrashic writings. The emphasis on the combinatory theory, which is only hinted at in the Talmudic passage on Bezalel, assumes a certain freedom in the usage of the letters, which are not seen as forming the fixed and sacred combination of the letters in the canonic Torah. Now God is not copying the content of the Torah, transposing it on another plane, but is creating freely. No wonder that this treatise does not touch the topic of commandments; the common Jewish religious concepts are rather marginal in comparison with the cosmogonical elements that pervade the entire book.[22]

I described the various versions of the ancient Jewish views of linguistic creation in order to allow a phenomenology of the role of language; when fixed in the specific structures of the Torah and the divine name, the archetypal role is central and a certain axiology, mostly a religious one, is involved. However, when the letters are mentioned as separate entities, as in the *Book of Creation*, the focus is a certain type of anomic knowledge, a certain type of gnosis that exposes the primordial processes.

In the first type of using language, the difference between the creator and the created is implicit. God transcends the material world, which emerges by an act that is basically different from the nature of the creature. No so in the type of creation as proposed by the *Book of Creation*: the letters enter the constitution of the world and became part of its fabric; God himself is portrayed as immersed in the process of creating the letters and in arranging them in the specific permutations that are the source of each and every created entity. The interest in the specific relationship between each letter and the peculiar astronomical, temporal, and human domain on which it is appointed, so characteristic of the *Book of Creation*,[23] contributed greatly to the process of atomization of language that became manifest in the later stages of Jewish mysticism. Regression—or, if we want, return—from the informative to the magical and mythic nature of language is triggered by the focusing of interest on the single letter as a topic in itself.

Finally, another way of understanding the nature of language, which includes elements central in the two models mentioned above, is to be found in the literature of the *Hekhalot* or the *Merkavah*. This ancient Jewish body of literature contributes the theory that the Torah, the divine names, and the alphabet in general are existing, apparently even preexisting, in the divine world as part of the divine retinue, sometimes even as inscribed on the divine body.[24] In one particular instance, God is described as comprised in His name, and His name as being in Him.[25] Angels are viewed as linguistic entities,[26] the divine names being described as having huge dimensions.[27] In one of the most important treatises of this literature, each and every letter is a divine name in itself,[28] a view that had substantial reverberations in later Jewish mysticism; combined with the *Sefer Yeẓirah* emphasis on the peculiar nature of individual letters in the creational process, the view of the *Hekhalot* literature provides an important element to the magical understanding of the nature of the Hebrew language. According to a recent study, the *Hekhalot* literature includes a theology of the divine names that can be arranged hierarchically so as to provide a relatively coherent scheme. The divine pleroma has, according to this theology, conspicuous linguistic characteristics, a fact that considerably reduces the distance between the creator and the creature, their common denominator being the elements of the Hebrew language.[29]

A primary typology of the various understandings of the creative functions of language seems to emerge from this discussion; letters were seen as energy that may directly trigger the creation when they are pronounced by God, or in their arrangement as Torah, they constitute archetypes of creation. It seems that only in the *Book of Creation* are the letters explicitly considered as the components of the created world.

All the later conceptions of the mystical nature of language are the offshoots of one of these views or a mixture of the various mystical interests presented in some of them.

Language in Theosophical Kabbalah

In the mainstream of Kabbalah, the theosophical-theurgical one, the graphic facet of the letters is considered to symbolize the configuration of the divine attributes, the *Sefirot*. According to a late-thirteenth-century kabbalist:

> All the letters of the Torah by their shapes, combined and separated, swallowed letters, curved ones and crooked ones, superfluous and elliptic ones, minutes and large ones, and inverted, the calligraphy of the letters, the open and closed pericopes and the ordered ones — all of them are the shape of God, Blessed be He.[30]

No wonder that this kabbalist, explicitly referring to the Torah as the picture of the divine, considered any alteration of the shapes of letters in the Torah as distorting the divine image. Another kabbalist in his entourage envisioned the study of the Torah as a way to know the "Supernal Form."[31] What transpires from these views is the paramount importance of the visual facet of the alphabet and the special arrangement of the letters in the scroll of the Torah. The encounter with the text consists of not only a study of its meaning, or even infinite meanings, but also a contemplation of its peculiar formal structure. We are here at the verge of the symbolic conception of a text, or of written language, and at the beginning of the hierogrammatic perception of letters as directly conveying a certain type of content by their very forms. The distance between the symbol and its *signatum* is substantially reduced, if not completely effaced. As Umberto Eco aptly described "the Kabbalistic drift": "Language can be the place where things come authentically to begin: in Heidegger's hermeneutics the word is not 'sign' (Zeichen) but 'to show' (Zeigen)."[32] By this reification of letters, a "deification" of their status is attained.

The previous stand represents a basic conception of theosophical Kabbalah regarding language; Hebrew letters, mainly their visual form, constitute the image of the divine, and this feature bestows, according to the kabbalists, a unique character of holiness on Hebrew texts in general. On this assumption, in the middle of the fourteenth century an anonymous kabbalist composed a classic of kabbalistic literature, *Sefer ha-Temunah* (*Book of the Image*), a treatise devoted to a detailed explanation of the theosophical significances of the forms of each and every letter;[33] all of them were considered to constitute the image of one of the ten *Sefirot*.

The conception of language that dominates the theosophical-theurgical Kabbalah is reminiscent of Platonic thought; both consider the ideal source to be the higher world, whence everything comes down. Indeed, this resemblance indicates a certain historical affinity, which nevertheless seems to be limited. Although language is considered as descending from the high and therefore as having some natural connection with its source, in Kabbalah the function of language differs from what we may have expected in a strictly Platonic universe of discourse. Platonic ideas are conceived of as static entities, as archetypes that, according to Neoplatonic theories, emanate from the lower entities; although the *nexus* between cause and effect does not disappear during the emanative process, the possibility that the lower entity will affect the higher one is not accepted by Platonic or Neoplatonic thinkers.[34] However, according to kabbalistic theosophy, the Sefirotic realm is dynamic, its dynamism prone to being influenced by the deeds of men in the mundane world. Language, as an emanated entity and at the same time as a kind of human activity, was regarded by kabbalists as a major instrument man can use in order to affect the divine. Because of the correspondence of the various components of language with the supernal powers, the proper use of language may effectively change the processes taking place on high. Consequently, we may define the main function of language in this type of Kabbalah as theurgical; its components reflect the supernal domain while affecting those elements. This impact can be regarded as linguistic theurgy. Basically, the facets of language do not differ from any other entity in the world, all of them being emanated, but due to the flexibility of this medium, and the easy way it may be used by the expert, it represents an appropriate means of exercising an influence above. Let me adduce one instructive passage illustrating this approach to language. According to the sixteenth-century Safedian kabbalist Rabbi Moses Cordovero:

> There is no doubt that the letters that compose each and every pericope of the pericopes of the Torah, and every *Gemara* and chapter [*Pereq*] someone is studying, which concern a certain *Miẓwah*, have a spiritual reality which ascends and clings to the branches of this sefirah, namely that [peculiar] sefirah that hints to that *Miẓwah*, and when the person studies the [corresponding] *Miẓwah* or the chapter or the pericope or the verse those letters will move and stir on the high, on this reality [*Meẓiut*], by the means of a "voice" and a "speech," which are *Tiferet* and *Malkhut* and *Maḥashavah* and *Re'uta deLibba*[35] . . . since *Maḥashavah* and *Re'uta deLibba* are like a soul to the "speech" and to the "voice," which are the [lower] soul [*Nefesh*] and the spirit [*Ruaḥ*]. And behold, the voices and the realities of the letters [produced by] the twist of the lips bestow on them a certain act and movement [like that] of a body. And the reality of the letters ascends and it is found everywhere on the way of their ascent from one aspect[36] to another, following the way of the [descending] emanation from one stage to another.[37]

This kabbalistic master presents a comprehensive theory that involves the letters and voices together with their sources in the lower domain of the Sefirotic realm, *Tiferet* and *Malkhut*, and their supernal sources, two higher *Sefirot*, *Maḥashavah* and *Re'uta deLibba*. On the psychological level, they correspond to the two lower spiritual functions. This concatenation of the psychological and linguistic Sefirotic conceptions explains, according to Cordovero, the possibility of affecting the higher *Sefirot* by the ascending letters. This dynamism of the letters—that is, their ascending capacity and the impact they may have on the various *Sefirot*—stems from the impetus conferred by human thought and will, which correspond to divine thought and will. Intentional speech is an ascending human creation complementing the descending divine speech.[38] Although in these instances there is no reason to speak about a dialogue in the Buberian manner, basically here is a dialectic of the relationship between the human and the divine, language serving as a major vehicle, though in some instances only as a metaphor. I would like to emphasize this quality of language because it seems to complement, and perhaps also modify, the way Scholem presented the kabbalistic conception of mystical language as especially focused on nouns. Although in theosophical Kabbalah words and letters do function as symbols, and therefore as nouns, it is their dynamic, flexible quality that is basically significant for the way kabbalists understand the role of language.[39] If theosophy contributed to the transformation of language into a body of symbols, it is the theurgical aspect of Kabbalah that changed these symbols into living entities, which possess specific qualities beyond that of representing the higher realities.

As an extension of the divine in the world, a way for man to return to the divine, and a major constituent of the mystical path, language, according to theosophical Kabbalah, encapsulates the role of the instrument. At the same time, it embodies the purpose of the mystical quest, the infinite light that, according to Hasidic texts, dwells in the linguistic material.

Language in Ecstatic Kabbalah and Hasidism

The vocal aspect of language is a vital component of the mystical technique cultivated in the ecstatic Kabbalah. Rabbi Abraham Abulafia, the major exponent of this brand of Jewish mysticism, emphatically distinguishes his type of Kabbalah from the more common one, the Sefirotic Kabbalah, exactly on this ground. The other kabbalists, he assesses,[40] are undergoing experiences of light, sent down by the divinity, whereas his own Kabbalah is based on the hearing of "speech"—that is, primeval speech—that would be identified by Abulafia with the Agent Intellect of medieval Aristotelianism. The ecstatic kabbalists use linguistic devices, pronunciation of the divine names, in order to attain a basically acoustic experience.[41] The affinity between the technique and the results in both Sefirotic and the ecstatic Kabbalah is obvious. According to the former, a major concern of the kabbalists is the nature of the revealed aspect of the Divinity, the Sefirotic realm; this realm is reflected in the type of experience they underwent, since the light that descends on the mystic is to be related to the ten *Sefirot* understood as translucent or illuminating entities.[42] The ecstatic kabbalist was interested, from the very beginning, in a more linguistic subject—the divine names—and, as a result, the nature of the experience is related to the nature of the concern and of the technique appropriate to this type of experience. This difference splits the techniques used by those two types of Kabbalah and the results of those techniques, and it is one of the most basic distinctions between the two major brands of Kabbalah. Indeed, Abulafia seems to be the only kabbalist who formulated all the "principles" of Kabbalah in linguistic terminology; his Kabbalah was described as the Kabbalah of Names, and its three principles are "letters," their "combinations" (*zerufei 'otiot*), and the vowels (*neqqudot*) that are seen as causing the movement of the combinations of letters, which are, actually, purely consonants.[43] This brief description of the "divine Kabbalah" evinces the distinctive linguistic feature of the ecstatic Kabbalah in comparison with the Sefirotic one, which seems to emphasize more the meaning of the words as they appear in the canonic text rather than the free, associative combination of letters cultivated by ecstatic Kabbalah. This is not the place to describe the details of the mystical techniques used by Abulafia in order to reach a mystical experience; such a description appears elsewhere.[44] However, the historical dimension of the practice proposed by Abulafia requires consideration.

The attempt to cultivate a vocal technique and to strive for an auditive response from the divine, or from the Agent Intellect, seems to be a continuation of earlier types of Jewish mysticism—such as the *Hekhalot* literature and Ashkenazi Hasidism, which were more interested in achieving mystical experience than in making theosophical speculations.[45] Therefore, the vocal aspect of language in Jewish mysticism apparently enjoyed a long history, in conspicuous distinction from the more visual type of mysticism that, ancient as it is in, for example, the Ezekiel vision, seems to move to the center for a rather shorter period with the emergence of the Sefirotic Kabbalah. If the emanational theories were pernicious for the development of Jewish mysticism, as Scholem noted,[46] it is vocal mysticism that enabled Jewish mystics to experience revelations, in addition to visions; vocal techniques were instrumental in allowing mystics to receive prophetic messages instead of contemplating the theosophical structures, using techniques centered on the *Sefirot*. As an alternative to the emanational system that centers on metaphysical questions regarding the nature of the *Sefirot*, the ecstatic Kabbalah is much more involved in experience than in the mythology of the divine powers; thus the latter may rescue Kabbalah from the pit of Neoplatonization, which may ontologize, and has ontologized, the theological concepts by projecting them onto the Sefirotic firmament.

Indeed, an important characteristic of the ecstatic Kabbalah and the eighteenth-century Polish Hasidic conceptions of language is the emphasis they put on the emitting aspect of the letters, which is comparable to their concern about the auditory aspect of their mystical conception of language. Generating sounds is considered as important as hearing, and I include in this category even the phenomena of auditory revelations. In the case of Abraham Abulafia, as in those of some other Jewish mystics, mostly in the Maggidic tradition—those mystical phenomena in Kabbalah where the source of inspiration is an angelic mentor[47]—the mystic himself is articulating not only those linguistic elements that form his mystical techniques, but also the linguistic revelations he strives to attain. Although these phenomena have several features in common with automatic speech, it seems that not every instance of revealing through the voice of the mystic is easily reducible to automatism. In the case of pronouncing the sounds that are part of the techniques, we witness a mystical interpretation of a Halakic requirement; according to the Talmudic view, the words of the regular prayers have to be pronounced in a distinct way, so as not to reduce prayer to a mental activity. This basic assumption reverberates in the Hasidic conception of the mysticism of language, barring the mentalistic possibilities that characterize some Jewish mystical phenomena and some non-Jewish types of mystical prayer.

The previous remarks open the way to a comparison between

the positive attitude of Jewish mysticism toward language and the negative conception of language in Christian mysticism. It is language, or languages, that are to be surpassed in order to reach the acme of mysticism, according to a highly influential statement of Saint Augustine.[48] The mentalistic and introvert mood that characterizes nonlinguistic mystical experiences seems to be exceptional in Judaism. Conceiving Hebrew as the perfect and the divine language, there was no reason to attempt to transcend, attenuate, or obliterate its use. "Generating" Hebrew was understood by some kabbalists and by most of the Hasidic masters not as a hindrance but as a mode of *imitatio Dei*, an assimilation to the divine activity and thus coming closer to Him.[49] If language is the main way to bridge the gap, or to communicate between God and man, it is the same vehicle that enables man to restore the connection with the divine. Although the Hasidic mystical theologies still indicate the superior state of the "World of Thought" as higher than the "World of Language," both designating divine universes, it is the latter that constitutes the main scene of activity of these mystics.[50] Let me present one example of this bridging the gap between God and man by means of language:

> In the Chapters of *Hekhalot*[51] it is written that when God dwells upon the throne, a fire of silence falls upon the heavenly beings [ḥayot]. It means that when God dwells upon the speeches [of prayer] then a silent fire falls upon the vitality [ḥiyut] of man, namely a great awe . . . and he does not know where he is, and he does not see and he does not hear since the power of [his] corporeality was obliterated. And its meaning is that happy is the king who is praised in his house, so that the body of man will become the house of God, since it is incumbent upon man to pray with all his power so that his corporeality will be obliterated, and he will forget himself. . . . [A]ll this happens in the flash of an instant, as he is in the state of *devequt*, beyond the world of time.[52]

The concentrated articulation of the words of prayer causes an anesthetic experience, an experience of union during which man transcends time and bridges the distance between God and humanity. Words become the throne on which the deity dwells, ensuring the closest contact between the two entities.

Moreover, the importance of the emission of sounds even at the revelatory level of mysticism implies an activist attitude that is still maintained when the technical stage has been surpassed. This is obvious in the ecstatic Kabbalah, when the mystic, as part of the revelatory process, is supposed to answer the questions he himself was interested in. Language becomes the instrument of a dialogue, or we may even regard it as a monologue, where the human throat is playing the role of both the human and the divine speakers. In the case of some Hasidic types of linguistic mysticism, the emission of the sounds is considered as creating the vessels wherein the divine influx dwells, or wherein it was attracted, and therefore enables the union or the communion with the "light of the infinite"[53] here "below." Whereas the ecstatic Kabbalah implies a two-stage linguistic process, the technical and the revelatory, Hasidic linguistics views the mystical phenomena as taking place during the same linguistic process that is part of ritualistic prayer. In other words, the Hasidic mystic is not so much interested in a dialogic situation, as Buber argued, as in a one-stage process that induces the divine into the humanly created sounds, resulting in *devekut*. Strangely enough, Kabbalah, which was regarded by Buber as a nondialogic type of mysticism,[54] seems to supply examples of stances where dialogue seems to be more manifest than in Hasidic mysticism.

Oral language in the Hasidic milieu became important precisely because the mystical teachings were transmitted directly by the master to the community or by the master to the disciples, who were supposed to attend the sermons or the lessons of the spiritual leader. But during most of the period when Kabbalah was creative, the few kabbalists were dispersed in several distant centers; living far from one another, they were obliged to communicate and transmit their teachings in ways different from those of the masses of Hasidim, who frequently gathered around their *Ẓaddiq* in order to hear his speeches. Moreover, the complex theosophical theories of the kabbalists could be better communicated in written form, which allowed the perusal necessary for the digestion of their complexities, whereas the more simple Hasidic teachings could be absorbed when attending a sermon of the *Ẓaddiq*. Therefore, the turn from the higher evaluation of the written language to the oral one is also the result of a deep sociological restructuring of the European segment of Jewish mysticism, which implies also a reevaluation of the already existing theories, preferring the ecstatic Kabbalah over the theosophical Kabbalah as far as their conception of language is concerned. Let me turn now to the last of the important views of language in Jewish mysticism, which indeed emphasized the centrality of the articulated form of the letters.

The Talismatic Conception of Language

Language was, finally, conceived to be not only an important avenue of expression, a great symbol, an instrument of creation, but also a talismatic entity. In several kabbalistic sources in the medieval Spanish Kabbalah, the Hebrew letters were understood to be vessels into which the divine influx could be captured and used in a certain way. Basically, it is a magical perception of language, more accurately of its components, the pronounced letters. Although similar to the Hermetic and Neoplatonic magic of late antiquity,[55] language, as envisioned by the fifteenth-century kabbalists, was a self-sufficient instrument that could be influential even without adding the complementary rites and materials that are characteristic of pagan magic.[56] The development of this talismatic interpretation of language is a very complex one, and it cannot be described in this context; I would like to mention here only the most important stages of this approach to language and offer some examples.

The first clear-cut instance of this understanding of language occurs in the writings of an early-fifteenth-century Spanish kabbalist, Rabbi Shem Tov ben Shem Tov. In his *Sefer ha-Emunot*, a work ignored by the fifteenth-century Kabbalah but important in the sixteenth century, Shem Tov indicates that voice letters were formed from Moses and that these letters "are like a body to the inner, spiritual and holy intellects, the names of God, which are like drawing deep waters by means of a vessel: so was Moses drawing by his form [*zurato*], by the means of that voice, the innerness of the intellects . . . the building of the letters, which are vessels of the inner intellects."[57]

Under the influence of this work, some Safedian kabbalists elaborated on Shem Tov's conception, the most important of them being Rabbi Moses Cordovero. In a highly influential compendium of Kabbalah, *Pardes Rimmonim*, Cordovero asserts that "the prayer using mystical intentions [*Kavvanah*] has to draw the spiritual force from the supernal level downwards into the letters he [the prayer] is pronouncing so as to be able to elevate those letters up to the supernal level, in order to fasten his request."[58]

Cordovero describes the letters as containers of the influx attracted from above by the mystical intention of the prayer, this attraction enabling the ascent of the letters to their source on high, in order to attain his request. Here letters are regarded as vehicles of the intention of the mystic, who is able to infuse in them the supernal force. Since the propagation of the Cordoverian Kabbalah, mostly through the printing of *Pardes Rimmonim* with it commentaries, and indirectly by the books of Cordovero's disciples, the talismatic conception of language became widespread, its most important impact being the Hasidic conception of letters as "palaces"—that is, "places"—where the mystic who pronounces the holy sounds thereby captures the divine presence.[59]

At the end of the fifteenth century, seemingly without any direct relation to *Sefer ha-Emunot*, the same view is found in the writings of Rabbi Yohanan Alemanno, a Renaissance figure who expressed it several times in his works; one interesting example will suffice in order to demonstrate the affinity of Alemanno's views to that of the Spanish kabbalists. Speaking, like Cordovero later would, on prayer, the Italian kabbalist wrote on the prayer of the simpletons: "[These prayers] receive the influxes which descend onto them because of the existence of human voices, which are arranged [i.e., the letters] in such a manner, that they are worthy of receiving the influxes, which are ready to descend upon them, even if the performer does not prepare them with [the proper] intention."[60]

With Hasidism, the magical implications of this view were sometimes attenuated, though not totally obliterated. As a mystical means, language enables the Hasid to reach an experience of *devekut*, or communion, and sometimes even union, with the divine light that is present in the pronounced letters. According to a tradition in the name of the Besht, "the main purpose of the study of the Torah and of the prayer is to cleave to the innerness of the spiritual force[61] of the light of the *Eyn Sof*[62] which is in the pronounced letters of Torah and prayer."[63]

Language, in the form either of prayer or of the loud study of Torah, was transformed from an instrument for achieving a type of relationship to God in a personal way, as Buber would have us believe, into the main avenue for mystical experience.

Monadic and Emanative Conceptions of the Letters

Already in the ancient Jewish mystical sources we find the view that each and every letter is a divine name in itself.[64] This view was reiterated by a series of mystic authors throughout the Middle Ages, testifying thereby to its importance.[65] I would like to deal here with the kabbalistic metamorphosis of this view. According to one of the earliest kabbalists, the Provençal author Rabbi Isaac the Blind:

> In each of the letters all the [other] letters are [inherent]. However each of them has an essence of itself. And all the ten *sefirot* are [present] in each and every letter . . . since how may they be combined if each of them does not comprise everything; for example in *Alef* the first ten *sefirot* . . . and in each of them [there were] a resemblance of essences, fine and subtle, hidden and comprehending everything that will originate from them, there was there [just] as all the generations were in Adam. So was in each letter.[66]

The whole divine universe and all the future creations are present in each and every letter. Following the teaching of Rabbi Isaac, Rabbi Jacob ben Sheshet, a kabbalist from Catalonia, describes the letters as the archetypes of creation: "The essence of the letters is that they are the forms of all the creatures,[67] and there is no form which has not a likeness in the letters or in the combination of two or three of them or more."[68]

Ben Sheshet goes on to say that every letter hints at the divinity. The emergence of the letters is described by the kabbalists as an inner process in the divine pleroma, as part of the process of emanation, mostly the transition from the *Sefirah* of *Ḥokhmah* to that of *Binah*. Following this understanding of the divine revelation as the articulation of the inarticulated through the emergence of the letters, the same kabbalist proposes an interesting manner of imitating God. According to ben Sheshet, the Talmudic imperative to articulate the words of prayer is meaningless if its intention was merely to pronounce the words; God knows even the hidden things so He does not need the act of pronunciation in order to understand the intention of the prayer.[69] However, ben Sheshet continues, it is incumbent to worship God according to "what He is, namely to generate all the forms [*leẓayyer kol ha-ẓurot*], as it is written,[70] "There is no Rock like our Lord."[71]

According to this conception, the inner mental process, since it seems to be only a potential state, cannot be completed by the act of articulation. Language, that is to say, not only is a means of expression, an inferior form of externalized thought, as the medieval philosophers considered the relation between "inner speech" — reason — and "outer speech,"[72] but also is thought on its creative level. According to another statement of this kabbalist, letters contain everything that can be spoken of, since no issue can be expressed unless we use letters.[73] This assessment assumes that only the expression of thought, not thought itself, is dependent on the letters. This understanding of the language-thought relationship is evidently different from the expression Scholem gives to language as the "mother of thought."[74] On the contrary, as we shall see, thought finds its expression in the articulate language, envisioned as the lowest stage of the Sefirotic realm.

The aforementioned ideas, developed at the very beginning of the Kabbalah, have laid the foundation of the symbolic-monadic conception of letters as composing the whole reality. This is the reason for the appearance of a new literary genre, the mystical commentaries on the form of the letters, an endeavor to decode the theosophical significance of the letters. Beginning with the *Book of Bahir*,[75] and until the end of the thirteenth century, there are several commentaries on this issue that betray a profound interest in the hidden content of the letters.[76] In other words, the Hebrew letters were now seen as hierograms because of their intrinsic value, which transcends any communicative function characteristic of the regular function of letters.[77]

Following the emanational scheme of theosophical Kabbalah, the early kabbalists focused their discussions on the passage from the *Sefirah* of Ḥokhmah, the locus of the undifferentiated letters, to that of *Binah*, where the letters emerge as full-fledged entities. Indeed, this *Sefirah* is also symbolized by the symbol of language.[78] However, in the late thirteenth century, the kabbalists completed the description of the emanational process using linguistic symbolism. So, for example, Rabbi Moses de Leon, an important Castilian kabbalist, conceived by modern scholarship as the true author of the *Zohar*, envisaged the third *Sefirah* as the place of the expansion of hidden thought — in other words, the emanation of the *Sefirah* of Ḥokhmah[79] — but at the same time the *Sefirah* of *Binah* is considered to be a "great voice" (*Qol gadol*), which is—paradoxically enough—identical with the "subtle and inner voice" (*Qol Daq Penimi*) mentioned in the revelation to Isaiah.[80] *Binah* is the place of transition of thought into the very beginning of speech. The more articulated speech symbolizes, however, the subsequent stages of the Sefirotic world. According to de Leon, "the fine voice" is transformed into an audible entity as it descends from the third to the sixth *Sefirah*, that of *Tiferet*.[81] There alone the hidden thought begins its metamorphosis into an intelligible linguistic phenomenon. Although still meaningless, this voice is the substratum, or the hylic matter, of the speech itself, *Dibbur*, which is represented by the tenth *Sefirah*, *Malkhut*. Only with this last *Sefirah*, which completes the emanational process, is articulated speech generated.[82] The entire emanation takes place between "Thought" and "Speech." Whereas the starting point of emanation is the totally hidden realm, imperceptible even to human thought, the final point is the place where revelation takes place, where the distinct formulations emerge. This seems to be the significance of the correspondence of the level of the inarticulated voice, identical with the *Sefirah* of *Tiferet*, with the Written Torah, whereas Speech corresponds to the Oral Torah.[83] This later corpus is considered in Judaism as the most explicit form of revelation in comparison with the Written Torah, whose ultimate meaning is accessible solely through the agency of the Oral one. The superiority of the oral to the written, which reflects at the same time the superiority of the audible to the seen, is to be understood as refracting the needs of the mundane realm; on the supernal plane, the vision of the Torah is sometimes preferred as the most important one, as the mystical descriptions of Abraham Abulafia, Isaac of Acre, and Shem Tov ibn Gaon testify. Moses was portrayed as copying from a written book, the primordial Torah, which, as the Midrashic sources indicate, was the source of the contemplation by God when He created the world. Even higher is the primordial Torah as understood by the kabbalists, which is identical to the Divine wisdom and, as such, is an infinite entity.[84]

Human speech is considered to be the starting point of the mystical ascent; the journey to the occult is possible, a theosophical kabbalist would assert, only by understanding that Hebrew and its contents are expressions of the hidden entities. The mystic must, according to this type of mysticism, transcend articulated speech in order to reach the highest levels of the divine, but this fact does not imply a negative attitude toward language. Far from being the predecessors of Ludwig Wittgenstein's suggestion to transcend language, viewed as a ladder, the kabbalists considered their mystical contemplation as a recurring event, which must occur time and again with language, texts, and ritual as indispensable starting points. Although phenomenologically different from the ecstatic Kabbalah, the theosophical Kabbalah strives to surpass the common experience governed by informative language in favor of a monadic perception of letters, the ultimate meaning of which is the destruction of our language. The effort of the theosophical kabbalist to reach the level of the third *Sefirah*, where letters are stored as distinct entities, is similar to the technique employed in the ecstatic Kabbalah, where the final stage of dealing with language is the contemplation of single letters as worlds in themselves. Coming to that point, the kabbalist approaches the state of God who began the creational acts with distinct letters that entered a certain type of combination. Escaping the lower world is tantamount to the escape of the conventional usage of language that is representative of the articulated forms of existence.

According to Rabbi Abraham Adrutiel's *Avnei Zikkaron*,[85] a kabbalistic treatise compiled at the beginning of the sixteenth century in North Africa, each and every letter of the Tetragrammaton includes or hints at, or both things simultaneously, the names of several angels, which are specified in the discussions referring to the various *Sefirot*. The author, apparently following the views of the famous kabbalistic book *Brit Menuḥah*, put into practice the theory found in the ancient sources that each letter is a divine name, though he seemingly limited himself to the elaboration of the angelic names he could extract from the letters of the divine name alone.

Rabbi Menahem Mendel of Vitebsk, one of the most mystically adept masters of early Hasidism, combined Lurianic concepts with pre-Lurianic views in order to account for the appearance of the Hebrew language in the primeval processes of creation. He asserted that

> the totality of the *Ẓimẓum* is [formed of] the letters, and from my flesh I shall see God;[86] just as a person will contemplate at

the beginning of his thought, [and] it roams and does not rest at all, and the vitality [is running] in an intermittent manner, divesting itself from a form and assuming another, all [these forms] are the form[s] of the letters. Since it is impossible to grasp thought without letters, without them thought is simple, and in its great simplicity it is incomprehensible and it is not designatable as thought, [only] by the concentration of its simplicity does it divest a form and assume the form of other letters. Wisdom[87] is a crucible. Then he understands something by his understanding, and Knowledge[88] is revealed, which was hidden and it preponderates between Wisdom and Understanding. After the revelation [i.e., emergence] of Knowledge, the attributes of Love and Judgment[89] emerge. . . . [s]ince the quintessence of Knowledge is to preponderate and combine the two into one, this is the reason why Knowledge is referred to as the Holy Language, since it preponderates between Wisdom, which is called Holiness, and the preponderating entity is called Language.[90]

The appearance of articulate letters at the very first stage of intellection indicates the linguistic nature of any concrete mental activity. Only after the concretization of diffuse thought into forms — that is, letters — are the more advanced forms of apprehension possible. Then the vocal form of language appears, as the reference to language testifies.

Let us compare this basic view of language articulated by theosophical Kabbalah with that propounded by Lurianic Kabbalah. The Lurianic notion of contraction is applied here to the process of passing from the mental, prelinguistic stages to linguistic activity, the former being conditioned by the latter. At the same time, this process is presented as symbolizing the emanational event in the bosom of the Divinity, all the above concepts conspicuously indicating the gradual emanation of the *Sefirot* in the line presented by classical Kabbalah. However, in comparison with the text of Rabbi Jacob ben Sheshet, and with similar stands in the *Zohar*, the emergence of letters precedes the beginning of the emanational process; it is not merely one stage of it. Rabbi Menaham Mendel, using the Lurianic concept of *Zimzum* and the Sarugian concept of *Malbush* (the garment constituted by combinations of letters that precede emanation[91]), not only propels language to a higher ontological plane than classical Kabbalah, but also proposes a different psychology by elevating letters—in the vein Scholem envisioned the kabbalistic perception of language—to the level of the strictly necessary elements of any mental activity.

For reasons already noted in this essay, a turn from a preference for the written to the oral took place. One of the most articulate expressions of this shift was that of Rabbi Levi Isaac of Berditchev, who mentioned the classical kabbalistic works dealing with the forms of the letters, such as the anonymous book of *Temunah*, the views of Rabbi Isaac Luria, and even the view of the Besht, whose discussion of the mystical significance of the forms of letters is not explored in other sources. After listing this impressive array of authority regarding the mystical interpretations of the forms of the written letters, the Hasidic master indicates that

> it is known that there is an image of the letters as it appears in a book. And there is the language of the speaker, who speaks what is written in the book. And the image of the letters as written in the book is [tantamount] to the world of making, the world of nature since they have a limit and an image whereas the language of the speaker who speaks what it is written in the book, his very speech is spiritual, something that has no limit and it corresponds to the world of Thought.[92]

The axiological principle inherent in this description is clear to anyone cognizant of the kabbalistic and Hasidic ontology; the world of making is the lowest one in the hierarchy of the four worlds, whereas the world of thought is the highest one. Indetermination is the central characteristic of human speech in comparison with the limited nature of written expression. Speech is spiritual in comparison with the natural—that is, the material—world. It is possible that we witness here a conclusion drawn from the early kabbalistic description of the vowels as the spirit that dwells in the consonants.[93] If the consonants are the sole letters expressed in written form, the vowels are regularly not committed to writing. Implicitly, the vocalized version of the Bible was, however, considered by kabbalists like Rabbi Jacob ben Sheshet, Rabbi Joseph Gikatilla, and Rabbi Joseph of Hamadan as the articulated and therefore limited form of the Bible, whereas the unvocalized form of this book—the way in which it is written in the scrolls of the

Torah—was considered as the unlimited, actually the infinite form of the Bible.[94] It seems that the Hasidim regarded the articulated expression as more spiritual than—and therefore superior to—the written one.

I assume that there is a certain relationship between an elaborated theosophy, which consists of a complex hierarchy of divine powers, and the understanding of language that sees in language a series of symbolic meanings that relates each and every linguistic element to a specific aspect or level of the intradivine realm. However, the plethora of symbolic meanings that is characteristic of the theosophical-theurgical Kabbalah vanished in other types of Jewish mysticism that later emerged. To the extent that the theosophical system has lost its centrality or was, sometimes, totally obliterated, the symbolic feature of language became marginal. That is the case in ecstatic Kabbalah and in Hasidism, where language serves more as a ladder to reach the divine in a unitive experience and less to contemplate It or decode Its structure. Language, when retreating from its symbolic function in one brand of Kabbalah, commenced another career playing a more technical role, similar to the role language plays in Hindu and Muslim mysticism. The magical nature of language becomes more and more conspicuous as the divine realm becomes simpler: in ecstatic Kabbalah, the Aristotelian theology was dominant, this type of Kabbalah viewing God as the supreme intellect; in Hasidic mysticism, a more personal theological conception became prevalent, though some important features of the theosophical Kabbalah were still influential. As those types of theology came in lieu of the complex theosophy of the Sefirotic Kabbalah, it was natural to simplify the whole symbolic system that transformed the language of the sources in a radical way. The magical role of language is obvious, since it functioned not as a means of expressing the mystical experience of the mystics, but as a means of showing the way to attain such an experience. Language was conceived as a *preparatio experientis* rather than as its expression. Meaning, not only in its symbolic aspect but also in its common informative function, was attenuated as the discrete components of language were invested with a surplus of meaning. While the separate letters were more likely to be regarded as polivalent morphemes, interest in the entire word waned. In these types of theologies, the conventional or informative function of language disintegrated as individual letters were conceived of as monads consisting of an infinity of meanings.

The Ascent of Letters

A recurring idea in some ancient and medieval Jewish texts is that the words of prayer pronounced by the people of Israel are ascending on high and there are transformed by the angel Sandalfon into a crown of the Divinity.[95] This ascent is understood as embellishing the divine pleroma and confers on this ritual a peculiar importance as a theurgical operation, an act that affects the divine realm. Commonly, this view refers to entire words and reflects the desire to strengthen the importance of performing the prayers exactly as they are required by the liturgical canon.[96] According to medieval versions of this idea, mostly in Ashkenazi Hasidism, the divine name formed of forty-two letters takes the place of the words of prayer in the earlier texts.[97] The two versions, similar as they are, reflect differing spiritual concerns. According to the second view, what is portent is not the meaning of our acts—that is, the significance of our words—but the magical power inherent in the letters of the divine name.

With the emergence of Kabbalah, another possibility inherent in still more ancient views was exploited: the individual letters became the object of meditative activity. Although these letters are part of the canonic liturgy, kabbalistic prayer, according to several kabbalistic texts, has to concentrate on the symbolic meaning of each and every letter—that is, on the Sefirotic significance of a specific letter. Moreover, each letter is to be visualized in a certain color that corresponds to a Sefirotic force on high.[98] This concentration of the spiritual force of prayer gives a certain ontological status to the letter, which is conceived of as ascending to the divine world in the way Cordovero had already indicated. In other words, the pronunciation of the letter is to be accompanied by the production of the form of the letter in a certain color and the projection of this imaginary form into the divine realm. The view of the late-thirteenth-century kabbalists—who subscribed to the conception that mystical prayer involves visualization of the letters, mostly the Tetragrammaton, which subsequently will ascend to the divine realm—underwent an important change after the Safedian Kabbalah. Beginning with Cordovero, kabbalists began another mystical understanding of the ascent of the words of prayer on high. Although still accepting the visualization technique, Cordovero emphasized the importance of the vocal aspects of the letters of the prayers. By emitting the sounds of the word of prayer, the kabbalist attracts the supernal influx onto the material substratum created by the pronunciation of the letters. By the impetus of the spirituality of this influx, the words ascend to the *Merkavah* or, according to other texts, to the various Sefirotic stages, and they affect the transmission of the influx in accordance with the request of the prayer. Thus we witness a twofold motion caused by the generation of the vocal aspect of language: the first one is the quality inherent in the sounds to attract the flow descending from above. As mentioned earlier, words are viewed as temples or palaces where the divine power is supposed to come to dwell. The second move is the ascending one, the elevation of the sounds by the force of the divine that has descended. Finally, a third motion, now independent of language, is causing the channeling of the flow in accordance with the request of the prayer. In the first two stages, language functions as a material substratum that is transformed into an entity that affects the divine.

The implications of the shift from the emphasis on visualization to pronunciation are numerous, and they cannot be presented here. It is sufficient to mention the most important one, the possibility of presenting the mystical prayer as a desideratum for popular circles and not an esoteric technique practiced by the few—that is, by an elite. Indeed, it is this transformation that reinstaurated the importance of the vocal aspect of language—and not mental or imaginary constructs—as the center of mystical activity, thus enabling the dissemination of Hasidism as a mystical movement. Although this novel approach to prayer, and implicitly to the status of language, was initiated by Cordovero, it seems that the importance of the recitations of the divine names in ecstatic Kabbalah was instrumental in the formation of the new direction.[99] However, whereas Abulafia posited the vocal performance of the recitation on a level higher than the combination of the letters in written form, at the same time he posited the mental combination of the letters as higher than their combination orally. With Cordovero, the importance of the mental activity seems to have been attenuated in comparison to Abulafia, this attenuation affecting the subsequent development of Jewish mysticism. Language, in Abulafia's view, does not represent the divine graphically, as the classical kabbalists would assess, but is seen as the locus of the encounter between humanity and the divine. The descent of the divine presence facilitates also the mystical contact with the divine.[100] *Devequt*, the experience of communion or union with the divine, became dominant in Hasidism, and the importance of the mystical quality of the ritualistic sounds was instrumental in Hasidism's renewed emphasis on mystical experience, as we have seen in the citation in the name of the Besht.

Interestingly, mystical prayer returned to the vocal dimension, which seems to have been crucial in the ancient mystical sources that form the *Hekhalot* literature and which was canonized by the Halakhic regulations. In the mystical sources, the mystic — the person who undertook the dangerous ascent to the divinity — was doing it while he was reciting the hymns and the divine names that function both as protective means and as a certain type of vehicle to ensure the ascent.[101] As far as we can determine, the graphic facet of the letters was not employed in the techniques of *Hekhalot* literature, as it was later utilized by medieval kabbalists, and the return to the importance of the recitation of liturgical texts in Hasidism, including in this category the Hasidic conception of the study of the Torah, is reminiscent of the centrality of this phenomenon in ancient Jewish mysticism.

Already in an early important document of Hasidism — the epistle of the Besht, Rabbi Israel Ba'al Shem Tov, to his brother-in-law, Rabbi Gershon of Kutov — the letters of prayer are conceived as ascending on high, and the Besht recommends integrating one's soul into those letters in order to attain an experience of cleaving with the divine.[102] Let me conclude this part of our discussion by citing Rabbi Meshullam Phoebus of Zbaraz, a Hasidic master who wrote in the second half of the eighteenth century:

> The quintessence of the intention to study [Torah] is identical to that of the intention of prayer: The soul cleaves to, and comes nearer to God, Blessed be He, by [he means of] the letters of the

Torah. Then the letters ascend, and likewise the vapors, up to God, Blessed be He, and He has a great pleasure in it.[103]

Letters become entities that enable the mystic to come in direct contact with the divine in the mundane world, while at the same time they are viewed as vehicles for an ascent to the divine in the transcendental world. They serve as intermediaries for contact with the immanent and transcendent divine.

Hebrew as a Vehicle of Intellectual and Mystical Knowledge

According to a view expressed in a work of ecstatic Kabbalah, the holy language is tantamount to the efflux originated by the divine presence, the *Shekhinah*. Rabbi Isaac of Acre wrote in his mystical diary that

> the holy language comes onto the souls of the mystics of Israel from the radiance of the glory of the *Shekhinah*. And before the generation of the Tower of Babel, there was only the holy language alone, as it is said: And all the earth was [speaking] one language and the same words. And understand that "language" is the secret of *Shekhinah*, and "words" allude to the divine name formed of 72 [units] whose letters are 216.[104]

The secrets hinted at in this text are the numerical equivalencies of the words language, *Safah*, and *Shekhinah*, both of which total, according to their numerical value, 385. Thus the linguistic material of the Hebrew is tantamount to the intellectual forms that flow from the divine presence. Speaking Hebrew is, accordingly, the corporeal articulation of the divine overflow. Now so much a creation of the human vocal organs, Hebrew emanates from above. Apparently, this kabbalist has in mind a rabbinic dictum, whose sources are rather obscure, that states that "*Shekhinah* spoke from the throat of Moses." This conception differs from the understanding of Hebrew as divine because of its origin as a creation of God. It is divine because it flows from the divine realm onto the mystic, and the speaking of this language may possibly be understood also as experiencing the presence of the divine. We witness an attempt to ontologize the language by comparing it to, and even identifying it with, the Neoplatonic emanation that descends on the mundane realm. Actually, Jewish Neoplatonic thinkers, such as Solomon Ibn Gabirol and Isaac Ibn Latif, and some theosophical kabbalists, such as Rabbi Jacob ben Sheshet, had already compared the emanative process to the emission of speech;[105] however, for them this comparison was, apparently, only a simile, whereas for Rabbi Isaac of Acre this metaphor was exploited in order to view language as an overflow descending on the souls of the mystics of Israel.

No wonder that ecstatic kabbalists regarded the knowledge of the principles of kabbalistic linguistics as the core of Kabbalah; according to Abraham Abulafia, "whoever does not know the combinations of letters and is a very 'examined' and experienced person in this lore, and in the counting of letters and their division and in the changing of their order and permutations according to what is written in the *Book of Creation*, does not know the Lord, according to our way."[106]

The kabbalist distills the content of the language that reaches us from above by using exegetical principles of the linguistic Kabbalah, and in this way ensures the knowledge of God. Just as the knowledge of the philosophers constitutes the reception of the intellectual overflow from above and its transformation into distinct statements with metaphysical significance, the kabbalist uses his "superlogical" exegetical techniques in order to attain another, higher, type of connection with God, an experiential one that is achieved through the permutation of letters.[107]

The preceding discussion affirms that the dispersion of languages at the Tower of Babel is to be obliterated in order to reach the messianic age; based on hints in biblical verses, Abulafia maintains that the coming of the Messiah will change all the languages into one, and the nations will worship God together. This is a normative view, to be found in many postbiblical Jewish texts. However, it is reasonable to assume that such a statement meant much more when it was articulated by someone who considered himself to be the Messiah.[108] By the unification of languages into one, I assume that Abulafia means that his Kabbalah will serve as a means for the attainment of this ideal state of things; as he indeed did in his extant works, this kabbalist considers the linguistic material to be found in the languages of the Gentiles to be a distortion of the original Hebrew, the primordial intellectual language that is a powerful means of worshiping God.[109]

Abulafia's view of language found its way to a number of individuals active during the Renaissance; it reverberates in the works of Rabbi Yohanan Alemanno, the companion of Pico della Mirandola. In a highly interesting passage dealing with the relationship of the biblical Joseph to Pharaoh, probably an allegory of his own situation in comparison with Pico's, Alemanno asserts that notwithstanding either the Egyptian ruler's great wisdom or his familiarity with seventy languages, Pharaoh was unable to master Hebrew, though he made attempts to learn this language "artificially." His failure is due to the fact that the knowledge of Hebrew has a prophetic quality, which is reserved to Jews alone. Alemanno, following the lines of Abulafia's theories, understood the very usage of Hebrew as fraught with mystical value.[110] No doubt this emphasis on the knowledge of Hebrew was, in the case of Abulafia, connected to his messianic and prophetic pretensions, which conditioned the attainment of higher experiences with the usage of Hebrew by the ancient Jewish prophets, and the assumption that at the end of days Hebrew will become the unique language of mankind. It seems that this language preserved for certain types of Jewish mystics the essential role of the "divine thing," that very particular core of Jewish being posited by Rabbi Judah Ha-Levi, or again that peculiar Jewish "soul" referred to in the mystical anthropology of Rabbi Joseph Gikatilla. Accordingly, the Jews were the repository of a uniquely powerful instrument whose use ensured a mystical status unattainable otherwise.[111]

As we have seen, the written form of the letters in the scroll of the Torah was regarded by the theosophical kabbalists as the avenue by which to apprehend the form of the divine pleroma; again, a certain type of knowledge transpires behind the very formal structure of language, bestowing on it a surplus of information concerning issues that transcend the common contents of the intrahuman communicative role of language.

Some Mystical Conceptions of Language in the Twentieth Century

At the final stage of this study, I would like to comment briefly on the attitude toward language of some leading figures in modern mysticism, both as mystics and as scholars and thinkers. One of the most picturesque figures in the last generation was Rabbi David ha-Kohen, the prophet who flourished in the land of Israel. His most important work, *Qol ha-Nevu'ah* (*The Voice of Prophecy*), constitutes a detailed survey of the most important Jewish texts that support his main thesis: that speech, much more than vision, was the channel of revelation in Judaism. This survey, which seems to have personal implications regarding the mystical life of ha-Kohen, is an impressive collection of texts that invites a more meticulous and subtle analysis, but nevertheless demonstrates the basic thesis of the centrality of hearing over seeing in Judaism.

Two other important figures—Martin Buber and Franz Rosenzweig—emphasized the importance of the auditive part of the Hebrew Bible, and they attempted, in their joint project of translation of the Bible into German, to put into sharp relief this aspect of the translated text.[112] It seems probable that at least Buber was sensitive to this facet of the text, given his study of Hasidism.

Their contemporary Gershom Scholem, however, was much more impressed by the written form of language; in a letter of his, published recently, he expresses fears regarding the transformation of Hebrew, a sacred language, into a spoken tongue. As early as the late 1920s, he predicted that this shift, which turned the ancient language into a vernacular, would have bizarre repercussions, since this "resurrected" language would haunt those who used it without being aware of the entire range of religious significance immanent in a sacred language.[113] It seems that Scholem, a famous scholar of Kabbalah, preferred the written over the oral form of language, under the influence of the classical kabbalistic axiology concerning language, as we have tried to explain it in this essay.[114]

Notes

1. Genesis 1: 1.
2. These are the consonants of the word *Bereshit* (In the Beginning). The whole treatise named *Tiqqunei Zohar* is a plethora of interpretations of the various meanings of the significances of these consonants. See, for example, *Tiqqunei Zohar*, ed. R. Margaliot (Jerusalem, 1978), fol. 24a, *Tiqqun* VII.
3. Psalms 118: 22.
4. See *Sefer Yezrah* 4,4. Compare with R. Zeev Wolf of Jhitomir, *Or ha-Meir*, fol. 5b-d.

5. These two activities are envisioned by Hasidism as almost identical, since the Hasidim emphasized, as we shall see, the importance of the vocal acts for their linguistic mysticism. See the quotation with note 63 of this chapter and *Or ha-Meir*, fol. 5c.

6. In Hasidic literature, the word *Mishkan* was seen as the locus of the divine presence; the term *Teivah* means in Hebrew both the word and the actual ark where the scroll of the Torah is deposited. This double meaning was exploited several times by Hasidic authors. See, for example, the quotation in the name of R. Israel Ba'al Shem Tov, in R. Abraham Hayyim of Zlotchov, *Orah Le-Hayyim* (Jerusalem, 1960), fol. 98a; and *Or ha-Meir*, fol. 5bc, 248ab.

7. Psalms 118: 22.

8. R. Moses Elioqim Beriah, *Qohelet Moshe* (Lublin, 1875), fol. 8a.

9. M. Idel, *Kabbalah: New Perspectives* (New Haven, Conn., 1988), pp. 53-54.

10. See note 6.

11. The phrase *'Olam ha-Otiot* (the world of the letters), which mediates between the Sefirotic world and the material one. See M. Idel, "The Magical and Neoplatonic Interpretations of the Kabbalah in the Renaissance," in B. D. Cooperman, ed., *Jewish Thought in the Sixteenth Century* (Cambridge, Mass., 1983) p. 235, n. 95, and *Language, Torah, and Hermeneutics in Abraham Abulafia* (Albany, N.Y., 1988), p. 132, n. 1.

12. See note 6 and the words of R. Menahem Mendel of Vitebsk, quoted on pp. 62-63.

13. Idel, *Language, Torah, and Hermeneutics in Abraham Abulafia*, chap. 1.

14. Such a view, apparently, occurred in Egyptian thought. See John A. Wilson, "Egypt," in H. Frankfort, H. A. Frankfort, J. A. Wilson, T. Jacobsen, and W. A. Irwin, eds., *The Intellectual Adventure of Ancient Man* (Chicago, 1964), pp. 59-60.

15. See *Avodah Zarah*, fol. 3a, and Idel, *Kabbalah*, p. 171.

16. *Berakhot*, fol. 55a. See also E. Urbach, *The Sages: Their Concepts and Beliefs*, trans. I. Abrahams (Jerusalem, 1979), p. 197.

17. G. Scholem, "The Name of God and the Linguistic of the Kabbala," *Diogenes* 79 (1972): 71.

18. See, for example, the tradition mentioned by R. Jacob ben Sheshet, *Sefer ha-Emunah we-ha-Bittahon*, in D. Chavel, *Kitvei ha-Ramban* (Jerusalem, 1964), vol. 2, p. 363, and Urbach, *Sages*, pp. 197-98.

19. Urbach, *Sages*, pp. 197-213.

20. See Idel, *Kabbalah*, pp. 112-22.

21. Scholem, "Name of God," pp. 72-74.

22. See Scholem, *Kabbalah* (New York, 1974), pp. 23-26.

23. See Chapter 5.

24. See M. Idel, "The Concept of the Torah in Heikhalot Literature and Its Metamorphosis in Kabbalah" (in Hebrew), *Jerusalem Studies in Jewish Thought* 1 (1981): 43-45.

25. Idel, "Concept of the Torah," p. 67.

26. M. Idel, "The World of Angels in Human Form" (in Hebrew), *Jerusalem Studies in Jewish Thought* 3 (1984): 2-10.

27. Idel, "Concept of the Torah," pp. 39-40.

28. Idel, "World of Angels," p. 6.

29. See K. E. Groezinger, "The Names of God and Their Celestial Powers: Their Function and Meaning in the Hekhalot Literature," in J. Dan, ed., *Early Jewish Mysticism, Studies in Jewish Thought* 6 (1987): 53-69.

30. Quoted in M. Idel, "Infinities of Torah in Kabbalah" in G. Hartman and S. Budick, eds., *Midrash and Literature* (New Haven, Conn., 1986), p. 145.

31. Idel, "Concept of the Torah," pp. 64-65.

32. U. Eco, *Semiotics and the Philosophy of Language* (Bloomington, Ind., 1984), p. 154.

33. Scholem, *Origins of the Kabbalah* (Princeton, N.J., 1987), pp. 460-75.

34. The Neoplatonic theurgist can, indeed, attract the gods in statues here below, but they seem to ignore a supernal pleroma whose dynamics can be affected by the ritual of the theurgist.

35. Divine thought and divine will, which correspond to the two highest *Sefirot*.

36. The term *Beḥinah* is characteristic of Cordovero's writings, and it refers to the reflections of the features of the ten *Sefirot* in each of them.

37. R. Moses Cordovero, *Or Yaqar* (Jerusalem, 1983), vol. 12, p. 147.

38. See pp. 59-66.

39. Idel, *Kabbalah*, pp. 222-31.

40. See also M. Idel, *The Mystical Experience in Abraham Abulafia* (Albany, N.Y., 1987), pp. 77-79.

41. Idel, *Mystical Experience in Abraham Abulafia*, pp. 83-95. Abulafia also had visual experiences (pp. 95-98), but he himself emphasized the importance of the acoustic or linguistic components of the experiences that characterize ecstatic Kabbalah.

42. Idel, *Mystical Experience in Abraham Abulafia*, pp. 78-79.

43. Abraham Abulafia, *Ḥayei ha-'Olam ha-Ba*, Ms. Oxford, Catalog Neubauer 1582, fol. 45b.

44. Idel, *Mystical Experience in Abraham Abulafia*, chap. 1.

45. This issue has to be explored in more detailed studies; until then, see Idel, *Kabbalah*, chap. 5.

46. G. Scholem, "Zehn unhistorische Saetze über Kabbala," in *Geist und Werk: Festschrift zum 75 Geburtstag von Dr. Daniel Brody* (Zurich, 1958), p. 213, sec. 7.

47. On this phenomenon, see R. J. Z. Werblowsky, *Joseph Karo, Lawyer and Mystic* (Philadelphia, 1977), pp. 257–86.

48. Augustine, *Confessiones*, IX, 10. See Idel, *Language, Torah, and Hermeneutics in Abraham Abulafia*, p. 143, n. 52.

49. See pp. 59–66.

50. See notes 6 and 92. According to *Or ha-Meir*, fol. 37d–38a, "there is a 'voice' (*qol*) that precedes even the 'primordial thought'" (*Qidmat ha-Sekel*), the latter being the source of regular voices and speeches. There are, however, some important instances when Hasidic masters, following kabbalistic statements, conceived the state of silence as superior to that of speech. See M. Hallamish, "On Silence in Kabbalah and Hasidism" (in Hebrew), in M. Hallamish and A. Kasher, eds., *Religion and Language* (Tel Aviv, 1981), pp. 79–89. See also "World of Thought" and "World of Speech," in Rivka Schatz Uffenheimer, *Quietistic Elements in 18th Century Hasidic Thought* (in Hebrew) (Jerusalem, 1968), pp. 121–128, which emphasizes the superiority of the spiritual—that is, the mental—world over the vocal one. One the basis of this material, the relationship between the two realms seems to be much more complex, since even the world of thought includes linguistic elements.

51. See *Shi'ur Qomah*; cf. Martin Cohen, *The Shi'ur Qomah: Liturgy and Theurgy in Pre-Kabbalistic Jewish Mysticism* (London, 1983), pp. 283–342.

52. *Or ha-Emet* (Jhitomir, 1911), fol. 4c. The passage is based on a pun in which the word "Ḥayyot" (heavenly beings) is reinterpreted as "Ḥyyiut" (vitality), which stands in Hasidic writings for the presence of the divine force in man. This play on the *Ḥayyot-Ḥyyut* seems to stem from the Besht himself. See G. Scholem, *The Messianic Idea in Judaism* (New York, 1972), p. 219.

53. See pp. 58, 68–69.

54. Michael Oppenheim, "The Meaning of Hasidut: Martin Buber and Gershom Scholem," *Journal of the American Academy of Religion* 49 (1971): 410–11. However, Buber's phenomenology of Kabbalah is based exclusively on Lurianic Kabbalah, seemingly ignoring the ecstatic Kabbalah, where some elements of dialogical states are to be found. See Idel, *Mystical Experience in Abraham Abulafia*, pp. 86–95.

55. Idel, "Magical and Neoplatonic Interpretations of the Kabbalah in the Renaissance," pp. 212–15.

56. Idel, "Magical and Neoplatonic Interpretations of the Kabbalah in the Renaissance," pp. 198–99, 207–9. See also M. Idel, "Jewish Magic

from the Renaissance Period to Early Hasidism," in J. Neusner, E. S. Frerichs, and P. V. McC. Flesher, eds., *Religion, Science, and Magic* (New York, 1989), pp. 82-117.

57. R. Shem Tov ben Shem Tov, *Sefer ha-Emunot* (Ferrara, 1556), fol. 98b.

58. R. Moses Cordovero, *Pardes Rimmonim*, Gate 32, chap. 3.

59. See my detailed discussion of the significance of the palaces as words in "Perceptions of Kabbalah in the Second Half of the 18th Century," *Jewish Thought and Philosophy* 1 (1991): 88-95.

60. R. Yohanan Alemanno, *Collectanaea*, Ms. Oxford, Bodleiana, Catalog Neubauer 2234, fol. 3b. For the context of this quotation, see Idel, "Magical and Neoplatonic Interpretations of the Kabbalah in the Renaissance," pp. 207-8.

61. *Penimiut ha-Ruḥaniut*. On the meaning of *Ruḥaniut* and its sources, see Idel, "Perceptions of Kabbalah," pp. 84-87, and "Magical and Neoplatonic Interpretations of the Kabbalah in the Renaissance," pp. 201-7.

62. Or *Eyin Sof*.

63. See R. Jacob Joseph of Polnoye, *Toldot Ya'akov Yoseph* (Korez, 1780), fol. 25a.

64. Idel, "World of Angels in Human Form," p. 6, n. 16.

65. Idel, "World of Angels in Human Form," p. 6.

66. R. Isaac the Blind, *Commentary on Sefer Yeẓirah*, appendix to Gershom Scholem's lectures, *Ha-Kabbalah be-Provence*, ed. R. Schatz (Jerusalem, 1963), p. 12. For more on R. Isaac's theory of language, see Scholem, "Name of God," pp. 166-69. For parallels to this text, see R. Azriel of Gerone, *Commentary on the Talmudic Aggadot*, ed. I. Tishby (Jerusalem, 1945), pp. 14-15, and the editor's footnotes there.

The view that everything is included in the Hebrew letters has an interesting parallel, and perhaps even its source, in Islam. See Louis Massignon, "La Philosophie orientale d'Ibn Sina et son alphabet philosophique," in *Opera Minora* (Beirut, 1963), 2, pp. 591-605. See also the view of R. Yehudah ben Solomon ha-Cohen, a Toledan thinker with some mystical leanings, who indicated, in the first half of the thirteenth century, that "from our letters everything existing is explained, from its beginning to its end" (*Literaturblatt des Orients* 10 [1849]: 730, n. 24), and note 76.

67. "In the letters are all the entities having a form, included" (R. Jacob ben Sheshet, *Meshiv Devarim Nekhoḥim*, ed. Georges Vajda [Jerusalem, 1969], p. 155). See also note 66.

68. ben Sheshet, *Meshiv Devarim Nekhoḥim*, p. 154.

69. ben Sheshet, *Meshiv Devarim Nekhoḥim*, p. 154. See also Georges Vajda, *Recherches sur la philosophie et la Kabbale dans la pensée juive du Moyen Age* (Paris, 1962), pp. 356-71.

70. 1 Samuel 2: 20; *T. B. Berakhot*, 10a. The Talmudic statement, which envisages God as shaping everything, is understood here as referring to the divine articulation of all the letters, conceived as forms.

71. ben Sheshet, *Meshiv Devarim Nekhohim*, p. 154.

72. On the critical attitude of ben Sheshet to the intellectualistic approach of the philosophers, see Vajda, *Recherches sur la philosophie et la Kabbale dans la pensée juive du Moyen Age*, pp. 356-71.

73. ben Sheshet, *Meshiv Devarim Nekhohim*, p. 157.

74. Scholem, "Name of God," p. 62.

75. See Gershom Scholem, *Das Buch Bahir* (Darmstadt, 1970), pp. 13-41. There are some pre-Kabbalistic interpretations of the Hebrew alphabet in the Talmudic and Midrashic literature; however, in the first 150 years of kabbalistic writings, kabbalists produced more discussions of this issue than the entire Jewish literature preceding historical Kabbalah.

76. This kabbalistic literary genre has not received due attention from the scholars of Kabbalah. See the interesting treatment of Elias Lipiner, *Ideologie fun Yidishn Alef-Beis* (Buenos Aires, 1967), and especially the expanded Hebrew version (Jerusalem 1988.) See also Colette Sirat, "La Qabbale d'après Juda b. Salomon Ha-Cohen," in G. Nahon and C. Touati, eds., *Hommage à Georges Vajda* (Louvain, 1980), pp. 191-212.

77. Idel, *Language, Torah, and Hermeneutics in Abraham Abulafia*, pp. 138-39, n. 20.

78. Language (*Lashon*) as a symbol of the *Sefirah* of *Binah* is a commonplace of kabbalistic symbolism. However, this term may point, in some rare cases, to the *Sefirot* of *Tiferet* and *Malkhut*, which, as we shall see, articulate the linguistic material.

79. Gershom Scholem, "Two Treatises by R. Moses de Leon," *Qovez 'Al Yad*, n.s., vol. 8 (1976): 335-36. Compare with pp. 346 and 370, and with the Zoharic material noted by Scholem in his footnotes.

80. 1 Kings 19: 12.

81. R. Moses de Leon, *Shoshan 'Edut*, pp. 335-36.

82. de Leon, *Shoshan 'Edut*, p. 336.

83. de Leon, *Shoshan 'Edut*, pp. 335-36.

84. de Leon, *Shoshan 'Edut*, p. 335.

85. R. Abraham Adrutiel, *Avnei Zikkaron*, Ms. New York, JTS 1659, fol. 96a, 97a, etc.

86. Cf. Job 19: 26. This verse is the *locus probans* of the kabbalistic discussions of the anthropomorphical structure of the Sefirotic realm; here, the Hasidic master transposes the human linguistic process to the intradivine world.

87. *Mazref la-Hokhmah*. I assume that this phrase, translated here literally, refers in this context to the combination of letters at the highest level of the divine realm. See also *Or ha-Meir*, fol. 248ab.

88. *Da'at*. In certain kabbalistical systems, there is a *Sefirah* that mediates between the *Sefirot Ḥokhmah* and *Binah*; this author is obviously referring to this peculiar status of Knowledge as a mediator between Wisdom and Understanding.

89. The two *Sefirot Ḥesed* and *Din*, which are located "below" *Da'at*.

90. R. Menahem Mendel of Vitebsk, *Peri ha-Areẓ* (Jerusalem, 1969), fol. 9a.

91. On this concept, see Scholem, "Name of God," pp. 181-82, and M. Idel, "Differing Conceptions of Kabbalah in the Early 17th Century," in I. Twersky and B. Septimus, eds., *Jewish Thought in the Seventeenth Century* (Cambridge, Mass., 1987), pp. 179-86.

92. R. Levi Isaac of Berditchev, *Qedushat ha-Levi* (Jerusalem, 1972), fol. 117ab. See also R. Menahem Mendel of Vitebsk, *Peri ha-Areẓ*, fol. 9a. The implicit identification of the "World of Thought" with "speech" is found also elsewhere in the school of the Great Maggid. See *Or ha-Emet*, fol. 4d: "It is as if the first thought is called also speech."

93. See Scholem, *Das Buch Bahir*, pp. 87-88, 168.

94. See Idel, "Infinities of Torah in Kabbalah."

95. Idel, *Kabbalah*, pp. 191-97.

96. Idel, *Kabbalah*, p. 192.

97. Idel, *Kabbalah*, pp. 192-95.

98. Cf. M. Idel, "Kabbalistic Prayer and Colours," in David Blumenthal, ed., *Approaches to Judaism in Medieval Times* (Atlanta, 1988), vol. 3, pp. 17-27.

99. See Idel, "Perceptions of Kabbalah," pp. 94-95.

100. Idel, "Perceptions of Kabbalah," pp. 94-95.

101. Idel, *Mystical Experience in Abraham Abulafia*, pp. 14-17.

102. J. Mondshein, ed., *Migdal Oz* (Kefar Habad, Isr., 1980), p. 124; R. Jacob Joseph of Polnoye, *Toldot Ya'akov Yoseph*, fol. 25a.

103. R. Meshullam Phoebus of Zbaraz, *Yosher Divrei Emet*, para. 39 (printed with *Liqqutim Yiqarim* [Jerusalem, 1981], fol. 133a). See also *Or ha-Meir*, fol. 239b.

104. R. Isaac of Acre, Ms. Moscow-Guensburg 775, fol. 79a.

105. See S. O. Heller-Wilensky, "R. Isaac ibn Latif: Kabbalist or Philosopher?" in Alexander Altmann, ed., *Jewish Medieval and Renaissance Studies* (Cambridge, Mass., 1967), pp. 208-9, and the numerous sources referred to in the footnotes.

106. Abraham Abulafia, *Sefer Sitrei Torah*, Ms. Paris, BN. 774 fol. 163a.

107. Idel, "Infinities of Torah in Kabbalah," p. 149.

108. Cf. M. Idel, "Abulafia on the Jewish Messiah and Jesus," *Immanuel* 11 (1980): 70-72.

109. Idel, "Abulafia on the Jewish Messiah and Jesus"; Scholem, "Name of God," pp. 190–91.

110. R. Yohanan Alemanno, *Ḥeseq Shelomo*, Ms. Oxford, Bodleian, Catalog Neubauer 1595, fol. 66a.

111. The Hebrew language is, therefore, parallel or similar to Kabbalah and Oral Law as an important factor that ensures, according to the kabbalists, the superiority of Judaism.

112. See Grete Schaeder, *The Hebrew Humanism of Martin Buber* (Detroit, 1973), pp. 340–41. Rosenzweig emphasizes the superiority of the spoken word over the written one in "Die Schrift und das Wort!" Compare here Rosenzweig's observation that Scholem regards the written word as revelation and the spoken one as art.

113. See "A Confession on Our Language" (letter, G. Scholem to F. Rosenzweig, 26 December 1926), *Molad* 9 (1985–86): 118–119. On the importance of the mysticism of writing, see Scholem, "Name of God," p. 167.

114. For a survey of Scholem's view of language, see David Biale, *Gershom Scholem: Kabbalah and Counter-History*, 2nd ed. (Cambridge, Mass., 1982), pp. 112–42. See especially pp. 119 and 133–34, where Biale points to the affinity between Scholem's mysticism of language and that of the kabbalists and stresses the influence of Walter Benjamin on Scholem's view of language.

3

Literal and Nonliteral in Reports of Mystical Experience

WILLIAM P. ALSTON

The Category of Mystical Experience

I will term "mystical" any experience that is taken by the subject to be a direct awareness of (what is taken to be) Ultimate Reality or (what is taken to be) an object of religious worship. I realize that the boundaries of application of phrases like "Ultimate Reality" and "object of religious worship" are by no means crystal clear. More to the point, it is by no means crystal clear when a person could be properly said to take an object of experience to be Ultimate Reality or an object of religious worship, especially the former. Just what sort of ultimacy is in question here; and as for people who do not habitually engage in metaphysical talk about ontological ultimacy, what is it for them to make such suppositions? Nevertheless, I will assume that there is a wide enough area of unproblematic application to render these concepts useable.

Another problem for my approach is that the term may fail to stretch over some forms of Buddhist mystical experience and may not cover "naturalistic" mystical experience. This difficulty is, of course, intimately connected with its predecessor. Is *nirvāna*, or a merging of natural things into a supreme unity, taken to be "ultimate reality" or an object of religious worship? In this respect, my criterion may be regarded as inferior to a familiar criterion in terms of the experience and/or its object being an *undifferentiated unity*.[1] But even if we lose some cases by doing it my way, we also gain some, since, as will become evident from our examples, by no means all experiences selected by my criterion are, phenomenologically, experiences of an undifferentiated unity.[2] In any event, it is reports of this class of experiences that I want to scrutinize. And since I am writing the paper, I get to do it my way!

Let me spell out a bit more how I am thinking of the category of mystical experience here. I take that category to range over any experience of the specified sort, whether lay or professional, and however Ultimate Reality or the object of religious worship is being construed. However, I am going to confine myself to theistic mystical experience, in which the object is taken to be a personal deity or at least a deity conceived in personalistic terms. (Correspondingly, I will speak of what mystics take themselves to be aware of as "God.") Indeed, a majority of my examples will be drawn from a subregion of that territory, the tradition of Catholic mysticism. Admittedly, this narrowness of focus will prevent me from drawing any unrestrictedly general conclusions from my survey. But, as will be made explicit in a moment, I do not aspire to any such conclusions in this paper. Rather, I will be seeking to combat certain unrestrictedly general claims by providing counterexamples from the Catholic mystical tradition. If this were a tiny group on the fringes, these counterexamples would be of little moment; but it is, on the contrary, a subregion that bulks large in the total picture. Hence it will be quite suitable for my purposes here.

Can Mystical Experience Be Described Literally?

I am now in a position to specify the contentions I will be endeavoring to support in this paper. While theorists of mysticism recognize that familiar claims of ineffability are overblown, since obviously something is done to describe the experiences, and that some more modest and more discriminating position on the language of mysticism needs to be taken, they still commonly hold that the possibilities for reporting mystical experiences are radically different from those in other realms of thought and experience. We may distinguish two broad classes of such views. (1) Since mystical experience and/or its objects are radically different from anything we encounter in "ordinary" experience, on the basis of which and for application to which most of our conceptual resources and our vocabularies have been constructed, we are forced into stretched or extended uses of language in order to capture, so far as possible, the features of this alien world. Domestic terms are pressed into foreign service by such devices as analogy, metaphor, and symbolism.[3] (2) A more extreme view is that no *statements*, not even rough, imprecise ones, are possible with respect to mystical experience or its objects. In mystical literature, language is limited to evocative or expressive uses. Mystics should be understood as saying what they do in order to *evoke* in the hearer some faint echo of the mystical experience and/or to *express* that experience or their reactions thereto.[4] Both these positions imply that it is impossible to make straightforward literal uses of words in reporting mystical experiences or in describing what one encounters therein. The overblown allegations of ineffability are then diagnosed as misguided expressions of the fact that language is put to special, unusual uses in mystical literature.

Now far be it from me to deny that we are severely limited in the extent to which we can articulate in language the nature of mystical experiences and their objects. Nor have I any inclination to deny that metaphor, symbols, and images loom large in attempts by mystics to tell us what it is like. But I do wish to, and will, deny that straightforward literal assertions, with straightforward truth values, play no role in mystical reports. It will be the main task of this paper to identify those aspects of mystical reports involving the literal use of language.[5] The aforementioned views, though less crude and undiscriminating than the unqualified ineffability view, are still much too simplistic to match the facts. As we will see when we differentiate the variety of linguistic jobs undertaken by mystics, literal statement is involved in different ways in some of them, while not available or hardly available in others. It is the failure to realize the variety of tasks confronting one who sets out to report the mystic state that leads theorists to simplistic reductions of the sort that I am seeking to counter.

A Perceptual Model

As a background for the distinctions I will draw between various components of reports of mystical experience, I will explain how I am thinking of the structure of that experience. In a word, I employ a *perceptual* model. Negatively this means that I do not construe the experience as purely subjective, or purely a matter of feeling, affect, or emotion. Positively, I am thinking of it as essentially involving a relation to one or more object(s) in basically the same way sense perception does. That summary formulation requires some unpacking.

First, in saying that it essentially involves a relation to an object, am I implying that all mystical experience is *veridical*, in the sense that the subject is, by virtue of having the experience, cognitively related to the kind of object he or she takes herself to be experiencing? *No*. Even if the subject is directly aware of something, it may be radically different from what the subject supposes it to be and from how it presents itself experientially to the subject. It may not even be something objective. It may feel to the subject like the presence of God, while in fact it is only some passing autonomic physiological arousal.

Although, I claim, the experiences with which I am concerned have the same kind of structure as sense perception, there are important differences as well. I am not suggesting that mystical experiences typically involve *sensory* content, an awareness of basic sensory qualities like colors, shapes, sounds, tastes, and smells. Quite the contrary. Where such material is involved, there is good reason for denying that the subject is directly aware of God. At most, this would be an indirect awareness of God through the awareness of some (real or hallucinatory) physical object(s). Thus I will consider only experiences without sensory content.

Then just how is the structural isomorphism to be construed? That depends on our account of sense perception, more specifically the experiential aspect thereof; and this is a hotly debated topic among philosophers and psychologists. Sensory experience has been thought by some to be a matter of the direct awareness of *sense data*—nonphysical objects, the crucial role of which is to be the bearer of the basic sensory qualities of which we are directly aware in sense perception. Others hold that sensory experience is "adverbial," a way of sensing rather than the direct awareness of any *object*. When I perceive a ball as round and red, the sense datum theorist would say that my sensory experience is a direct awareness of a red, round nonphysical entity, the nature of which is exhausted by such qualities, while the adverbial theorist would say that the experience is a matter of sensing redly and roundly.

Since I cannot go into the pros and cons of the various theories of perception here, I will have to content myself with dogmatically putting forward my own position, the theory of appearing. According to this theory, a sensory experience is essentially a matter of something's *appearing* or *presenting* itself to one as so-and-so, or being *given* to one's experience as so-and-so; that is, it is a matter of something's *looking* red or round, *smelling* acrid, or *sounding* loud. The something that presents itself as bearing certain sensory qualities will, when the perception is veridical, be an externally existing physical object; in hallucination it will be something else, perhaps a vivid mental image. So the theory of appearing treats the qualitative content of sensory experience differently from the other two views. Whereas the sense datum theory takes this content to have the status of qualities of sense data, and the adverbial theory takes it to have the status of the *way* or the *manner* of one's sensing, the theory of appearing takes the content to be the *way in which the object one is directly aware of appears to one* — how it looks, smells, tastes, or whatever. The theory of appearing makes it possible to hold that in normal sense perception we are directly aware of the physical objects we are perceiving, while recognizing that those objects may not actually possess the qualities they present themselves as having. I take the theory of appearing to be the view that corresponds most closely to our natural and spontaneous construal of sense experience. Thus if it does not fall prey to fatal difficulties, as I believe it will not, it will clearly be the theory of choice.

The theory of appearing seems to me to give just as natural a construal of mystical experience, and I will use it to make explicit the isomorphism of structure between the two realms.[6] In mystical experience, too, something is presented experientially to the subject as so-and-so, as *powerful, loving, beautiful*, or whatever. Because of this identity of structure, I shall feel free to think of mystical experience (when veridical) as a *perception* of God. Here are some samples of reports of theistic mystical experience that are naturally understood in these terms, with various so-and-sos, various ways of appearing, involved.

> [I.] . . . all at once I . . . felt the presence of God—I tell of the thing just as I was conscious of it—as if his goodness and his power were penetrating me altogether. . . . I thanked God that in the course of my life he had taught me to know him, that he sustained my life and took pity both on the insignificant creature and on the sinner that I was. I begged him ardently that my life might be consecrated to the doing of his will. I felt his reply, which was that I should do his will from day to day, in humility and poverty, leaving him, The Almighty God, to judge of whether I should some time be called to bear witness more conspicuously. Then, slowly, the ecstasy left my heart; that is, I felt that God had withdrawn the communion which he had granted. . . . I asked myself if it were possible that Moses on Sinai could have had a more intimate communication with God. I think it well to add that in this ecstasy of mine God had neither form, color, odor, nor taste; moreover, that the feeling of his presence was accompanied by no determinate localization. . . . At bottom the expression most apt to render what I felt is this: God was present, though invisible; he fell under no one of my senses, yet my consciousness perceived him.[7]

> [II.] I was in prayer one day . . . when I saw Christ close by me, or, to speak more correctly, felt Him; for I saw nothing with the eyes of the body, nothing with the eyes of the soul. He seemed to me to be close beside me; and I saw, too, as I believe, that it was He who was speaking to me. Jesus Christ seemed to be by my side continually. As the vision was not imaginary, I saw no form, but I had a most distinct feeling that He was always on my right hand, a witness of all I did. . . . For if I say that I see Him neither with the eyes of the body nor those of the soul—because it was not an imaginary vision—how is it that I can understand and maintain that He stands beside me, and be more certain of it than if I saw Him? If it be supposed that it is as if a person were blind, or in the dark, and therefore unable to see another who is close to him, the comparison is not exact. There is a certain likelihood about it, however, but not much, because the other senses tell him who is blind of that presence . . . but in these visions there is nothing like this. The darkness is not felt; only

He renders Himself present to the soul by a certain knowledge of Himself which is more clear than the sun. I do not mean that we now see either a sun or any other brightness, only that there is a light not seen, which illumines the understanding, so that the soul may have the fruition of so great a good.[8]

[III.] At times God comes into the soul without being called; and He instills into her fire, love, and sometimes sweetness; and the soul believes this comes from God, and delights therein. But she does not yet know, or see, that He dwells in her; she perceives His grace, in which she delights. And again God comes to the soul, and speaks to her words full of sweetness, in which she has much joy, and she feels Him. This feeling of God gives her the greatest delight; but even here a certain doubt remains; for the soul has not the certitude that God is in her. . . . And beyond this the soul receives the gift of seeing God. God says to her, "Behold Me!" and the soul sees Him dwelling within her. She sees Him more clearly than one man sees another. For the eyes of the soul behold a plenitude of which I cannot speak: a plenitude which is not bodily but spiritual, of which I can say nothing. And the soul rejoices in that sight with an ineffable joy; and this is the manifest and certain sign that God indeed dwells in her.[9]

[IV.] That which the Servitor saw had no form neither any manner of being; yet he had of it a joy such as he might have known in the seeing of the shapes and substances of all joyful things. His heart was hungry, yet satisfied, his soul was full of contentment and joy: his prayers and hopes were all fulfilled. And the Friar could do naught but contemplate this Shining Brightness; and he altogether forgot himself and all other things. Was it day or night? He knew not. It was, as it were, a manifestation of the sweetness of Eternal Life in the sensations of silence and of rest. Then he said, "If that which I see and feel be not the Kingdom of Heaven, I know not what it can be: for it is very sure that the endurance of all possible pains were but a poor price to pay for the eternal possession of so great a joy."[10]

[V.] But as I turned and was about to take a seat by the fire, I received a mighty baptism of the Holy Ghost. Without any expectation of it, without ever having the thought in my mind that there was any such thing for me, without any recollection that I had ever heard the thing mentioned by any person in the world, the Holy Spirit descended upon me in a manner that seemed to go through me, body and soul. I could feel the impression, like a wave of electricity, going through and through me. Indeed, it seemed to come in waves and waves of liquid love; for I could not express it in any other way.[11]

Aspects of Mystical Reports

In this paper I will be looking at the use of language in reports of mystical experience. The mystical literature contains a great variety of linguistic performances, and many of them do not fall under this rubric. There are various sorts of autobiographical materials (in addition to reports of mystical experiences); practical directions to those engaged in the mystic quest; expressions of sentiments toward God and oneself; metaphysical speculations; theological constructions; and so on. We will not be concerned with any of that. Instead, we will be discussing those passages in which mystics tell us about their direct perceptions of God. What is involved in that? We can usefully distinguish the following aspects. On the *subjective* side there is (1) the account of the mode of consciousness involved, what it is like to be directly aware of God; and (2) conscious reactions, largely affective. On the objective side there is (3) the identification of the object; and (4) a specification of how the object appeared to the subject, what the subject experienced the object *as*, or, as we shall call them, *modes of appearance*.

The Use of Language in Aspects 1 and 2

Now let us survey the four aspects I have distinguished with an eye to the semantic status of each, particularly with respect to the distinction between literal and figurative uses of language. To begin with aspect 2, there is no particular difficulty in a literal interpretation. There is absolutely no reason to deny that Henry Suso, in excerpt IV, was speaking literally when he reports being *joyful, satisfied*, and *full of contentment*, and experiencing *sensations of silence and of rest*, or to deny that in excerpt III, Angela da Foligno is speaking literally in reporting *delight* and *joy*. These are relatively unspecific descriptions; our subjects believe, no doubt, that the joy they felt is specifically different from more familiar joys, and they do not really try to specify just how it is different. Angela just signals that it is quite special with her phrase "ineffable joy." Nevertheless, they do succeed in telling us something about their affective state; being joyful, satisfied, or contented is markedly different from being morose, angry, or upset. And so they can, and do, go some distance toward reporting their reactions by using words in a straightforward, literal way.

Aspect 1 is a somewhat different story. But first let me make sure I have sufficiently explained the distinction between aspects 1 and 4. Aspect 4 has to do with what God is presented to the subject's experience as being or doing. Reports of aspect 3 are thus confined to attributes or actions that are conceivably attributable to God. In our passages, the following constitute a sample of these "modes of appearance" as we shall call them: *goodness* and *power* (excerpt I), *plenitude* (III), and *love* (v). On the contrary, aspect 1 is the subjective side of the experience; it has to do with the way the appearances "come to" the subject or are "presented to" her. The mention of penetration by Bonnet (as we may call the anonymous French Swiss in excerpt I), obviously comes under this rubric, along with the talk in excerpt v of "waves of liquid love," indicating a certain periodicity and an ebb and flow in the appearances. It is clear that these specifications involve analogy and/or metaphor, though my partial unpacking of the "wave" metaphor indicates that something might be done in the way of more literal speech. In any event, most of the attempts to contribute to aspect 1 in these selections involves the use of terms for sensory modalities. In the second of Angela's three stages in excerpt III, she speaks of *feeling* God (and since God speaks words to her, she also plainly implies that she *hears* Him). In the third stage she *sees* Him, and it appears that she distinguishes the third from the second stage primarily by this distinction between feeling (and hearing) on the one hand, and sight on the other. Suso also speaks of "that which I see and feel." Here our informants are employing the doctrine of "spiritual senses," of which we hear quite a lot in the Catholic mystical tradition.[12] The sensory terms are being applied here analogically. Our subjects are telling us that there are different ways of being directly aware of God, the differences between which can be grasped only (or best) by considering the differences between sense modalities as a model. Thus some ways of being conscious of the presence of God are related to other ways, as touch is to sight. The major mystics in this tradition are often quite explicit in denying that they mean to be speaking literally of the bodily senses when they report seeing, hearing, feeling, or tasting God. Thus Saint Teresa:

> It [the soul] perceives a fragrance, let us say for now, as though there were in that interior depth a brazier giving off sweet-smelling perfumes. No light is seen, nor is the place seen where the brazier is; but the warmth and the fragrant fumes spread through the entire soul and even often enough, as I have said, the body shares in them. See now that you understand me; no heat is felt, nor is there the scent of any perfume, for the experience is more delicate than an experience of these things; but I use the examples only so as to explain it to you.[13]

And in the last part of excerpt II, we find Teresa struggling to explain the sense in which she "saw" Jesus Christ by her side. Much more could and should be said about the "spiritual senses," but we shall have to forgo that here. Like the talk of "permeation" and "waves," this talk of spiritual senses is analogical or metaphorical; but unlike the former, it would seem to be an irreducible metaphor. Until or unless a mystical linguistic community is established in which terms for "spiritual senses" can become publicly established, there will be no alternative to using metaphorical language to refer to these modes of consciousness. For more on this, see the discussion of aspect 4.

Modes of Appearance

As for the objective side of the matter, it is best to begin with aspect 4. Here we come to what is most basically learned from mystical experience, that which serves as the basis for anything further we can glean from these experiences. As a basis for this discussion, let us list the modes of appearance specified in the passages with which we are working: *goodness* (excerpt I), *power* (I), *presence* (I and II), *plenitude* (III), *brightness* (IV), *love* (V), *speaking* (I, II, and III), and *descending* (V). A careful scrutiny of this list will reveal a surprising fact: most of these terms clearly do not pick out phenomenal qualities that have the same status as simple sensory qualities like redness, roundness, roughness, or acridity; thus they would not seem to pick out qualities that something could present itself to our experience as bearing. Consider attributes like power, goodness, love, and plenitude, or actions like speaking. Power and goodness are complex dispositional properties or bases thereof, dispositions to act in various ways in various situations. To speak to someone is to engage in certain actions with a certain intention. How can something present itself to one's experience as *good* or *powerful*, or as *speaking*, in the same sense as that in which it can be experienced as red, round, rough, or bitter? How can our sources be telling us about how God *appeared* to their experience? Aren't they rather telling us what they *believe* about what appeared to them? We must clear up this perplexity before we can come to grips with the uses of language here. And this will require becoming more explicit about the notion of phenomenal qualities and their difference from what we may call "objective" qualities. Let us make the distinction in terms of concepts rather than qualities, since I do not want to assume that the same quality cannot be grasped both as phenomenal and as objective.

1. A *phenomenal* concept is a concept of the intrinsic qualitative distinctiveness of a way of appearing (looking, smelling . . .). When I use the word "red" in a phenomenal sense, in saying that something looks red, I am simply recording the qualitative distinctiveness of the way it visually appears to me, and that is all. I am saying nothing about its continuing powers and proclivities, its entanglements with other things, its intrinsic nature, or anything else that goes beyond the visually sensible character of its look. When, on the other hand, I use "red" in an objective, physical-property sense, I am saying something about the disposition of the object to look one way or another under one or another set of circumstances, and/or its physical structure, powers, or capacities.

Next, let us note that we frequently report how something looks, or otherwise appears, not by recording a phenomenal distinctiveness of the appearance, but by conceptualizing it in some other way. These "appears as . . ." concepts can be classified as follows:

2. *Comparative.* This is to say what sort of object can be expected to appear, in these circumstances or in normal circumstances, as this object is appearing. Thus to say "This tie

looks red (to me now)" could be to say "This tie looks to me now as a red tie would be expected to look under normal conditions." Here we are clearly not using a phenomenal concept of red or any other phenomenal concept. We are, rather, using objective concepts of red tie, normal conditions, and so forth, and characterizing this look by comparing it with other looks characterized in these objective terms.
3. *Doxastic.* This is to say something about the belief to which this appearance could be expected to give rise. According to the doxastic concept, the statement "The tie looks red" means "The tie looks so as to normally lead one to believe that it is red." Here, again, none of the concepts employed are phenomenal ones, even the concept of red, for the belief that the tie is red, to which the look is being said to normally give rise, is the belief that the tie has a certain physical property.
4. *Epistemic.* This is like the doxastic concept, except that the look is characterized in terms of what beliefs it can justify or provide an adequate basis for, rather than in terms of what beliefs it can be expected to engender. Here "The tie looks red" means "If one formed the belief that the tie was red on the basis of the way it looks, that belief would be justified."

Please note that we are not distinguishing different ways or modes of appearing (looking), but different ways of conceptualizing appearances. One and the same look of the tie to one and the same person at a certain time could be correctly reported in each of these four ways. It is important to note that a phenomenal concept is, so to speak, always in the background even when not explicitly employed. If I make a true report by using a comparative concept in saying "X looks red," I am really presupposing that there is some qualitative distinctiveness to the appearance that could be captured by a phenomenal concept, even though I am using no such concept at the moment. For I am supposing that there is some way in which an X like this looks under normal conditions, and this way would have its intrinsic nature captured by a phenomenal concept. The same comment applies to the doxastic and epistemic concepts.

Now for the bearing of all this on our perplexity. The critic was pointing out that such concepts as power, goodness, and love are not phenomenal concepts. And so they are not. However, that does not show that our sources could not be accurately reporting how God appears to their experience by using such concepts as these. We have just noted various alternatives to the use of phenomenal concepts in specifying how something looks or otherwise appears. In particular, there are comparative concepts that can be used to characterize a particular appearance in terms of how something of a certain objective sort could be expected to appear under certain conditions—for example, these conditions. To illustrate this with sense perception, I could correctly report that X looked like a house or a Porsche or Jason's Porsche or a bald eagle, or tasted like a white Burgundy, or sounded like Handel, thereby giving you an idea of how it looked, tasted, or sounded. And yet these are objective, nonphenomenal concepts. No doubt, in each of these cases there will be some complex pattern of visual, gustatory, or auditory qualia by virtue of the awareness of which I can recognize the object as a house, Jason's Porsche, or whatever. And, no doubt, it is in principle possible to form and use a phenomenal concept of just that phenomenal pattern. But we rarely make use of any such concepts, and for good reasons. The diversity of such patterns is enormous; nor do there seem to be any intuitively natural principles for classifying such patterns into types on the basis of intrinsic features. What we do instead is to group such patterns, such complex "looks," into types on the basis of extrinsic features, most usually on the basis of how a certain sort of objective thing (event, state of affairs) will look under certain frequently recurring types of conditions. Thus we group the phenomenally heterogeneous looks of houses, under not unusual conditions of observation, into a general concept of "looks like a house." Moreover, and this is the point I have been leading up to, we typically report all but the most elementary ways of perceptual appearing in these comparative terms. Except for basic sensory qualities like color, shape, size, loudness, softness, and bitterness, we report how a thing looks or sounds by specifying some objective thing that could be expected to look or sound the same way. This is not due to laziness or an excessive interest in the objective as opposed to the subjective. As we have seen, there is really no alternative. Even where we set out to explain what it is about the look of something that leads us to classify it as, say, a tree, we rarely have recourse to phenomenal concepts. I am likely to point out that it has the look of something with branches, leaves, and so forth. But these part-looks are also being reported in comparative terms.

And so it is here. Our sources could quite well be using comparative concepts to specify how they are being appeared to, just as we typically do with sense perception whenever the mode of appearance is complex. They can be interpreted as saying something like: *I was aware of God as presenting the kind of appearance it would be reasonable to expect a supremely powerful (good, loving) being to present.* And so from the premise that they are not using phenomenal concepts, it does not follow that they are not reporting how God appears to their experience. To be sure, this is not the only possible way to understand them. They could conceivably be using terms like "power" and "goodness" to pick out a distinctively mystical *phenomenal* quality. However, on that construal we cannot understand what they are saying, whereas on the one I have suggested, we can. Since they are addressing their remarks to the world at large and not just to highly developed mystics, there is a presumption in favor of an interpretation that renders what they are saying intelligible to their audience.[14]

So far, so good. But we have still not specified the basic phenomenal qualities of spiritual perception. We have spoken in a holistic way about how a loving being might characteristically appear to one. This will presumably involve some pattern of simple phenomenal qualities. But are those qualities the spiritual analogues of color and shape and other simple sensory qualities?

It must be confessed that we are quite incapable of enumerating the basic phenomenal qualities of which "divine phenomena" are configurations. That's the bad news. The good news is that we can understand why this should be the case. Let us consider what enables us to carry off this job for sense perception. We have gone some distance in discerning the ways in which sensory experiences of various sorts depend on physical, physiological, and psychological conditions. Thus we have discovered quite a bit about the stimulus conditions of various sensory qualities, and so we have been able to subject the experience of those qualities to a considerable degree of stimulus control. The more rudimentary forms of these accomplishments predate recorded history; this is why we have had an intersubjectively shared language for sensory qualities since time immemorial. This knowledge and control has been greatly extended in the past 150 years by physiological psychology, and as a result we have been able to dimensionalize and study various sensory qualities and gain much more understanding of them and their role in perception. But nothing like this has happened with respect to the perception of God, nor is it likely to happen. We know nothing of the mechanisms of such perception, if indeed there are such things; nor can we grasp any useful regularities in the conditions under which God will appear in one or another qualitatively distinctive way to one's experience. Perhaps such conditions have to do with God's purposes and intentions, but if so, that gives us no handle for prediction and control. Thus we lack the most elementary prerequisites for analyzing divine appearances into their phenomenal elements, cataloging them, associating them intersubjectively with names, dimensionalizing them, and so on. The reason this is good news is that it explains why we would be in a position of almost complete ignorance here even if there are basic phenomenal qualities that make up the character of divine appearances.

The Use of Language in Aspects 3 and 4

The preceding discussion might leave the reader with the impression that mystics use only comparative concepts to report modes of appearance, leaving completely unspecified the phenomenal qualities out of which divine appearances are composed. But that would not be accurate. Think back to the earlier reference to the doctrine of "spiritual senses." This way of thinking has definite implications for what might count as basic phenomenal qualities in the perception of God. In supposing that "seeing" God is related to "feeling" God in a way analogous to that in which seeing is related to feeling, we are thereby supposing that the phenomenal qualities one is aware of in the former way of perceiving God are related to the qualities of the latter way in a fashion analogous to that in which visual qualities are related to tactile qualities. And, in fact, our sources invite that implication by using sensory quality terminology (as well as sensory modality terminology) to specify, metaphorically, how God appears to them. Thus Suso refers to a "Shining Brightness" and "sweetness," thereby implying that the way God appeared to him was much more like the way something bright looks than the way something dim looks, and much more like the way something sweet tastes than the way something sour tastes. Compare also Teresa's talk about "perfumes" in the passage quoted earlier. Thus some of our sources are using sensory terms analogically or metaphorically to specify spiritual phenomenal qualities. Just because we cannot forge senses for spiritual phenomenal terms in an established language, this is their only recourse. Our talk about feelings provides a useful analogue. The shadings and nuances of feelings are much too variegated and subtle to be captured in distinct terms. Often the best we can do to get across to someone else (or even to ourselves) how we felt on a given occasion is by analogy or metaphor. "I felt as one does when seeing the first crocus peeping up in the garden in early spring"; or "I felt something like the way one feels when just awakening out of a sound sleep." Perhaps it is this inability to specify phenomenal qualities in a more direct way that is chiefly responsible for the frequency of complaints of "inexpressibility."

But the fact remains that most of the talk about how God appears to one's experience is in comparative terms, with the distinctive content contributed by terms for objective rather than phenomenal properties. We will look at the implications of this for linguistic questions after we take a look at aspect 3, the identification of the object, which, we will see, raises similar questions.

Aspect 3 is unlike the other factors in the way in which it "goes beyond" experience. In identifying what one is aware of as God or as Christ, one is neither simply reporting that one's experience has a certain feature or is of a certain sort, as in aspects 1 and 2, nor simply making explicit how something appears to one's experience, as in aspect 4. To be sure, in reporting that I felt the presence of God, I was speaking of what I am aware of; but in identifying that *what* as God, I was going beyond anything this object presents itself as being to my experience. The word "God" carries a lot of theological freight for our informants. Or if that is not the right way to put it, if "God" is a proper name and does not have meaning but only a reference, we can still say that in using that name to refer to what one is experiencing, one is thereby taking oneself to be aware of the presence of the creator of heaven and earth, He who spoke to the prophets, He who became incarnate in Jesus Christ for our redemption from sin and death, and so on. And even if X presents itself to one's experience as goodness, power, or a shining brightness, X could hardly be presenting itself to me as the creator of heaven and earth or the redeemer of mankind. In being aware of the presence of God, I am *not* aware of Him bringing heaven and earth into being, nor am I aware of Him sending His son into the world. How could I be?[15] Even if I am aware of God as "saying" to me that He created heaven and earth, what I am experientially aware of is the communication of that message, not the creation in question. Of course, there is a sense in which I can experience X as the creator of heaven and earth. That is, I can, while being experientially aware of X, think of it as the creator. But that is something I bring to the experience rather than something I glean from it. I am not experientially aware of the creation the way I may be experientially aware of God's love.[16]

An analogy with sense perception may help here. A house can present itself to me as square, red, rough-textured, and even having dormer windows and siding. But how about its being *your* house? Of course, it can present itself to me as bearing your name on the front. But that is not the same thing. Its being *your* house is a matter of legal ownership, and that legal status is not something that can be displayed in experience the way sensory qualities can, or even in the way *being a house with certain kinds of doors and windows and walls* can. Note that in both sense perception and mystical perception, X can be perceptually recognized as something that bears certain properties that cannot be presented in experience. I may have come to know that a house that looks a certain way is the house that enjoys the legal status of belonging to you, and so by virtue of knowing that truth I can tell by the way the house looks that it is your house—even though the latter is not something presented to me in experience. And similarly for being God, or, more specifically, being creator, redeemer, or judge. I may have come to know (or be justified in believing) that anything that exhibits certain features to my experience (supreme lovingness or plenitude) is the creator of everything other than itself, and by virtue of this knowledge I can tell by the way something is experienced that it is the creator. But, again, this is not something that can itself be displayed to anyone's experience.

But why suppose that the identifying characteristics of God differ from ways of appearing like *power* and *goodness* by virtue of "going beyond" what is given in experience? After all, we have seen that power and goodness are objective rather than phenomenal properties; they, too, go beyond the qualitative distinctiveness of any experience. The crucial difference is this: for properties the terms for which can be used in comparative concepts of appearances there is a distinctive look, feel, or whatever that things with such a property normally present, even where this is not part of the meaning of the term. Thus though being a knife is not just (or perhaps at all) looking a certain way, still there is a distinctive look to a knife; and so *being a knife* is something that, in that way, can be displayed in experience. But for the terms we have been tagging as "going beyond experience," the objective property is not tied to any distinctive appearance; it does not look, smell, or feel any characteristic way. This is true of legal statuses like ownership, social statuses like being the president of a certain company, and relational statuses like being the judge or redeemer of mankind. We are hard put to envisage any distinctive experiential "feel" associated with such statuses or activities. Thus these features "go beyond experience" in a stronger way.

Without more ado, let us consider how terms are being used both in employing comparative concepts of appearances and in identifying God. The most basic point is that there is nothing about mystical experience that enforces a metaphorical or other nonliteral interpretation here.[17] There is nothing here comparable to the constraints we felt with respect to aspect 1 and with respect to basic phenomenal qualities. The objective terms used in reports of aspects 3 and 4 are not themselves directly descriptive of experience, mystical or otherwise. They are "brought to" the experience rather than stemming from it. Hence the fact that they are being used in mystical reports has no tendency to show that their use is any different from what it is in any other context. Thus the question of how they are used *is* the general question of how terms are used in application to God. If no term can be literally applied to God, these terms are not used literally here. If, on the other hand, it is possible to speak literally as well as metaphorically and otherwise of God, that possibility is open here as well. There is nothing about mystical experiences to foreclose that possibility.

But let us not go too rapidly. The foregoing is, I think, quite adequate for aspect 3, assuming that, at least for the most part, the identifying characteristics of God are brought by the mystic to the experience rather than read off of them in any way. But aspect 4 is more complicated. The terms themselves are objective ones, but in being used to express comparative concepts of *experiential appearances*, they are being put to a special use. Since they are used to specify, indirectly, the way God appears to the subject's experience, does that shake us out of a literal interpretation? I do not see why it should. Here the distinction between the comparative concept and the (possible) phenomenal concept in the background is crucial. We have already seen that we (and they) are without resources for literally denominating the distinctive phenomenal quality of the experience, whether in terms of simple phenomenal qualities or in terms of some larger phenomenal gestalt. But that is not what we aspire to do in using comparative concepts of appearances; in fact, we use those concepts just because we are unable to do the former. Let us go back to sense perception to help clarify the point. I say "It tastes like pineapple"; here I am using "pineapple" in as literal a way as it can be used, *even though I am not using any terms literally to specify the distinctive phenomenal quality involved*. I am not using any term literally to do this because I cannot. Unable to deploy a term for the intrinsic quality of the taste, there being none, I have recourse to an indirect maneuver: I specify what biological kind would taste that way under normal conditions. In doing so, I use the biological kind term just as literally as I would if I were simply identifying an object as a pineapple.

And so it is here. In using a comparative concept like *appears to my experience the way a very good person could be expected to appear*, I employ the term "good" to specify the kind of external object the experience of which would normally yield the phenomenal complex to which I am referring. And, again, that use is or can be just as literal as if I were to say of a particular human being that she is a good person. To be sure, these terms *could* be used metaphorically in such applications, but there is nothing about the fact that they occur in comparative specifications of divine appearances to imply that they are. They can be used literally and, I think, often are.

Let us spell out these points in application to some of the terms with which we have been working. To take an extreme case, why suppose that Teresa is not speaking literally in saying that she felt

Christ "by my side" and "always on my right hand." The passage gives every indication that she meant "on my right hand" in the same way as she would if she were speaking of an embodied human being on her right hand. True enough, in the latter case she would discern this with the eyes of the body, and in the former case it is rather an "intellectual vision." But that is not to say that "on my right hand" is used any differently in the two cases. Of course, one *could* use a phrase like that metaphorically or symbolically, as when the Nicene and Apostles' creeds speak of Christ as "sitting on the right hand of the Father," but Teresa, who does literally have a right hand, is presumably not using the phrase in that way. Indeed, most of the terms on our list seem to be used literally rather than figuratively. Why suppose that Bonnet was not using "power" and "goodness" literally? Did he mean to be saying not that God appeared to his experience the way a good and powerful person in the ordinary senses would, but that God appeared to him as a person who had some analogue of these characteristics would? I see no reason to suppose so. Similar remarks apply to the use of terms like "plenitude" and " beauty" in comparative concepts.

How about the action attributions: "reply, " "speak," and "descend?" We have to keep reminding ourselves (at least I do) that we are not discussing a direct application of these terms to God, in which case "speak" would presumably not be used literally, since no vocal chords are involved. Now I do not wish to deny that Teresa and Angela did mean to be making such a use; they presumably believed, and were saying, that God did speak to them. But what we are considering is the use of these terms to specify, comparatively, how God was appearing to them.[18] And here the considerations of the previous paragraph apply. In saying that God appeared to her (somewhat) as a human being speaking would, Teresa, it seems clear, meant "as a human being *literally* speaking would," not "as a human being *metaphorically* speaking would." Again, the term is being used to specify the basis of the comparison for the comparative concept. It is not being used, in this application, to directly describe the experience; nor is it being directly applied to the object of the experience. Hence even if God does not speak in the literal sense of the term, the term may well be used literally in expressing a comparative concept of a mode of appearance. And so for the other action terms, including any that may be literally applicable to God, like "reply" (which does not carry any restrictions to the use of vocal chords).

Thus as far as objective terms are concerned, the upshot is this: there are no pressures from anything distinctive of mystical experience that push us in the direction of a nonliteral interpretation. If these terms are being used nonliterally it is because of more general considerations that constrain us to use terms nonliterally in any talk about God, whether in reporting mystical experience or otherwise. With space and time enough, I would now go into that more general question of the status and interpretation of theological predication. But since I have reached the end of the editor's tolerance, and the reader's patience, I shall merely refer you to some of the works in which I have discussed this issue at length.[19] The general conclusion is that certain relatively abstract and unspecific terms can be used literally of God, and indeed can be used univocally of God and creatures. But this abstract and sketchy core must be supplemented by healthy doses of metaphorical, analogical, and symbolic language before we have what is needed for a functioning religion. Within the literal core are some terms we have seen in our sample reports: "power," "goodness," and "plenitude."

This paper has addressed only a fragment of the total problem of the use of language in mysticism. But however tiny that fragment, it is of the first importance, I believe, to get straight as to where language may be used literally in such reports, so as to free ourselves of the undiscriminating view that everything in such reports is to be understood analogically, metaphorically, or symbolically.

Notes

1. See, for example, W. T. Stace, *Mysticism and Philosophy* (Philadelphia, 1960), chap. 2.

2. Some of my sources, such as Henry Suso and Angela da Foligno, also report unitary experiences, but that does not alter the fact that some of their putatively direct awarenesses of God, and many experiences of others, are not of that character. It may be argued, of course, that the unitary experiences are more "highly developed," but even if that is true by some standards, my point remains. In *Mysticism and Philosophy*, Stace

tries to show that the experiences of Saint Teresa that do not appear on the surface to be unitary really are, but I find his attempt unconvincing.

3. See, for example, Evelyn Underhill, *Mysticism* (New York, 1955), chap. 6.

4. A good example of this is W. T. Stace, *Time and Eternity* (Princeton, N.J., 1952), chap. 6. In *Mysticism and Philosophy*, chapter 6, Stace recants these views.

5. Although this view is unusual it is not unprecedented. In chapter 6 of *Mysticism and Philosophy*, Stace also claims a place for literal language, though he does not go into the distinctions I will be drawing between the places where it is and is not useable.

6. I could make the same linguistic points I will be making in this essay if I used another theory of perception to construe mystical experience. Since I have to do it in some particular way, I use the theory I believe to be the most adequate.

7. This is an anonymous report quoted in William James, *Varieties of Religious Experience* (1902; reprint, New York, n.d.), pp. 67-68.

8. Saint Theresa of Avila, *Life*, chap. 27, quoted in Underhill, *Mysticism*, pp. 284-85.

9. Angela da Foligno, "Livre de l'experience des vrais fidèles," quoted in Underhill, *Mysticism*, p. 282.

10. Henry Suso, *Leben*, chap. 1, quoted in Underhill, *Mysticism*, p. 187.

11. Quoted in James, *Varieties of Religious Experience*, p. 250.

12. For a good presentation of this doctrine, along with quotations from a wide variety of figures in the Catholic mystical tradition, see Augustin Poulain, *The Graces of Interior Prayer*, trans. L. L. Yorke Smith, ed. J. V. Bainvel (St. Louis, 1950), chap. 6.

13. Saint Teresa of Avila, *The Interior Castle*, Fourth Mansion, trans. Kieran Kavanaugh and Otilio Rodriguez (New York, 1979), chap. 2, sec. 6.

14. Of course, in using a comparative concept of *looks like a P* to characterize an experience, S is assuming that he knows what a P looks like (in normal conditions or whatever), and this assumption may be challenged. How does Bonnet know how a supremely good being would present itself to his experience? Presumably, his experience with more or less good human beings has given him some idea as to what it is like, experientially, to be interacting with a good person manifesting his goodness, as contrasted with what it is like experientially to be interacting with an evil person manifesting that quality.

15. Am I being too narrow here? What if God brought it about, by a supernatural elevation of my faculties, that I did behold His act of cre-

ation? I do not have any sense of how this would go, but that is presumably not much of an argument for its impossibility. But I can dismiss it from consideration on the grounds that in the sorts of cases on which we are concentrating the subjects do not report any such thing. I am interested in understanding the normal cases in which in identifying the object of one's awareness as God one is supposing this object to have various properties and to have performed various actions that are not then and there displayed to one's experience.

16. The fact that the perceptual recognition of God is largely based on what one brings to a particular experience, rather than on what is displayed therein, poses an obvious epistemic problem for the supposition that beliefs about God can be based on mystical experience. For it would seem to imply that the basing can be partial at best. But that is not our concern in this paper. Here our interest is limited to the bearing this has on the way these characteristics can be articulated in language.

17. In saying this I am presupposing the point made earlier that not all mystical experiences, and in particular not the kind reported in our chosen passages, are experiences of an absolutely undifferentiated unity. If all mystical experiences fit the "undifferentiated unit" model, the linguistic story would be different.

18. It may, of course, be argued that there is no such use of the actions terms in these passages, and such a position would be more plausible than would a like position with respect to attributive terms like "power" and "goodness." Nevertheless, it seems overwhelmingly plausible to me that they also meant their talk of God's speaking to give us some idea of how God appeared to their experience.

19. William P. Alston, "Can We Speak of Literally of God?" in A. Steuer and J. McClendon, eds., *Is God GOD?* (Nashville, Tenn., 1981); "Irreducible Metaphors in Theology," in E. T. Long, ed., *Experience, Reason, and God* (Washington D.C., 1980); "Functionalism and Theological Language," *American Philosophical Quarterly* 22 (July 1985); "Divine and Human Action," in T. V. Morris, ed., *Divine and Human Action* (Ithaca, N.Y., 1988). All these essays are included in my *Divine Nature and Human Language* (Ithaca, N.Y., 1989).

4

What Would Buddhaghosa Have Made of *The Cloud of Unknowing*?

NINIAN SMART

This essay is in a self-evident way concerned with the relation between mysticism and language. It makes use of ideas first expressed in my essay "Interpretation and Mystical Experience" (1965). It takes two texts from different cultures, reflecting highly diverse religious assumptions—one could hardly get a greater contrast than Theravada Buddhism and medieval Christianity, save that both traditions took contemplation seriously. It tries to get at the phenomenology behind the language. It uses methods sketched in my 1965 article. It argues that there are phenomenological similarities between the differing practices despite the contrast in language and style between Buddhaghosa and the author of *The Cloud of Unknowing*. It appears to me that the best mode of dealing with the issues of mysticism and language is to be found in the comparative treatment of texts. While I have long argued for the importance of context in analyzing doctrinal systems and mythic schemes and, indeed, have devoted a good deal of attention to this in my book *Reasons and Faiths* (1958), written in the analytic or linguistic philosophical tradition and under the influence of J. L. Austin, my

Oxford supervisor, I hold that there are genuine phenomenological comparisons to be made cross-culturally, especially in relation to mystical experience. This I hope is something that emerges from this essay.

One of the major obstacles to the thesis of a commonality between mystical or contemplative states in differing religions lies in the very diversity of contexts in which some of the most important treatises are written. Thus the whole atmosphere of the *Visuddhimagga* (*Path of Purification*) differs greatly from that of the English *Cloud of Unknowing*. Among other divergences is the way in which the *Path* is full of rather detailed instructions on the nitty-gritty of contemplative practices, while the *Cloud* is more poetic and allusive. Then there are the assumptions of the two religions. The *Path* urges recollection, for instance, of the Buddha (VII.2ff.) and the various epithets applied to him, such as "accomplished," "fully enlightened," "blessed," and so on. The contemplative therefore explicitly places himself or herself in the context of follower of the Buddha. The whole soteriology lying behind the contemplative's activities is therefore flavored with Buddhist concepts. But by contrast, the *Cloud*—though it has sometimes been accused by Christians of not being sufficiently Christocentric—is firmly planted in the tradition of Christ. Thus in chapter 4 the author says, "For in the love of Jesus shall be thine help. Love is such a power that it maketh all things to be shared. Therefore love Jesus, and all things that he hath it is thine." Consider, apart from matters of doctrine, the very different mythic ambience of the two figures: the one of royal birth, and trailing behind a whole chain of *Jātaka* stories, working out his own salvation, living to an old age, analytic in teaching, dying peacefully; and the other of artisan background, divine however, brief in public career, fiery in parables, ending his life violently with criminal execution, rising from the dead, a king, but poor. It is obvious that the meaning of contemplation must have been very different for Buddhaghosa and the author of the *Cloud*.

But there are limits on particularism. If we so emphasize the difference of context that we have room only for diversity, then no activity can be properly compared as to likenesses across culture or between traditions. But this is obviously wrong, for several reasons.

1. There are no absolute divides between traditions (e.g., between Judaism and Christianity), still less between subtraditions.
2. The thesis would destroy the possibility of using a common language to write about two traditions.
3. Good comparative studies—for example, of sacrifice in diverse traditions—have been written.

All this does not mean that we should facilely overemphasize similarities. In some ways the situation is like the one that exists between individuals. Every person has a nose, but the shapes differ and their organic placement differs. The good artist captures the generality of noses, but, more important, also captures the individual particularity of the portraitee's nose. The methodological rub is how to find a way of discerning similarities beneath the great diversities of context and conceptual cultures. In "Interpretation and Mystical Experience," I suggested using the notion of ramification in trying to resolve the problem. Less ramified language is likely to be closer to immediate experience because more ramified language—like the above references to the Buddha and to Jesus—suggests a wider epistemological context.

If one were to imagine Buddhaghosa reading the *Cloud*, the most accessible part would, from this perspective, be related to the moral qualities required of the contemplative. Although the author of the *Cloud* is conventional in listing the seven deadly sins (chap. 10), the relatively straightforward application of the ideas, uncomplicated by doctrinal presuppositions—even if doctrinal selectively lies behind their being spotlighted—would make the relevant passages intelligible. There would indeed be some matching between anger, envy, sloth, pride, covetousness, gluttony, and lust and the relevant bad attitudes found in the *Path*, themselves arising from an old Buddhist tradition. Thus Buddhaghosa treats greed, ill will, grief at privation, cruelty, joy at success, aversion, and resentment as the enemies of the four great "abidings," or *brahmavihāras*. These attitudes surely cover much of the first five deadly sins, and there are plenty of references to gluttony (e.g., I.47) and lust (I.144). So though the way virtues and vices are described varies somewhat, there appear to be fairly broad agreements about the behavior required of a person undertaking the Christian or the Buddhist life. The fact that the *Cloud* arose in a culture where great importance was attached to the monastic life helps to close the gap between Sri Lanka and medieval England.

There is, of course, a usage that might have caused problems for Buddhaghosa: the identification of the highest virtues with love. The usual story is that for Buddhism the central virtue is compassion, or *karuṇā*. This has a different flavor from that of *agape*, or reverential love of other beings. But the proper comparison would be with the four *brahmavihāras*, which could cover both love and justice in the Christian tradition. For *metta, karuṇā,* and *mudita* — that is, loving kindness, compassion, and gladness of others' successes — cover love, while *upekkhā* (equity) covers the idea of the impartial treatment of others. Of course, there are doctrinal underpinnings of love, as there are of the *brahmavihāras*: on the one hand, the Trinity as an exemplar of loving solidarity, and, on the other, the impermanence and suffering that characterize the lot of living beings.

In principle, then, there is not a huge gap between the ethical requirements of the two paths, though the Buddhist account is more detailed and analytical, and is not negatively concerned with the concept of sin, which figures prominently in the language of the *Cloud* (e.g., the heading of chap. 10: "How a man shall know when his thought is no sin; and if it be sin, when it is deadly and when it is venial"). There is, however, quite a different analysis of our troubles, more to do with original ignorance than with original sin in the Buddhist tradition.

Since in the *Path* the practice of the *jhānas* is very important, both with and without the use of devices, or *kasinas*, Buddhaghosa would have had no trouble in understanding what was sometimes strange and even shocking to English commentators — the idea of the "cloud of forgetting." Consider some things that the *Cloud* says on this matter:

> Thou art full further from him [God] when thou has no *cloud of forgetting* betwixt thee and all the creatures that ever be made. (chap. 7)

> Surely this travail is all in treading down of the thought of all the creatures that ever God made, and in holding of them under the cloud of forgetting named before. (chap. 27)

> And try to smite down all knowing and feeling of aught under God, and tread all down full far under the *cloud of forgetting*, And thou shalt understand that in this work thou shall forget not only all other creatures than thyself, or their deeds or thine, but also thou shalt in this work forget both thyself and thy deeds for God, as well as all other creatures and their deeds. (chap. 43)
>
> Thou shalt find, when thou hast forgotten all other creatures and their works—yea, and also thine own works—that there shall remain yet after, betwixt thee and thy God, a naked knowing and feeling must always be destroyed, ere the time be that thou mayest feel verily the perfection of this work. (chap. 43)

It is quite clear from these passages that the author urges readers to do something active about the various objects of their attention. They are to suppress thought and feeling about all entities. Moreover, they must suppress even the bare consciousness of self. This doubtless would remind Buddhaghosa of the higher *jhānas*, in which the adept passes beyond the contemplation of boundless consciousness and ascends to the realms of nothingness and neither-perception-nor-nonperception (*Path*, X.36ff.). It is obvious that putting away the thoughts and images of things does not imply that they have to be seen as creatures of God. So from the angle of unramified description, there seems to be a congruence between the procedures of the *Cloud* and the *Path*. Buddhaghosa is much more formal and detailed, as we have noted, but there is no reason to think that the two traditions point to differing systems of contemplation as such.

I stress the fact that the *Cloud* endorses activity. Despite the doctrine of grace, which the author mentions and makes use of, the follower has to make a strong effort because of the resistance of his normal self to the annihilation of self-consciousness, and because the giving up of everything and blotting it out runs contrary to his ordinary desires (chap. 29). This is analogous to the emphasis that Buddhism places on the wiping out of grasping or desire.

The *Cloud* suggests that the disappearance of the naked knowing and feeling of one's own being comes through grace, but it also depends on "ableness to receive this grace," which is "thought else but a strong and a deep ghostly sorrow." The author comments that readers have to be careful about this sorrow, so that they do not strain their body or spirit too rudely. They should "sit full still, as in a sleeping device." This perfect sorrow arises from the recognition that the person *is*. And yet "in all this sorrow he desireth not to un-be: for that were the devil's madness and despite to God" (chap. 44). Buddhaghosa would not worry too much about the devil, or Māra, but he doubtless would recognize here a parallel with the middle path. The adept desires neither to be nor to un-be. He hopes to lose consciousness of the self, but he does not wish for annihilation.

Incidentally, in the next chapter the *Cloud* makes reference to ways in which disciples can be deceived or deceive themselves, and among the delusory phenomena is an inclination "to have their breasts inflamed by an unnatural heat . . . or else they conceive a false heat wrought by the fiend, their ghostly enemy, caused by their pride and their fleshliness and curiosity of wit" (chap. 45). Here is some form of *tapas* (austerity, literally, "heat")!

The concept of the cloud of forgetting is not spelled out in detail, but there is little doubt that it refers to the systematic effort to blot out sense perception, memories, and imaginings of the world of our sensory environment and of corresponding inner states. For Buddhaghosa, this exercise would have been achieved through the *jhānas*. Thus in the *Path* there is the following interesting passage: "And when the kasina is being removed, it does not roll up or roll away. It is simply that it is called 'removed' on account of his [the contemplative's] non-attention to it, his attention being given to 'space, space.' This is conceptualized as the mere space left by the removal of the kasina" (X.8).

To explain a little: the first four stages of meditation, or *jhānas*, are the so-called *jhānas* of the realm of form because they make use of material forms as objects of concentration—for instance, a blue flower or a gray circle of clay. These so-called devices, or *kasiṇas*, are treated as sense data. The contemplative concentrates on the patch of blue or the patch of gray to the exclusion of everything else. Eventually, it is possible to see only the sense datum; the rest of the visual field is blank. In the next range of *jhānas*— which make use of increasingly refined formulas, such as "space, space," then "consciousness, consciousness," then "there is nothing," then "neither perception nor nonperception,"—the contemplative puts away even the sense datum, wiping out in his mind the perception of the patch of blue or gray. These formulas help to make the mind blank and, in effect, to purify consciousness. The aim is to achieve a state of consciousness that, looked at negatively, has none of its ordinary contents and even transcends the subject-object intentionality that is characteristic of ordinary human states.

It seems to me that this is how Buddhaghosa would have understood the idea of the cloud of forgetting, though he might have been a touch confused because of a different valuation on remembering, or *sati*, as he would have understood it. The notion of forgetting seems to run counter to that wide-awakeness that is typical of Buddhist spiritual manuals, in which the contemplative is super-clearly aware of his every state and is able to analyze the causes of his various feelings. This self-awareness is an important and impressive part of Buddhist techniques of self-control and self-direction. Is there a place for such *sati* in the *Cloud*? There is something parallel to it at least—the sense of the presence in them of stirring of love of the highest: "And if they think that there is no manner of thing that they do, bodily or ghostly, that is sufficiently done with witness of their conscience, unless this secret little love set upon the *cloud of unknowing* be in a ghostly manner the chief of all their work; and if they thus feel—then it is a token that they be called by God . . ." (chap. 75).

There is in the *Cloud* a kind of self-awareness in which particular qualities of the self are dismissed, and one is supposedly consciousness of one's own naked being. Although as we have seen there is not the desire to "un-be," there is an intent to paralyze the ordinary properties of the self. Perhaps the author is putting in a more positive form what in the Buddhist case is frequently seen in negative terms. That is, he may be alluding to something similar to the *anattā* doctrine. For Buddhaghosa, as for others, the purpose of recollection is to accomplish an alienation from the particular short-lived psychophysical properties pertaining to individual existence. At the same time, the Buddha wished to destroy the sense of a permanent something underlying these states, since one could also get attached to such a self. The *Cloud* does not share this way of looking at matters; but it does suggest that the individual contemplative should detach herself or himself from the usual events and concerns of inner and outer life—hence the language of "naked being." Psychologically or phenomenologically, it could be that the purification of consciousness (Buddhist) is equivalent to the attainment of nakedness of being (the *Cloud*).

It must be remembered that the *Cloud* was written within a medieval cultural context in which scholastic philosophy was the norm, and with it came the whole substance-metaphysics of Aristotle as modified somewhat by the negative theology of Dionysius the Areopagite. Pseudo-Dionysius had a great influence on the *Cloud*. But Pseudo-Dionysius nevertheless exercised his negative notions on a structure of substance. His paradoxes occur within the framework of a philosophy of being. (Thus God is said to be both being and nonbeing. To say this, however, is to deny on the surface the applicability of the term "being," but at a deeper level it is to accept that way of talking: Dionysius does not move to some radically alternative mode, such as the idea of events as point-instants, in the mode of Scherbatsky and the Theravadin tradition.) In brief, the *Cloud* was written, naturally enough, from within Western orthodoxies, even if its message was stated somewhat problematically and paradoxically. Given its substance-metaphysic, its concept of "naked being" was a radical one.

It would seem that the author envisaged, with his twin ideas of naked being and the cloud of forgetting, a contemplative attainment in which all particularities in consciousness, even self-consciousness, were put aside. Although this would have been in line with Buddhist meditative procedure, the author of the *Cloud* goes further, as can be seen in the "Epistle of Privy Counsel" (chap. 4).

> For know thou right well, that in this work thou shalt have no more beholding to the qualities of the being of God than to the qualities of the being of thyself. For there is no name, nor feeling, nor beholding more, nor so much, according unto everlastingness (which is God), as is that which may be had, seen and felt in the blind and the lovely beholding of this word *is*. For if thou say: "Good" or "Fair Lord" or "Sweet," "Merciful" or "Righteous," "Wise" or "All-witting," "Mighty" or "Almighty," "Wit" or "Wisdom," "Might" or "Strength," "Love" or "Charity" or what other such thing that thou say of God: all it is hid and enstored in this little word *is*.

In short, the various characteristics of God are ignored. I think this is an indication of what may be called the contextual nature of

God in the *Cloud*. By this I mean that of course God serves as a powerful focus of the whole life and practice of the mystic, and in this way God is a looming part of the mystic's context. But God as such is not—at least not in detail, that is, with his relevant properties—part of the higher inner experience of the mystic. We shall return to this point in discussing the so-called cloud of unknowing. But it seems quite possible that the author of the *Cloud* emphasized the absolutely nondiscursive character of the state of consciousness; he was aiming at its being free even from the more "elevated" thoughts such as of the nature, goodness, and power of God. Put linguistically, the language of theism is imposed on the experience.

There is in the *Cloud* a thesis related to this "nakedness" of experience, and of the intent that impels the person on his quest, which might have interested Buddhaghosa as indicating a parallel with Buddhist ethics. In the Buddhist case, we note a mysterious solidarity between insight and compassion (which in the Mahayana was embodied in the figure of the compassionate Bodhisattva). In an important sense, the *Cloud* is about the love of God. But whereas many writers think of love as related specifically to a person, so that loving God is loving a Person, the *Cloud* has an interesting and paradoxical twist. For true love is identified with "naked intent." This links up, as William Johnston has pointed out, with Thomas Aquinas's doctrine of perfect love, which is not inspired by any "mean,"; that is, it is not inspired by the remembrance of the goodness of God, but simply arises from the loveliness of God in Himself (p. 108). From this perspective, the love of God is the love of X, because all the particularities of the Christian myth and doctrine fall away in the cloud of forgetting. So paradoxically, it is God considered without those attributes that constitute personhood for us, which is the "object" of perfect love. The ineffable character of the focus of the mystical quest thus helps to explain the nature of perfect love. Buddhaghosa would, of course, have used very different language, but he might easily have failed to see any stateable distinction between *nirvāṇa* and God as considered nakedly, so to speak. Is there a distinction phenomenologically? I do not think it can be denied that at least the possibility of the congruence of the two experiences exists. If they are congruent, we still of course have the problem of why, outside of ineffability, such very different "trailers" were left dangling by the two concepts. That issue would take us far afield, but we may note that the numinous dread of God is something that courses down salvation history in the Jewish and Christian traditions but has no strong place in the Theravada. Naturally, too, one can point to the divergence of philosophical theory or worldview and hence of language between the two cultures. All this can be summed up by saying that while Buddhaghosa would have rejected the contextual language of the *Cloud*, he would have made sense of the notions of naked intent and pure or perfect love.

The notion that the mystic must blot out the attributes of God leads him to some passages that seem antidogmatic, as if he were heretical. Thus he writes: "Yea, — and if it be courteous and seemly to say — in this work it profiteth little or nought to think of the kindness or the worthiness of God, nor of our Lady . . ." (chap. 5). The author of the *Cloud* is a devout and orthodox Christian, but even from within the tradition there are forces that make a mystic go beyond doctrines. Buddhaghosa might consider this a kind of confirmation of the Buddha's reluctance to define or describe, except in metaphors, the nature of *nirvāṇa*.

One might add an aside here that helps to reinforce the point made about the contextuality of belief in God and the Trinity in the life of a contemplative such as our author. Given the nature of his upbringing in medieval times, how else could he conceive of his highest quest than as drawing close to or becoming united with God? But if it is the case that the essential character of the higher mystical experience is to be devoid of perceptions of images, even of God, and to rise beyond conceptualization, then there is bound to be a split between the conventional doctrines concerning God (and biblical language), on the one hand, and the mode in which the mystical experience is expressed, on the other. The teaching of the church and the Bible were based substantially on a prophetic and sacramental religion, stressing the dread character of the Almighty, the coming to earth of His Son, and the infusion of the Holy Spirit in the work and sacraments of the church. All these items — the numinous, the incarnation, the ritual dimension of the faith — can exist without the element of mysticism — that is, without the contemplative life. Indeed, there have been periods and phases in the church's history when the contemplative life has been substantially ignored (e.g., in much of Presbyterianism, in periods of

Anglicanism, and so on). The mystical tradition of Christianity has certainly been very important, and the fusion of Neoplatonic thought and practice with Christian doctrine and life has been very fertile. But the main structure of Christian thinking and experience has not derived entirely from contemplation. Hence the question must be asked: How have these noncontemplative elements affected the contemplative, and vice versa? By contrast, it is hard to think of Buddhism appearing in the varieties of Pure-Land Buddhism — and it is impossible to think of Buddhism without contemplation in the context of the Theravada of Buddhaghosa. The *Path* itself expresses the heart of Theravadin spirituality; notably absent is a sacramental kind of ritual and the very idea of a numinous supreme creator. There is no "Thus spake the Lord" prophetism in this tradition. Buddhaghosa would, then, have continually wondered how it was that the author of the *Cloud* had to import such alien ideas as God and Christ into his description of the path that led into the cloud.

So far we have concentrated on the ideas of forgetting and nakedness. But we have to deal with the cloud of unknowing itself. For Buddhaghosa it would have seemed a paradox for a special reason: Buddhism always saw the root of our problem to be, in the last analysis, ignorance—that is, lack of (existential, living) knowledge. It would have seemed strange to have valued a cloud of unknowing so highly. But of course for the *Cloud*, unknowing is, after all, a kind of knowing. The author quotes Dionysius, to whom he is much indebted (though his understanding of him was perhaps imperfect): "And therefore it was that Saint Denis said: The most godly knowing of God is that which is known by unknowing." His reasoning is: "For have a man never so much ghostly understanding in knowing of all made ghostly things, yet he may never by the work of his understanding come to the knowing of an unmade ghostly thing: the which is nought but God. But by the failing it may. Because that thing that it faileth in is nothing else but only God" (chap. 70).

Buddhaghosa acknowledges that higher wisdom, or *paññā*, differs from ordinary knowledge (*Path*, XIV.1-3). It is a penetrative understanding that differs, however, from the kind of understanding or knowing alluded to by the *Cloud* in that it involves reflection, after the highest *jhānic* experience on the nature of events in the world, revealed by contrast with the unmade, the permanent, and so forth, that characterize *nirvāṇa*. We may say that Buddhist knowledge is cyclical in character: the analysis of the world and the possibility of liberation set the scene for treading the path of purification. The worldview is used in describing and categorizing the various states and attitudes of the individual searcher. But the search ends at a higher level that, reflecting back on the world as previously analyzed, penetrates to a deeper level in discerning the nature of things. This process of beginning with a worldview and then returning to it more deeply in the light of mystical experience is less evident in the *Cloud*.

Let us now pass to the cloud of knowing, itself. How does this look from a Buddhist perspective? I think there are three points that we need to consider, which I shall take in reverse order: the nature of the cloud considered in itself; the reference in the *Cloud* to the ray of light said to pierce the cloud; and the notion of a kind of union with God. A major text here, in regard to this last, is found in chapter 67:

> Above thyself thou art: because thou attainest to come thither by grace, whither thou mayest not come by nature. That is to say, to be oned to God, in spirit and in love and in accordance of will Beneath thy God thou art: for although it may be said in a manner that in this time God and thou be not two but one in spirit — insomuch that thou or another that feeleth the perfection of this work may, by reason of that onehead, truly be called a god, as Scripture witnesseth — nevertheless thou art beneath him. For he is God by nature without beginning; and thou sometimes wert nought in substance; and afterwards, when thou wert by his might and his love made aught, thou willfully with sin madest thyself worse than nought. And only by his mercy without thy desert art thou made a god in grace, oned with him in spirit without separation, both here and in the bliss of heaven without any end. So that, although thou be all one with him in grace, yet thou art full far beneath him in nature.

This is indeed a striking passage. We may note how the author is sensitive to possible criticisms. To say that you are God would be *tout court* unacceptable in the Christian tradition. The great gap between God and humanity, bridged by Christ, must be maintained. And yet the author can figure that he is like Christ, who offers himself to God — and so, in the mystic's self-consciousness, his naked being turns out to be the being of God, and so it is God offering himself up to himself (or worshiping himself). The suffering implicit in giving up one's natural desires and impulses can be likened to Christ's suffering. The language of martyrdom, incarnation, and self-giving can thus be melded.

Yet it is fairly clear that when the *Cloud* avers that "thou art less than God" this is not based on the experience itself. There is nothing phenomenological here in the contrast between nature and grace. The exposition of the distinction owes itself to the author's general theological background and linguistic schemata, and if there is anything that is phenomenologically like grace, it arises in the idea of the ray of light, to which I shall come shortly. The distinction that the author makes comes from a prior belief in the everlastingness of God, compared with the finite character of the individual. It should be noted by the way that the assumption that the individual previously was nought in substance is not one that Buddhaghosa would make, since he believes in the preexistence of the individual (*Path*, XVII.253ff.). Given that the author of the *Cloud* believes in a divine creator, then it is easy for him to make the nature-grace distinction, and this softens the alarming character of his claim that we are "oned with God."

It is also fairly clear that in order to be oned, there have to be at least two conceived of as different. It is because the *Cloud* holds to a God over against us that it can naturally enough talk of union. In the case of Buddhaghosa there is nothing out there, though there is the unmade, unconditioned State — *nirvāṇa*. For him it does not make sense to say that the individual is united with something — but there is the vision of *nirvāṇa*, the realization of the unborn condition. This notion was put into the language of emptiness in the Mahayana tradition. There is considerable testimony in the mystical literature that the highest state is without distinction of subject and object, or is nondual (*advaya*). The description that the *Cloud* gives of the cloud itself and the highest experience is consistent with there occurring a nondual experience, which is naturally enough seen ex post facto as being oned with God. But Buddhaghosa might reflect that if we confine our attention to the naked realization of being, in a nondual way, and if we substitute a different ontology for that of being and substance, then there is no incompatibility between the *Cloud* and the *Path* as to the highest state and realization of *nirvāṇa*. Rather than talking of mystical union—common for obvious reasons among theistic mystics and hedged about with qualifications to effect a compromise with the language of numinous Otherness—we might talk of mystical nonduality (I hesitate to use the term "nondualism" because of its association with a kind of monism, which is not the purport either of Theravada Buddhism or of Christian mystical theology).

But there seems to be more than the cloud in the cloud; there is the striking reference to the ray of light. Thus in chapter 26, the author writes:

> Then will he sometimes peradventure send out a beam of ghostly light, piercing this *cloud of unknowing* that is betwixt thee and him, and show thee some of his secrets, the which man may not and cannot speak. Then shalt thou feel thine affection inflamed with the fire of his love, far more than I can tell thee, or may or will at this time. For of that work that pertaineth only to God dare I not take upon me to speak with my blabbering fleshly tongue: and, shortly to say, although I durst I would not.

This experience of light is recorded by a number of mystics. Richard of St. Victor writes of it as *in modum fulguris coruscantis* (*Benjamin minor*, chap. 82). Various instances are recorded by modern Buddhists in Winston L. King's *Theravada Meditation* (pp. 126, 136–37, 159–60). The language of illumination has spread widely in English and other languages. The analogy to a sudden flash may be related to another interesting part of the *Cloud*, where the author writes:

> This work asketh no long time ere it be once truly done, as some men ween; for it is the shortest work of all that man may imagine. It is neither longer nor shorter than is an atom; the which atom, by the definition of true philosophers in the science of astronomy, is the least part of an hour. And it is so little that, for the littleness of it, it is indivisible and nearly incomprehensible. (chap. 4)

According to contemporary medieval calculations, there are over 20,000 atoms in an hour, making this unit equal to about one-sixth of a second. By the unrefined methods of medieval time, this was a tiny unit, perhaps less than the normal perceptions of time would be able to cope with. Perhaps the *Cloud* here signifies, as William Johnston suggests, that the experience is somehow outside time. There are remarks elsewhere indicating that time, place, and body should be forgotten or blotted out in the spiritual life. Somehow the experience of light then suggests something from "outside space and time." Buddhaghosa might note that *nirvāṇa* likewise is referred to as the "immortal place," no doubt hinting at an "event" that is outside of time (as distinguished from ordinary events, which are in time). In brief, the account of a timeless light is within the bounds of metaphors used in the Buddhist tradition.

The passage about the beam of ghostly light implies that somehow the ultimate illuminating experience is spontaneous. For the author, this is reinforcement of the feeling that here we see the operation of grace. The final consummation of the spiritual quest is something that seems given to us. This, of course, is a theme stressed in Zen, though it is less prominent in the Theravada tradition. But an event can be spontaneous without being caused by God and as such categorized as grace. The language of grace has far-reaching ramifications, here no doubt superimposed on the mystical experience.

In saying this I am not implying that the *Cloud* is wrong. In all our experience, we superimpose knowledge gained from elsewhere. I see a patch of red outside my window, out there where the lawn finishes; it is bougainvillea. How do I know that? Not simply by looking, but out of my complex learning in the past. It may be that the author of the *Cloud* is right to diagnose his experience in the cloud of unknowing as being a kind of contact and ultimately oneness with God. Whether he is right or wrong depends on a much wider set of conditions than can be drawn from the mystical experience itself, but it is a wider set that could be put on one side by Buddhaghosa.

We may draw certain conclusions about the cloud of unknowing itself. First, from Buddhaghosa's viewpoint, it can be the same "place" as *nirvāṇa*, provided that the mystic, having reached it, were then to cast his divine eye on the rest of the world in order to contemplate it *sub specie eternitatis* and thus gain insight, or *paññā*. Second, it takes the mystic "outside time" to perceive what is transcendent. Third, the experience involves the perception of a spiritual light, so that it contains the images of both light and obscuring (a point mentioned by some other mystics, notably Willem van Ruysbroeck). In my view, it is quite possible to conceive of the experience without applying to it the whole language of nature and grace, God and creatures, and so forth, that the author of the *Cloud* naturally uses.

But it is worth noting that though Buddhaghosa might wish to put aside all that language, he would be faced with the question of how it is that the whole Buddhist analysis is to be applied to the highest stages of meditation. Since, of course, Buddhism centers on the mystical quest, which is only one main element in the fabric of Christian experience and practice, it would be easier to justify the Buddhist than the Christian analysis of mysticism. Perhaps this is already brought out by the detailed and confident analytic style of the *Path* and other works. The question of whether the *Cloud* is right turns our attention to the whole language of God, built as it is on the numinous experience and the practice of worship that have only minor places in the Theravadin outlook. Yet we should not neglect the fact that mysticism such as that of the *Cloud* has had notable effects on the language of Christian theology. There is no doubt that the whole enterprise of negative theology (such as in Pseudo-Dionysius) is erected on the practice of mysticism, and the negative language arises from the transsensory nature of mystical experience. Where the mystical strand of Christianity has been absent, other motifs become stronger, as in *bhakti* varieties of the faith and nineteenth-century Methodism. This perhaps reinforces the claim that mysticism and *bhakti*, and mysticism and sacramental religion, are independent of one another. But that is a wider question.

I think Buddhaghosa would have found the *Cloud*'s invitation to the mystical path both intelligible and attractive, but the language of God highly indigestible. The reason, of course, is that built into the language of the *Cloud* are highly ramified conceptions of the divine. That is, the author assumes the truth of classical Western theism as mediated through the Jewish and Christian scriptures and subsequent Christian theologizing and philosophizing. It is a tradition that effectively blends Neoplatonism and Christian faith. By saying that it is highly ramified, I allude to a distinction that I drew in "Interpretation and Mystical Experience." A highly ramified description is one in which a number of propositions are presupposed as true, lying well outside what could be revealed by the experience itself. Admittedly, this is a rather informal distinction. It can be intuitively recognized through the contrast between "He saw a yellow patch" (low ramification) and "He saw a black cassock" (more highly ramified). In the latter case, we have to know what a cassock is, and its function as an ecclesiastical garment. In other words, highly ramified language postulates a fairly extensive context of belief and/or action. Although the existence of ramified language is a fact, it is something that is so because of a nonlinguistic state of affairs, in the sense at least that it is a state of affairs that includes much more than the linguistic. Thus the author of the *Cloud* was plugging into a context of monastic life lying within the historic Christian tradition. The strangeness of the language to Buddhaghosa lies not in the question of translation per se, for many of the problems lie in the divergence of assumptions. Perhaps, being formerly a Brahmin, Buddhaghosa might have recognized in the *Cloud* some pre-Śankaran form of Vedanta, a kind of system of the *Brahmasūtra*.

But the *Cloud*'s language has two levels to it because the author is keen on the negative theology of the Dionysian tradition. The quoted passage from the "Epistle of Privy Counsel" makes interesting reading in this connection. Bare being differs not a whit from bare nonbeing, save that it signals the commitment to a certain style of ontology. The effect of the author's appeal to the little word "is" in effect negates the more particular concepts that he alleges are contained in it. Now Buddhaghosa could have appreciated the negativeness, for that also characterizes emptiness (*sūnyatā*) and *nirvāṇa*. But could he have agreed that the other terms that the author of the *Cloud* draws forth from the ultimate do so derive? Such terms as "Strength," "Almighty," and "All-witting" (i.e., "Omniscient") simply cannot sensibly be predicated of *nirvāṇa*. The fact is that these various predicates are not contained in "is," which is a blank term in having no definitive descriptive function. This is one reason why Buddhaghosa might not find it too uncongenial, since in the higher echelons of the process of *jhāna* he looks for emptier and emptier characterizations of the ineffable state that the adept reaches. This is why for him the *via negativa* could prove to be congenial. Of course, Theravadin ontology is event-based, not thing-based. Yet the *via negativa* still leaves unexplained the connection between the negative descriptions (or non-descriptions) and the more positive language that is secretly there through the commitment and milieu of the believer who wants the negations to apply to her or his ultimate. This is a wider problem than one that is encountered in the *Cloud* or the *Path*. Let me digress a moment before expanding on this point.

Generally the negative way has its function from three sources. One is reflective on the intellectual reasons why the ultimate eludes our grasp. The second and third are existential. The notion of ineffability has a descriptive and a performative aspect. The descriptive aspect arises from the descriptive nullity of higher mystical states. To describe something as indescribable is in this way a minimal form of description, since most ordinary descriptions arise from determinate and discriminable contents of perception. The highest mystical experience passes beyond the ordinary sphere of description; but since it is an actual state, it has some minimum describability, and mystics use various methods to delineate its higher blankness. Third, ineffability is a performative, since the sublime character of the experience is "higher" — that is, of greater value — than other experiences. As in saying "I cannot express my deep gratitude," I express my gratitude, so in saying "My experience could not be put into words," I put it into words. Ineffability, indescribability, unutterability, indefinability — such terms and their relations have a performative aspect. And pregnant silence itself becomes a kind of utterance.

But, of course, the author of the *Cloud* approaches the ultimate from a certain angle. He comes from the direction of Christian theism. He projects into the formless "is" the concepts of Lordship and Omniscience and what have you, and then miraculously finds these terms encapsulated in the "is" and so easily to be drawn forth. This is not a criticism; it is the way the ultimate has to be seen — through the linguistic path by which it (or she, or he) is attained conceptually.

But Buddhaghosa does stand for something: he stands for the observation that the languages of unity, or of communion and love, of monism or theism, are not ineluctable, for the Theravada is not ontological absolutism or a kind of theism; there is not in it a great Being out there. It differs from all Vedantas and all Western theologies—indeed, from all theologies. This poses an important question about the mystical path.

To return to the negative way: it is obvious that a totally ineffable X is, so to speak, compatible with anything. Why should we, having trod the negative way, speak of the ultimate in one way rather than another? Why should we think that Śankara's ultimate is hitched to Brahmanical practices and the Vedas rather than to Christian theism and the sacraments? Insofar as the negative way often coincides at the intellectual level with the mystical path at the existential level, we can develop the question: How can we know that the goal of mysticism is one state (such as communion with God) rather than another? It may be that some forms of mysticism have a personal quality that suggests the language of God rather than that of *nirvāṇa*. But there seem to be some forms of mysticism that end in dazzling darkness, and these seem to be compatible with both Christian theism and Buddhist nirvanism. Any decision between the two interpretations must rest on other grounds. Or do we have to decide?

It will be seen from my discussion that we cannot divorce questions of language from doctrinal suppositions, living contexts, and phenomenology. In brief, very elaborate languages, but highly diverse, were evolved around the contemplative lives of the Theravada and of medieval Christianity respectively.

References

I have used the edition of the *Cloud* edited by Justin McCann, *The Cloud of Unknowing and Other Treatises* (Westminster, Md., 1952). I have cited Buddhaghosa's *Visuddhimagga*, trans. Bhikkhu Nyanamoli, 2 vols. (Berkeley, 1976).

Other works referred to:

John of Ruysbroeck. *The Adornment of Spiritual Marriage*, trans. C. A. Wynschenk. London, 1916.
Johnston, William. *The Mysticism of the Cloud of Unknowing*. St. Meinrad, Ind., 1975.

King, Winston L. *Theravada Meditation, the Buddhist Transformation of Yoga*. Philadelphia, 1980.
Knowles, David. *The English Mystical Tradition*. New York, 1961.
Richard of St. Victor. *Selected Writings on Contemplation*, ed. Clare Kirchberger. New York, 1957.
Smart, Ninian. *Reasons and Faiths*. London, 1958.
──────. "Interpretation and Mystical Experience," in Smart, *Concept and Empathy*, ed. Donald Wiebe. New York, 1986.

5

Mystic Analogizing and the "Peculiarly Mystical"

STEPHEN H. PHILLIPS

Can Nonmystics Understand Mystic Claims and Reports?

In this paper, the nature and limitations of nonmystics' ability to understand mystic claims are explored. The exploration uncovers a certain "open-endedness" and consequent radical "open texture" of key concepts in our worldwide religious heritage—for example, "God," "Brahman," and "Emptiness" (*śūnyatā*). The view of mystic language and communication that emerges reinforces the skepticism of those who would resist attempts to "read off" from mystical experiences detailed religious doctrines of individual traditions. But it also suggests that there is room for theoretical accommodations within a religious or "spiritual" domain, as have been attempted by such "universalists" as William James.[1]

Let me begin by formulating a few rough but working general characterizations (or definitions). A *mystical experience* is a psychological event of indefinite duration that the mystic herself *takes* to be a direct awareness of such "spiritual objects" as God, Brahman, or Emptiness, or of a "spiritual realm" that is not a matter of people's everyday acquaintance. (It is, of course, the crucial question whether the experience is indeed revelatory in the way the mystic takes it to be, but this is not our immediate topic.) In other words, a mystical experience is an awareness that the mystic herself *takes* to be "spiritually cognitive"—that is, an awareness taken to provide direct information about a "spiritual" object or state of affairs: God's present relatedness to the mystic, for instance. Then further, this experience taken to be spiritually informative is also an awareness that is either (1) not sense-mediated or, if sense-mediated, (2) not as sense perception normally occurs.[2]

Roughly, the *spiritual*, what mystical experiences are taken to reveal—their "objects," broadly understood—is to be conceived on analogy to human subjectivity: things spiritual, if there are any, would have such attributes as the old metaphysical dualists believed differentiated minds and matter—such as awareness, emotions, and the ability to think—or, again to speak roughly, would have characteristics—capacities for self-concepts and agency, for instance—that are appropriate to persons and higher animals and not to *merely* physical things. (God, Brahman, Emptiness, and the like are considered of course to have such characteristics in vastly superior modalities or degrees.)

A *mystic claim* is a proposition put forth on the basis of mystical experience. Mystic claims, like other empirical claims, range from the extremely abstract to the concrete and particular. Highly general and abstract beliefs standing at the center of entire religious worldviews may count as mystic claims as long as the body of theory is advanced at least in part on the basis of mystical evidence. An example of such a general or abstract claim might be, "Enlightenment reveals the Vibrant Void underlying all worldly phenomena." Other mystic claims are much more concrete. At the far extreme, we find putative "reports" of personal experience, reports that are roughly parallel to a (sense-mediated) "observation claim," such as, "I feel God embracing me now."

I wish to focus on the issue of nonmystics' ability to understand mystic reports. These reports of personal experience are claims that are low in the tiers of theory putatively built on mystical experiences. My contention is that the nature of and limitations on our ability (as nonmystics) to understand these reports carry important consequences for our ability to understand the more abstract claims and, indeed, much "religious" language in general. Oversimplifying and avoiding problems about memory, I offer the following rough characterization of a *mystic report*: a present psychospiritually perceptive judgment—for example, a claim about a spiritual object taken to be in the present mystically related to the (first-person) mystic perceiver and claimant.[3]

Why should it be thought that there is any special problem about the ability of a nonmystic to understand mystic reports? There is, after all, an extensive mystic literature that is not meant only for initiates. The problem arises when one reflects on the grounds of claims about meaning. Insofar as *ostension* is required within the realm of descriptions to define certain basic terms that cannot be defined adequately through other terms (as a long list of epistemologists and philosophers of language have held), and insofar as similarly basic, mystically descriptive terms appear in mystic reports, the lack of mystical experience appears an insuperable block to nonmystics' understanding them.[4] As, to quote David Hume's famous statement, "A blind man can form no notion of colours, a deaf man of sounds,"[5] so a nonmystic could have no idea of the "spiritual." D. W. Hamlyn writes:

> Even if terms like "red" cannot be defined purely by reference to experience, they could not be understood fully without experience, for example, by someone who does not possess and never has possessed sight.... A posteriori terms and concepts may thus be defined as those that directly require our having experience in order for us to apply them or those that can only be fully understood by reference to terms that directly require our having experience to apply them.[6]

Although these statements are made in a different context, their relevance for our concern is plain. How can we understand depictions made on mystic grounds, through means that we, the blind, do not have? According to some theologies, buddhologies, and other religious philosophies, there are claimed, to be sure, nonmystical means whereby a spiritual domain can be known to exist or to have a certain characteristic; yet we nonmystics ipso facto are not *mystically acquainted* with whatever it is that is putatively designated in mystic reports by such key terms as 'God,' 'Brahman,' and 'Emptiness.' Nor does it appear that we could know the meaning of predicates used in mystic descriptions of such "objects." Not having the experience, we are not in the right position to appreciate any potentially explanatory ostensions ("This is *nirvāṇa*," for example).[7] In the terms made popular by Bertrand Russell, knowledge by description depends on knowledge by acquaintance; similarly, understanding descriptive terms depends on an ability to relate them to one's own experiences.

The Language of Mystic Analogizing

But this reading of the issue is not quite correct, as I intend to show. To do better, let us consider the role of experience, of personal acquaintance, with respect to certain people trying to understand the following four claims, the last two of which are mystic:

1. The rains came to Delhi a month late this year.
2. A mango tastes like pineapple, pineapple blended with whipped cream.
3. In the innermost Mansion, the soul knows Heaven and salvation: free from disturbance as is a king in his private chamber, we receive from God the kiss for which the Bride besought him. (Saint Teresa)
4. This ["Emptiness"] is not fire, therefore it is fire. (Keiji Nishitani, echoing the *Diamond Sūtra*)

It is imaginable that Sam, an English-speaker who has never visited India or, let us say, witnessed a monsoon season anywhere, would nevertheless have little difficulty understanding statement 1. Having experienced rain and knowing some geography and the conventional measurements of time, it is imaginable that 1 would convey to him some information about the rains in India this year, though he has no personal acquaintance with such a season.

Imagine now two persons, Vic and Walt, told statement 2. Vic, let us say, has enjoyed many a ripe mango, and though he might quibble that the description is inexact, he surely would be able to understand 2—that is, as long as he were an English-speaker and had tasted pineapple and whipped cream. In fact, it would seem to be the analogue idea "pineapple blended with whipped cream" that would stretch most people's imagination—except dessert connoisseurs'. So to eliminate this complication, let us imagine that Vic is a fine chef who has himself prepared a pineapple blend that he shared with Walt the previous evening. Now Walt, unlike Vic, has never eaten a mango, but has, we are imagining, tasted Vic's pineapple-and-whipped-cream blend. Although it does not appear that he would understand 2 as well as Vic would—he has had less of the relevant type of experience to which to relate the claim—Walt is able to understand something about what a mango tastes like because he has tasted things whose flavor—he is being told—is similar to that of a mango. Therefore, as long as Walt were an English-speaker, there would be no special reason to suppose that even he could not understand 2.

Claim 2 is an explicit statement of similarity; in it an analogy is drawn. Thereby the attention of the person Walt, who has not tasted a mango, would be directed to a basis in his experience for understanding the taste of mangoes (and the meaning of 2). Since the explicit analogizing present in 2 is the key to Walt's understanding of the taste of mangoes, let us call 2 a *pedagogical* statement.

With 1, implicit analogies are key. It is by virtue of having experience of things similar to the particular rains referred to in 1 that Sam would be able to comprehend the statement. The similarity involved is actually of two types. The truth of 1 depends on a similarity in nature: it implies that the monsoon season this year is similar to those of previous years (despite the explicit denial of similarity in one respect).[8] But further, we must presume that a person's *experience* of rain at one time is similar to his experience of rain at other times, and that through memory he is able to recognize such similarities; otherwise, he would not be able to use tokens of "rain" appropriately on different occasions. Such implicit analogies, both between things and between experiences, are basic to communication in general.

Mystics' communication to nonmystics involves both these kinds of analogy, the implicit and the explicit. Yet comparisons of "things" that are largely unlike, and not groupings into common classes or abstractions of a single property, are distinctive in mysticism because of the importance of what I should like to call the "peculiarly mystical." As reported in the literature worldwide, mystical experiences are not just extraordinary in the sense that many people do not have them; the objects these experiences are thought to reveal are not just widely unknown, or less known than physical things. On the contrary, the "spiritual objects" are claimed to be encountered in a peculiar way. (Mystics could imaginably be in the majority.) As was mentioned earlier, it is sometimes said that God, Brahman, or Emptiness, a "supreme spiritual being," can be known in other, nonmystical ways, through "cosmological" inferences, or a priori. But it is typical of mystic testimony to claim a special means of encounter with whatever it is that such terms as 'God' are commonly, within specific traditions, taken to mean.

Mystic literature shows a certain kind of figurative speech to be typical of mystic reports, and it is my view that this reflects not just the rarity of the experiences but a "taking" of the experience to make something known in a *peculiar* and indeed superior fashion, somewhat as vision is better suited than audition to reveal colors.[9]

Let us now consider figurative analogizing in general, apart from mystic uses. And let us begin with metaphor as paradigmatic, though there are other tropes — simile and (what is called by rhetoricians) "analogy" — that are also important for our concern.[10] Metaphor invariably involves implicit analogizing. But the analogizing is implicit only in the suppression of certain comparison terms, such as 'like,' 'is similar to,' and 'as.' In this way, metaphor is distinct from simile, its most closely related species of trope. In sharp contrast, while general and abstract terms also set up implicit analogies, these are usually of such a "deep" sort — reflecting often, it seems, real joints of nature, or at least highly pragmatic conceptual slicings — that they are usefully distinguished from analogies that are comparisons across common categories. Sylvester is a cat *just* as Ferdinand is, and the general term 'cat' is used appropriately for what appears to be a "natural kind." But to say that a certain poem has the texture of sandpaper is to imply a resemblance of a much less fundamental order. Mystics do use general terms that transcend the mystical–nonmystical and spiritual–physical distinctions, as well as abstract terms that would similarly reflect what we may call a natural bridge. But figurative utterances occur very frequently. Metaphor and figurative analogizing are found in the texts of mysticism — in discourses, sermons, and autobiographies, and in the massive poetry — with the same high frequency that one would expect supposing the experiences to be "peculiar" in the sense I have outlined.

But let us note that though mystic language is highly figurative, this is no absolute block to nonmystics understanding mystic reports. Analogies (reflecting perceived similarities), whether set up by metaphors and similes or by general and abstract terms, are basic to all communication. We have the ability to comprehend analogies, even ones that are for us "open-ended" because, like Walt with claim 2, we are personally acquainted with only one of the two things compared. A personal acquaintance with X does carry certain epistemic and practical advantages concerning X, and I still have much to make of this point. But our ability to learn through analogies allows us from others' testimony to acquire information about things with which we are personally unacquainted. Thus we should not believe that a nonmystic is in general precluded from understanding a mystic's "spiritual" claims.

Let me analyze now the mystic statements 3 and 4, and show the role of metaphor and analogy in a more concrete way. Unpacking particular mystic figures is often a tricky business because of their context dependence. By "context dependence," I mean all of several types and dimensions of context and situatedness, some textual, some cultural, and some simply semantic (simply?). But there are theories of metaphor that are helpful. Among these, I find "pragmatic" analyses, such as those contributed by H. P. Grice and A. P. Martinich, the most acute.[11] According to the pragmatic approach, use of metaphor flouts a "conversational maxim" or common presupposition, and demands that the listener or reader appreciate a similarity beyond the usual senses of one or more of the terms employed.[12] Indeed, all figures of meaning appear to flout what Grice calls a "maxim of quality"—that one should try to say what is true.[13] Thus "The ship plows the sea" is a trope because a ship cannot really plow the sea, and in this case we are forced to appreciate an uncommon similarity by the flouting.

However, this ("The ship plows the sea") and other figures are "simple" in the sense that they are interpretable without a thorough knowledge of the immediate linguistic and larger cultural context of the utterance.[14] And while there are some rather "simple" metaphors in mystic literature, such as certain sexual ones,[15] many of the figures found in mysticism, and in literature in general, are quite complex, intended to suggest an association that is largely in the mind of the reader or hearer, whatever the ultimate basis in a person's experience for *its* meaning might be. So here a "semantic" approach, with an emphasis on a certain type of "context"—paradigmatically, internal relations of meaning within a single text—would appear to have merit. The difficulty of interpreting the more complex mystic tropes—those that trade on associations that are largely subjective—is that with these figures the entire belief system of the mystic, and his or her larger cultural context as well, is often relevant to their interpretation. Consider, then, claim 3.

This complex statement, which is a paraphrase and combination of several of Teresa's utterances,[16] exemplifies many of the points made thus far. Teresa's use of the term 'salvation,' among several others, is obviously figurative. Literally, the term means for her a state of grace that is actually known only after death. And she is not implying that she has died. She is saying that in her experience she felt an extreme peace, bliss, and "gentle rapture,"[17] *like* that which could be imagined to accompany an awakening to an actual state of salvation. This flouting of Grice's maximum of quality marks the usage as figurative, and in a straightforward way. No one is likely to take it literally. But a moment's reflection reveals how complex are the implicit analogies and how layered the associations raised with just this single term. 'Salvation' is an abstract noun derived from the verb 'to save': etymologically, "the state of being saved." Pressed for an ostensive definition, we might think of a person's being saved from drowning, though 'salvation' would unlikely be used now—after all the centuries of Christian thought—for such a mundane situation.

In one of the atomic propositions composing 3, a simile appears, introduced by the term 'as.' Here we have an explicit comparison—"[We are] free from disturbance as is a king in his private chambers." The statement as addressed to a nonmystic would be thus much like statement 2 as comprehended by Walt, the person who has not tasted mangoes. In this way, 3 would be, like 2, a *pedagogical* statement.

But even isolating the expressly analogical portion of 3, we would have a figurative statement, unlike what Walt has with 2, which is quite literal. The reason that this is so is, I hold, the very reason that figurative analogizing must be said to be typical of mystic language: mystical experiences, and the spiritual "objects" taken to be their indications, are considered sufficiently distinct from everyday experiences and objects to *require* mystics to use a special language, to employ common terms uncommonly—that is, figuratively.[18] The "spiritual" is to some degree irreducibly "peculiar." Nevertheless, there is no reason to suppose that a nonmystic could not understand 3 at all, since we do have the ability to understand analogies, whether figurative or not, as long as we have had experience of the analogue, or (as with "knows Heaven and salvation" in 3) of its analogue, down through possibly many layers of association, abstraction, or generalization.[19]

Consider now statement 4, which stands, I believe, among intelligible mystic utterances at a far extreme of difficulty. I may be unwise to take it up, since I shall be unable to make its meaning all that clear in a brief space. (Zen Buddhists are notorious for making apparently impenetrable statements.) But I believe that it is a good example of a mystic statement for our purposes because it is an extreme case of use of figurative speech to reflect experience that is "peculiar."

Statement 4 puts to use a special kind of trope, which I call "apparent paradox." The statement concerns the Buddhist concept, and "realization," of śūnyatā (Emptiness). The contemporary Japanese mystic philosopher Keiji Nishitani resorts to such apparent paradox in trying to explain śūnyatā, as have numerous Buddhists before him.[20] We are told that a nirvāṇa type of mystical experience involves becoming personally acquainted—in the direct way in which one is aware of one's own existence—with something, a "nothing," that though according to some brims with compassion and bliss has few other discernible characteristics: it seems hardly any particular thing. My view is that the frequent use of paradoxical language by Nishitani and others results from their sense that the experience, and what it indicates, is so extraordinary, so "peculiar," and so devoid of definitive marks—so unlike anything finite and physical—that language has to be used that does violence to common and firmly held suppositions. In other words, seemingly paradoxical language such as this represents within mysticism an extreme case of the point I made earlier about the prominence of figurative speech as reflecting the peculiarity of mystical experience and a corresponding peculiarity of the spiritual object(s).[21]

The use of apparent paradox, whether by mystics or by you and me, need not be understood as true paradox or nonsense and contradiction. For example, a principal of an "excluded middle" is commonly presupposed in conversation; we normally think that thing X has to be either F or not-F. Thus by flouting this rule, one can introduce a trope. Imagine two baseball fans, Jack and Karl, who are supporters of a team that is tied for first place near the end of a season. Jack reports to Karl, who is ignorant of the prior day's scores: "Last night's games? Not a celebration, and not not one either." Karl can be imagined to take this to mean that their team lost and that the other first-place team did, too. (If Jack had said, "Last night's games were both a celebration and a postponement," Karl would probably take him to mean that both teams had won.) Taking a mystic's claims seriously typically requires that one look beyond certain conversational presuppositions. "Apparent paradox," like all tropes, signals that one is supposed to.

Note that not just any paradox will do; Nishitani, for example, uses particular paradoxical language with a particular intent. When he asserts 4 (echoing, as he points out, the *Diamond Sūtra*),[22] he is trying to convey a particular idea: the transcendence of *śūnyatā* — the fact that it is not fire — permits its immanence; therefore, it is fire. Let me say just a few words about this.

Emptiness, as I read Nishitani, is thought to have a "logic" that while unlike that of any physical or finite thing may yet be compared with that of an infinite set. Only an infinite set can be mapped onto a proper subset of itself, as Robert Nozick has remarked.[23] Like Hegel's "genuine Infinite," Nishitani conceives Emptiness as including everything and as able to do so because it is nothing in particular, no finite thing. It is "no-thing" because it transcends all finite limitations. Nishitani believes that it is because Emptiness transcends fire — because it is not fire — that it is capable of being fire (and everything else). As I have argued elsewhere,[24] Nishitani does not show why Emptiness should come to be fire (or anything else). But he does intend, with 4, to convey a particular proposition. "This is not fire, therefore it is fire" is not nonsense or contradiction. The statement employs a trope.

Admittedly, I have provided only the briefest of glosses and explanations of statement 4. This is not the place to elaborate at length on the "Emptiness" idea. The point is that we should have some good reason — which could emerge only after patient study of a particular mystic worldview, typically a true conceptual tension — for supposing that the paradoxical language cannot be meaningful. Most mystic "paradoxes," I dare say, are really just tropes and special devices for communication, required by the peculiarity of the experiences and of their putative indications.[25]

The "Peculiarly Mystical"

To this point, I have defended the ability of a nonmystic to understand mystic testimony. I conclude that it is wrong to suppose that a nonmystic cannot in principle understand a mystic report. This I firmly believe, but I also believe that the degree of analogizing that is required for nonmystics to understand what the extraordinary *experiences* are like means that we should recognize that mystic usages of such spiritual terms as 'God,' 'Brahman,' and 'Emptiness' must remain for us nonmystics open-ended, that the "spiritual" is understood by us to a significant extent *only* analogically. My point here about the need for figurative speech to talk about things putatively mystically revealed is the truth behind much of the confusion of Western "negative theology" and of "anti-intellectualist" Eastern religious philosophy as well. But beyond its hermeneutic value, this recognition I am urging would also, I believe, promote accommodation among present and future "spiritual metaphysicians," enabling them to present views that are truly global and less tradition-bound.

Let me put the matter another way. In the arena of competing worldviews, traditional spiritual metaphysics (Buddhist, Christian, and so on) loses the advantage of its claims to mystically experiential foundations because of its squabbling with other views that also claim such foundations. Should not the nonmystic take all mystical experiences to be illusions, simply because mystic claims, indeed mystic reports, are in conflict with one another when viewed worldwide? Yet on the assumptions that (1) the mystics themselves are often not expert in high-tier interpretations of their experiences, and (2) precisely at issue are certain high-tier claims, what is "peculiarly mystical" has to be put into words. To take seriously the possibility that mystical experiences may provide significant support for spiritual beliefs, one needs to know what the experiences are like. This means that the "peculiarly mystical" has to be put into words. And these words, we have seen, must for nonmystics be irreducibly figurative, involving invariably open-ended analogies. Thus there would appear much room for theoretical accommodations. Open-ended analogies, unlike credos, are not set in stone.

To look again at our examples, though Sam could understand 1 and Walt could comprehend 2, neither of them is in any position to elaborate on the topics. Sam does not understand the Indian monsoon, or Walt the taste of mangoes, very well. In a phenomenological dispute, these are not the people we would consult, and they would be at a severe disadvantage in many imaginable *practical* pursuits.[26] Insofar as nonmystics need to know something about the "peculiarly mystical," that is to say, insofar as a belief about God, Brahman, Emptiness, or some comparably spiritual "object" would be a belief about something that, perhaps, is not altogether physical, and at least is not the sort of thing that is directly indicated by sense experiences, something for which the "peculiarly mystical" would be the best sort of evidence, or at least a significant dimension of whatever the "object" is, a nonmystic cannot hope to be confident about his understanding, just because he lacks the relevant experience.[27]

In a well-known paper, Friedrich Waismann terms "open texture" the feature of empirical concepts that they are subject to change and revision as we learn more about the way things are.[28] Experience—sense experience or mystical experience or whatever—comes with no guarantee that the evidence it provides is the complete and final story. All concepts derived from experience are subject to revision as we learn more. Waismann takes this "open texture," this essential revisability of empirical concepts, to follow from two ineradicable possibilities: "(a) that I should get acquainted with some totally new experience such as at present I cannot even imagine; [and] (b) that some new discovery [could be] made which would affect our whole interpretation of certain facts."[29] Now although these possibilities remain, it seems highly *unlikely* that what we call cats turn out to be anything other than animals. Common-sense and elementary groupings, such as whales as fish, have been discovered to be wrong. But on an assumption of the uniformity of nature, we may also assume that science has matured beyond the stage of salient classification of the "kinds" recognizable in everyday experience: such concepts as "cat" seem unlikely to be revised. The question is: Is there a similar maturity concerning things "mystically revealed" (if indeed anything is)? I contend that the essential open-endedness of mystic analogizing suggests a *radical* open texture for such traditional religious concepts as "God," "Brahman," and "Emptiness" (*śūnyatā*). There is no reason to suppose that a nonmystic cannot at all understand mystic testimony, including, to some degree, what the special experiences are like. But the nature of the communication makes it *likely* that much in traditional understandings of spiritual "things" needs revising. Further, the essential open-endedness of mystic communication helps explain why mystic language tends to be especially "theory-laden," a point that is now well established.[30] Mystic metaphors appear to have become fixed and reified in individual traditions, without what may have inspired their original forgings being clearly understood.

Let me test my positions now against a crucial case, a comparison of nonmystics' lack of mystical experience with the lack of sight on the part of the blind. To what extent can a person blind from birth understand statements employing color terms? My previous examples might be considered to fail to bring out the key role of ostension, or possible ostension, for understanding low-tier, "observation" statements and mystic reports, and I am afraid that all the talk of figurative speech may suggest that I am sweeping difficulties under a metaphorical rug.

Consider Lila, who has been blind from birth, trying to understand a statement employing the color term 'red.' My contention is that Lila could understand statement 5,

5. Red is the color . . . of the long-wave extreme of the visible spectrum. (*Webster's New Collegiate Dictionary*)

and through a knowledge of this and similarly theoretic and scientific statements would have an *intellectual* understanding of colors. The definition shows that much about colors is not so strictly phenomenological; an understanding of 'red' based on direct ostensions to, say, red apples, blood, and so forth is not all that is conveyed by some uses of the term. It is not true that Lila could understand no statement employing a color term. Not only do the blind understand such useful commonplaces as that a red traffic light requires vehicles to stop and that a red apple is a ripe one, a blind person *who learned the theories of optics* would understand *well* colors (or color) intellectually. We can imagine our Lila, blind from birth, to be a scientist mastering theories in optics and making contributions to the field. With a suitable genius, why could she not? It might be argued that to understand statement 5 and other information about optics, Lila would have to be able to discern the difference in her experience that its truth would make. But this could be mediated through instruments with dials in braille. (Perhaps only the sighted could design the instruments, but that does not alter the basic point.) Not only would Lila be able then to relate statement 5 to her experience, but 5 would mean for her *tangible* effects therein. And if she had mastered 5 and current theories in optics, she would have to be said to understand more about colors intellectually than most who can see, though she has no direct acquaintance. Lila's understanding of such expressions as 'visible spectrum' in statement 5 would indeed have to be fundamentally mediated by analogy. Her understanding of such expressions, expressions whose meaning involves directly the sense medium she lacks, would have to rely on *pedagogical* statements, like 2 for Walt, made by the sighted. These, of course, could be provided.

Someone might ask, "But how is it in the case of a blind person and colors that there is any relevant experience that could stand as the ultimate analogue?" The answer has already been implied. The blind do have other sorts of sense experience, mediated by other organs. Similarly, mystics communicate to the rest of us on the basis of the experiences that we have in common. Note that Lila could understand even more exclusively phenomenological visual terms on the basis of actual phenomenological similarities among the deliverances of the separate sense mediums. These her sighted teachers could appeal to. For example, colors "blend" phenomenologically in somewhat the same way that sounds do; thus one speaks of a "harmony" among the colors in a painting.

But in considering the blind and colors, it may seem that my principal thesis (a nonmystic is not precluded from understanding a mystic report) stands in opposition to my conclusion about the "open-endedness" of key spiritual terms: if a blind scientist can understand colors intellectually, then it seems that nonmystics would not have the reason that I have pointed to for considering descriptions of "objects" putatively mystically revealed to be irre-

could not be reduced to literal statements, could not be for her precise and "close-ended."

I have outlined an empiricist approach to mystic language. There are several further considerations both for and against this understanding that perhaps should, but cannot, be taken up here. Let me close by repeating just one advantage: by viewing spiritual terms and concepts as enjoying not only an "open texture," in the sense that we may want to make revisions when we learn more and to change traditional meanings, but also an intrinsic "peculiarity" (i.e., for nonmystics), we could then find *much* room for theoretic accommodations among spiritual philosophies worldwide. There may be nothing at all promising in an idea of the "spiritual." But if there is, it would seem that as dependent on mystic reports for our understanding of much that would be significant about it, we should recognize a *radical* open texture in particular instances—that is, in such concepts as "God," "Brahman," and "Emptiness," key traditional concepts about what is taken to be mystically revealed.[32]

Notes

1. William James, *The Varieties of Religious Experience* (Chicago, 1958), lecture XX.

2. This complication is necessary to include "nature mysticism" and "spiritually transformed sense perception." I confess that I am prone to restrict the characterization to the non-sense-mediated. But current studies of mysticism and typologies of mystical experiences do often include nature mysticism, and there is a substantial primary literature as well.

3. Compare Roderick Firth's characterization of a "present psycho-physical perceptual judgment," in Edward C. Carterette and Morton P. Friedman, eds., *Handbook of Perception* (New York, 1974), vol. 1, chap. 1.

4. E. Allison Peers, in his "translator's preface" to Teresa's works, complains at length of the difficulty of rendering the great Spanish mystic's talk of her experiences (*The Complete Works of St. Teresa of Jesus*, trans. and ed. E. Allison Peers [London, 1973], vol. 1, pp. xiv–xxii). This is not only a philosophical problem.

5. David Hume, *An Enquiry Concerning Human Understanding* (Indianapolis, 1955), sec. 2. Compare Hume, *A Treatise of Human Nature* (Oxford, 1978), bk. 1, pt. 1, sec. 1.

ducibly figurative. But such is not the case. The crucial difference between Lila's and a nonmystic Norma's cognitive situations, as I imagine that they might be with regard to, respectively, color terms employed in optics and mystic descriptions employed in spiritual ("religious") metaphysics, is that light is physical and there can be imagined a one-to-one correspondence between visual readings on spectrometers and ones in braille, while Norma, in my judgment, would typically need to understand something about the "peculiarly mystical." As has already been pointed out, Lila's understanding of terms such as 'visible spectrum' in statement 5 would have to rely on analogies made by the sighted. Note that this scientist, however much genius she might demonstrate concerning the physical nature of light, would not be able directly to pick out things by their color. Speaking roughly, I would say that an understanding of the "peculiarly mystical" is more important for the meaning of such key spiritual terms as 'God,' 'Brahman,' and 'Emptiness' than an understanding of the "peculiarly visual" would be for color terms, that is, (even) supposing the larger context in each case to be highly theoretic: in optics, there could be spectrometers with dials in braille, while it is difficult to imagine a similar correspondence between mystical and sensuous apprehensions. There are, after all, common indications of the separate senses, a fact that is best explained by the existence of physical objects that are sensed through different mediums.[31] Thus a blind person can know what Jim "looks like" from touching his face.

Now some "mystic claims" may appear to be similarly founded in an objective reality—God, Brahman, or Emptiness—that can be cognized through different mediums—through mystical experiences, on the one hand, and sense experiences, on the other. I cannot enter now into the theological (and buddhological, etc.) considerations called for here. But note that if sense experiences are restricted in their objective indications to things that are physical and if the "spiritual" ("religious") objects that mystics claim to encounter by peculiar and direct means are in any way intrinsically "spiritual," then understanding the peculiarly mystical would be far more important for Norma than understanding the peculiarly visual would be for Lila, (even) given a theoretical context. The peculiarly mystical must be expressed through irreducibly figurative speech that—unless Norma were to become herself a mystic—

6. P. Edwards, ed., *Encyclopedia of Philosophy* (New York, 1967), vol. 1, p. 141.

7. The point can also be stated in verificationist terms. A nonmystic, not being able to appreciate mystic ostensions, would not be able to check a mystic claim in the most appropriate way. Unable to understand what the experiences that would be entailed by the truth of the claim would be like because he has nothing to which to tie or relate the claim, a nonmystic could not be said to understand it, so the argument would go. Neither verification nor "ability to verify" is, I believe, precisely what is key here, but *relevant* experience is required to understand descriptive propositions, as it is to verify them.

8. Can one assert anything at all without implying at least one similarity relation? It would seem not. Even the statements "X is identical with Y" and "Z is unique" imply similarities: the identity of X and Y would be like other identities, and Z would be similar to other unique things in its very uniqueness. Bertrand Russell, considering and rejecting an ontology in which universals were eliminated, concludes (for similar reasons) that there is at least one universal that could not be eliminated: similarity (*An Inquiry into Meaning and Truth* [Baltimore, 1962], pp. 323-27).

9. This "taking" might perhaps be more accurately termed an "*ostensible* compelling by the Object."

10. There are two species of figures of speech: tropes, which concern meaning, and rhetorical devices, such as alliteration, which do not. Metaphor, analogy, and simile are closely related species of trope.

11. H. P. Grice, "Logic and Conversation," in Peter Cole and Jerry Morgan, eds., *Syntax and Semantics* (New York, 1972), vol. 3, pp. 41-58; A. P. Martinich, "A Theory for Metaphor," *Journal of Literary Semantics* 13 (April 1984): 35-56.

12. Grice, "Logic and Conversation," p. 53. See also Martinich, "Theory for Metaphor," pp. 39-41.

13. A similar view is expressed in the Naiyāyika literature (Indian "Logic"): "*mañcāḥ krośanti,*" "the stands are shouting." But the *stands* are not shouting; the *people* in the stands are shouting. Various Naiyāyikas develop a view of figurative speech, in discussing in particular *Nyāyasūtra* 1.2.14 (and a few other sūtras), and in focusing on this metonymy (given by an early commentator) and other tropes as well.

14. Is this metaphor so simple that it ceases to be a figure at all? Is the meaning of the term 'plows' here a general kind of action, a progressive splitting, not performed only by farmers or only on fields? Although I would say no, such cases as this suggest analogical origins for the meaning of many abstract terms. See W. V. Quine, *Word and Object* (Cambridge, Mass., 1960), pp. 9-12.

15. For example, Yājñavalkya's statement, *Bṛhadāraṇyaka Upaniṣad* 4.3.21.

16. *Complete Works of St. Teresa*, vol. 1, p. 58, and vol. 2, pp. 338, 343 in particular; compare vol. 1, pp. 119–20.

17. "They are no more afraid of death than of a gentle rapture" (*Complete Works of St. Teresa*, vol. 2, p. 340).

18. There could also be coinages, such as "hrim." Yet insofar as non-mystics are to have any understanding of these, analogies would have to be made.

19. Teresa's descriptions are much too long to examine without abbreviation. But it is easy to see that her writing excellently illustrates my theses. See, for example, the following quotation, and note how many analogies are explicitly drawn. (Statement 3, by the way, is a paraphrase of Teresa's descriptions of an experience that she takes to be more advanced than this one.)

> It is not a radiance which dazzles, but a soft whiteness and an infused radiance which, without wearying the eyes, causes them the greatest delight; nor are they wearied by the brightness which they see in seeing this Divine beauty. So different from any earthly light is the brightness and light now revealed to the eyes that, by comparison with it, the brightness of our sun seems quite dim and we should never want to open our eyes again for the purpose of seeing it. It is as if we were to look at a very clear stream, in a bed of crystal, reflecting the sun's rays, and shadowed by clouds. Not that the sun, or any other such light, enters the vision: on the contrary, it is like a natural light and all other kinds of light seem artificial. It is a light which never gives place to night, and, being always light, is disturbed by nothing. It is of such a kind, indeed, that no one, however powerful his intellect, could, in the whole course of his life, imagine it as it is. And so quickly does God reveal it to us that, even if we needed to open our eyes in order to see it, there would not be time for us to do so. But it is all the same whether they are open or closed: if the Lord is pleased for us to see it, we shall do so even against our will. There is nothing powerful enough to divert our attention from it, and we can neither resist it nor attain to it by any diligence or care of our own. This I have conclusively proved by experience.... (*Complete Works of St. Teresa*, p. 180)

20. Keiji Nishitani, *Religion and Nothingness*, trans. Jan van Bragt (Berkeley, 1982). See also, for example, Nāgārjuna, *Mūlamadhyamakakārikā*, trans. David J. Kolapahana (Albany, N. Y., 1986).

21. Note that (apparent) paradox is a feature of many mystic reports in other traditions as well. This fact has been emphasized by William James and W. T. Stace, two of the more prominent philosophers who have written about mysticism (James, *Varieties of Religious Experience*, lecture

XVI; Stace, *Mysticism and Philosophy* [Philadelphia, 1960], pp. 251–267). Neither, however, recognizes "apparent paradox" as a trope.

22. Nishitani, *Religion and Nothingness*, p. 118.

23. Robert Nozick, *Philosophical Explanations* (Cambridge, Mass., 1981), p. 603.

24. Stephen H. Phillips, "Nishitani's Buddhist Response to 'Nihilism,'" *Journal of the American Academy of Religion* 55 (January 1987): 75–104.

25. Another kind of extreme figure often employed in mystic writing is the symbol. The early-twentieth-century Indian mystic Aurobindo, for example, thinks of light as not just an analogue of spiritual phenomena but as "embodying" in its very materiality certain spiritual qualities that he intends his use of the symbol to suggest (*The Life Divine* [Pondicherry, 1973], pp. 945–46). Light, in his use, would be a symbol because the physical reality to which the term directly refers is thought to suggest (beyond itself) intrinsically spiritual qualities.

26. Let us suppose that Walt has been told that mangoes are a type of fruit as well as roughly what they look like, with the result that he would be able to pick out a mango when confronted with one in most situations. But is it imaginable that if asked to identify the bona fide mango among a lot of close fakes, he would be able to do so? As well as would Vic, the longtime mango-fancier? (*Ceteris paribus*, Vic would have the advantage.)

27. According to some theological views, God is never known directly, but is inferred form divine manifestations. Maybe, then, there is no mystical experience at all, but only a disposition of some to sense—really infer, probably in part on the basis of dubious suppositions, such as that nature exhibits design—the handiwork of God or even God's presence. But to be frank, I would simply exclude from the class of *mystic* claims assertions that were not in any way *about* something "spiritual," and "spiritual" in the strong sense that mystical cognition of it would be privileged as (likely) the most direct way of being personally familiar with it, like sight for objects with color, or at least, as I have said all along, as a particularly significant means to a personal knowledge.

28. Friedrich Waismann, "Verifiability," *Proceedings of the Aristotelian Society*, suppl. vol. 19 (1945) (reprinted in Ernest Nagel and Richard B. Brandt, eds., *Meaning and Knowledge* [New York, 1965], pp. 38–46).

29. Waismann, "Verifiability," p. 43.

30. See, in particular, Steven T. Katz, "Language, Epistemology, and Mysticism," Steven T. Katz, ed., *Mysticism and Philosophical Analysis* (New York, 1978), pp. 22–74.

31. John Locke puts forth this argument in *An Essay Concerning Human Understanding*, bk. 4, chap. 9, sec. 7.

32. Although hasty and imperfect—and perhaps downright wrong—on

more than one count, an example of the kind of theoretical accommodation this approach would promote is William James's most general conclusion in his wide-ranging study, *Variety of Religious Experience*

> He [the mystic of whatever tradition] becomes conscious that this higher part [of himself] is conterminous and continuous with a MORE of the same quality, which is operative in the universe outside of him, and which he can keep in working touch with, and in a fashion get on board of and save himself when all his lower being has gone to pieces in the wreck. . . . [But] what is the objective "truth" of their [the mystical experiences'] content? . . . Is such a "more" merely our own notion, or does it really exist? If so, in what shape does it exist? Does it act, as well as exist? . . . It is in answering these questions that the various theologies perform their theoretic work, and that their divergences come to light. They all agree that the "more" really exists; . . . They all agree, moreover, that it acts as well as exists, and that something really is effected for the better when you throw your life into its hands. It is when they treat of the experience of "union" with it that their speculative differences appear most clearly. (pp. 384–85)

6

Mysticism and Ineffability: Some Issues of Logic and Language

BIMAL KRISHNA MATILAL

I

"Mysticism" has been loosely used for an assortment of views. The salient feature of these views is that they envision an integrated picture of the cosmos and promote a special type of human experience that is at once unitive and nondiscursive, at once self-fulfilling and self-effacing. As William James has said, this experience has a "noetic" quality, the experiencer becoming directly aware of the ultimacy of the experience.[1] Some philosophers have questioned whether mystical consciousness takes us away from the realm of logical awareness and puts us within the realm of illogic. Does the mystical insight require us to look beyond the laws of logic, the so-called laws of noncontradiction and excluded middle? In connection with the word "language," the sense of the word "mysticism" acquires another dimension. The mystical reality is said to be beyond language, the mystic's experience uncharacterizable — even uncategorizable. Words cannot describe it. The famous Upanishadic line

> Wherefrom words turn back
> failing to reach, along with the mind

seems to coincide with another characterization of mysticism specified by James: ineffability.

To take the last point first: Is this claim to transcend ordinary language to be taken simply as a warning that the mystic's description of his experience is utterly inadequate? Or is it only a "marker" or indicator for transforming the ordinary meanings (of words) into mystical meanings? Or, again, is it a banal way of underlining the poverty of human language and the corresponding richness of mystical experience? This may well raise some further sets of questions: Can a very personal and intensely felt experience (e.g., love, hate, acute pain, agony) be properly described or expressed in language? Are pure sensations or sensory experiences effable? Can the expression "I am in pain" communicate exactly what it is that I am in? Or, as Al Ghazzali asked: How would one know what it is to be in a drunken state if one has never been drunk in his life? This is only an oblique way of asking: How would one know what it is to have a mystical experience if one has never had such an experience? An old Bengali poem puts the same point as follows: How can one understand the pain caused by a snakebite if one has never been bitten by a snake? The salient issue here seems to be that my experience, my pain, is mine, and yours is yours, and I cannot get "under your skin" to experience what you experience. Another triviality or banality.

Let us turn to a different set of questions. What is a language for? Is it solely a means of communication? Can we communicate our most private and intensely felt experiences in language? And, in contrast, does language not communicate information about a shared world? And shared experiences, perhaps? Can linguistic signs refer to unique particulars? Can uniqueness and particularity be captured by language? In raising these issues, we rise above banality, for they bring to the surface important and significant philosophical problems whose clarification may be advanced by a close investigation of like difficulties as they emerge in the study of mysticism. Indeed, this is one of the ways in which discussion of mystical experiences may contribute to our larger conceptual understanding of some fundamental philosophical dilemmas.

There is, for example, a well-entrenched philosophical position that argues that our direct sensory experience has an element within it that cannot be put into words. Whatever truth may lie in this view, it is implicitly at work as the basis of many of our epistemological disputes over sensation, perception, conceptualization, and knowledge. For example, some modern writers believe that when the Buddhist logicians (the *Dinnāga-Dharmakīrti* School)[2] define sensory perception as free from, or uncontaminated by, conceptual construction (*Kalpanā*) and describe the percept of such sensory awareness as "self-grasped" and ineffable, they appeal to a similar fact. Parallel views of sensory perception as "pure" sensation totally free from conception are also present in other systems and other places, but I will concentrate on the supposedly Buddhist version with which I am more familiar. The view that endorses the ineffable character of what is called "pure" sensation also endorses implicitly a particular view of language or "effability." That is, it should at least be required to explain what it is to be effable.

The alleged thesis is that what we grasp as the "epistemologically first" is characterized by such uniqueness that it is hardly conveyable to others in language. Language captures similarities and shared characteristics between experiences. Hence what is conveyed by a linguistic symbol is the shared or shareable part of the experience. Uniqueness belongs to the particularity of the experiencer.

II

Modern philosophers of language have enunciated a principle of expressibility, according to which it is held that for anything that a speaker wishes to communicate, there are words in the speaker's language that can express it. Succinctly, this principle means that what can be meant can be said. I shall avoid a strict or an elaborate formulation of this principle, as it is well known in the literature.[3]

Two comments related to the principle of expressibility, however, are relevant. First, the principle is in some ways reminiscent of Bhartṛhari's celebrated thesis that there cannot be any awareness that is not "interpenetrated" with words. Bhartṛhari was obviously talking about natural languages. His point was that expressibility constitutes the essence of any awareness (perceptual or otherwise) or any thought (a *pratyaya*). In fact, Bhartṛhari's thesis seems to be even more radical. He believed that as soon as a sensory reaction penetrates the cognitive level, it also penetrates the linguistic level, though this does not mean that we always have to use explicit verbal constructions. Cognizing is "languaging" (*śabdanā*) at some implicit level. Second, the principle may not imply that whatever can be said can be understood by others. For if it does, it would exclude the possibility of what Wittgenstein called a "private" language. But Wittgenstein's argument against a private language, against the possibility of such a language (a private "sensation" language in particular), a language that is logically impossible for anyone except the speakers to understand,[4] is that it is logically impossible to have such a language. The use of a language involves rule following, and there cannot be, as Saul Kripke has reminded us,[5] any "private model" of rule following; for obeying a rule, as Wittgenstein puts it, "is a practice,"[6] and therefore cannot be done privately. In other words, obeying a rule means doing the same as before, but what is meant by "the same" here can only be defined by a *practice*—it is a practice in which more than one person participates. In Sanskrit philosophical writings, the word *vyavahāra* is sometimes used exactly in this way—that is, as a *practice* in Wittgenstein's sense. These considerations do not eliminate the possible occurrence of private mental phenomena, but they certainly underline the intangibility or the indescribability of such inner phenomena. However, this is not the issue here. The point is that the principle of expressibility on a stricter interpretation would be taken to reject the possibility of a private language even in a Wittgensteinian sense. A loose interpretation of the principle, however, would not decide the issue for "private" language.

The principle of expressibility (in its nonstrict version) has been tacitly assumed to be a genuine characteristic of a natural language. Keeping this in mind, we may turn back and refer to our earlier questions regarding the alleged ineffability of mystical experience. It seems to us that this doctrine (call it IME), despite some resemblance, is not connected with the *Diṅnāga-Dharmakīrti* thesis about the nonverbalizable element in one's perceptual (sensory) experience. Even Bhartṛhari[7] would allow that there may be nonverbal sensory reaction (in fact, he gives an example of a man who, running along a village path, may have tactile sensation of the grass, which may be nonverbal).[8] But that is not the point of the mystic's claim. The only similarity lies in the fact that the mystic, much as the Buddhist, would regard verbalization or description by language to be a sort of "distortion" of what is experienced; that is, the direct object of experience is put under a theoretical construct that, as it were, contaminates its pristine purity. Words such as *prapañca* and *vikalpa* (verbal proliferation) are used to underline this disvalue.

On the other hand, the IME does not appear to suffer from the Wittgensteinian argument against the notion of a "private language," for he does not say that he has a *private* language that none but he can understand. It seems, however, more pertinent to ask whether the IME will clash with the principle of expressibility if this principle is in any way regarded as constituting the essence (or a necessary property) of all natural languages. Traditional mystics normally use a natural language, and hence if the IME is to be seriously entertained as a hypothesis, it is with regard to some natural language or other. This leads to another question about natural languages that arises as a consequence of recent studies in semantics and the persistence of semantical paradoxes.

III

The question is sometimes asked: Are natural languages universal in the sense that (roughly) what can be said *about* a natural language can be said *in* it? In other words, if a natural language is *universal*, then it can be used to say all there is to be said about its semantics. This is, very broadly speaking, the Tarskian formulation of the notion of the universality of a language. It is well known that in Alfred Tarski's view, "true in L" may not be defined in L, and no language is universal if there is any concept that is expressible in some language but cannot be expressed in the language in question. In this strict sense, then, as a consequence of a strict Tarskian notion of universality as well as of the preponderance of semantical paradoxes,[9] no language can be universal. This tends to cast doubt on the intuitive assumption that a natural language has enough, sometimes unexplored, expressive power in virtue of which it may be regarded as universal in the strict Tarskian sense. In fact, it has been argued by Hans Herzberger[10] that it is possible to show that with respect to a given language, there is a concept that is expressible somewhere but inexpressible in that language, by specifying a set of objects such that no term of the language has that set as its extension (but that some term of another language has that set as its extension). If this is proved, then no language (including a natural language) would be universal. This will have the rather counterintuitive consequence that even a natural language will lose its alleged universality on pain of harboring a contradiction. But Herzberger's proof has its own problems,[11] and we need not go into them here.

Even if we assume that for every language there is a concept (or a series of concepts) *not* expressible in that language (the unsettling difficulty is this: we do feel that we know and therefore can somehow express these concepts that our present language cannot express), it is still possible that a natural language can be deemed to express a significant portion (most, if not everything) of its own semantics. This might explain the guiding intuition that a natural language is sufficiently rich to reflect *almost* the whole of its semantics. But what happens to our IME doctrine in that case? Presumably, the nonuniversality of any language may allow that there are certain semantic truths that remain ineffable. But this will be an argument only in favor of the concept of ineffability. It will not lend any support in favor of IME.

IV

Before I deal directly with IME, I wish to mention another aspect of the semantic issue that is relevant to the discussion of the notion of ineffability. A language may lack a term for a given concept, but that would be only a trivial and accidental sort of semantic failure. For such an accidental deficiency can presumably be remedied through familiar means. But if we take our language to be a system of symbols and if symbolisms of language are such that they by their nature are constitutionally incapable of expressing certain ideas or concepts, this will be a serious and real semantic failure and will give credence to the notion of ineffability as a sound semantic concept. It has been argued by Paul Henle, for example, that a commutative symbolism can be such that the principle of commutativity is inexpressible in it.[12] The main point is that one's symbolism limits what can be expressed in it. Why should this be important for our discussion of IME? The answer lies in the fact that if words or concepts are like symbols and if our ordinary language is regarded as a system of symbols, then it may be that IME is based upon a claim that our present symbolism is inadequate or fundamentally flawed in its ability to express such experiences. Hence IME may be a valid doctrine from the point of view of semantics. But our natural languages are not closed systems (they are "creatively employable," they grow like living organisms, and they are self-referential), and hence the alleged inadequacy can be mended. I shall come back to this issue presently.

The general point so far analyzed has been that our language or the conceptual system of mankind is limited in the sense that not everything that is knowable is "sayable" within it. This is quite acceptable to an Indian Vedāntin for whom the Brahman experience is ineffable, or even to some Buddhists for whom the pure, translucent, *nirvanic* consciousness is such that the subject–object duality will completely disappear in it (hence it is completely free from "verbal proliferations" [*prapañca*] or "linguistic snares"). But the same point runs headlong into the basic thesis of the *Nyāya-Vaiśeṣika* School, according to which, whatever is knowable (*prameya* or *jñeya*) is "sayable" (*abhidheya*).[13] It seems that the Naiyāyikas put too much faith in the expressive power of language. But this is simply of a piece with the strong intuition we seem to have about our natural languages, that they are universal in the sense that they can talk about all languages, including themselves. The prevalence of semantical paradoxes, however, forces us to question this intuition, as we have suggested earlier.

It may be noted at this stage that some of the semantic paradoxes or near-paradoxes are also formulated in the Indian philosophical tradition. But the idea in the Indian tradition was not to regard them as antinomies. They were either used as *reductio ad absurdum* against an opponent's hypothesis or regarded as resolvable. For example, Nāgārjuna, in his *Vigrahavyāvartanī*, noted the following objection, presumably of his *Nyāya* opponent: the "Emptiness" is itself empty. The word "emptiness" is a predicate property; when it is said that every *bhāva* is empty, we mean it is empty of its own nature. According to Nāgārjuna, this is applicable to all metaphysical statements about reality. But if all such statements are empty, then the statement "All such statements are empty" is itself such a statement and has to be empty. But if this statement is empty to begin with, then what can show that all statements are empty? A Nāgārjunian would happily agree that it is a dilemma but would not accept the consequence that it is inconsistent with his original position. But how (and this is a big *how*)? Let us see. In response, he would argue that the so-called statement "All such statements are false" is actually not a *proper* statement (i.e., it is a nonasserted statement), and hence the predicate "is empty" can be applied to it only in a manner of speaking. In fact, Nāgārjuna admits as a consequence of his argument[14] that if all such statements are actually empty, it is still *unsayable* that all such statements are empty. For to say it is to falsify it. We have come back to the notion of ineffability in another way.

V

It was Bhartṛhari who said that there is no *expressive* word in our language for the word-object relation. This might be interpreted as asserting that this relation can only be *shown* but not *said* in our language. This point can be developed into a paradox, as has been done with great ingenuity by Hans Herzberger and R. Herzberger. We come back to ineffability again. This is particularly intriguing because it was Bhartṛhari himself who explicitly propounded the strong thesis that we cannot be (properly) aware of something without the "interpenetration" of word in it (that is, if there is no *expressive* word, there is no *proper* awareness). It is, however, still logically compatible to contend that there may be ineffable objects, but we cannot cognize such objects even if they exist; and if we somehow become aware of such an object, it would be in some way effable, though something else may still be ineffable.

The IME doctrine, therefore, can be taken with a grain of salt. The notion of ineffability may be a sound semantic concept, as has been discussed above. But our natural language is a very powerful tool, and whether or not it can be regarded as "universal" strictly in the Tarskian sense, it does seem to have not only the provision for expressing much of its own semantics (Martin), but also a great deal of unexplored expressive power. Even if we regard our natural language as a system of symbols (Henle) that restricts what we can say in it, it is possible for us (for at least some of us) to devise a better system or modify the present system and to use some ingenuity in order to express such concepts as we happen to be aware of, as well as to express our felt experience (insofar as such experience can be expressed or communicated). Thus I believe there are several ways by which our mystic authors may (and actually do) *present* the so-called ineffable. Going through the mystical authors of India, I can identify at least three broad ways by which they accomplish it. This does not mean, however, that the mystics have been lying or deceiving themselves when they have been claiming IME. I take the IME doctrine to be a warning signal to the readers (or hearers) to alert them against a facile understanding (a misunderstanding) of what the mystics say, such an understanding being based on the too literal interpretation of their words. The words of the mystics are generated by a flash of inspiration, and a similar sympathetic feeling may be needed in order to fully grasp their message.

The description of the alleged mystical experience in ordinary language, when treated as a description of just another (ordinary) experience, appears to be banal or even nonsensical. A poetic expression, if it is treated as a "prosaic" description of some ordinary state of affairs, would appear to be equally banal: "If my beloved is with me, the scorching rays of the sun would be as cool as the moon. But if my beloved is away, the moonbeams are as scorching as the sunrays." If we take the emotional content away, this becomes almost a nonsensical statement. But in the context of poetry, where the emotion is transmitted to the readers, this expression dons a new cloak of meaning, which is both beautiful and enjoyable. The language of the mystics has to be contextualized in the same way.

An improvised version of the statement of an Indian mystic (Sri Ramakrishna Paramahamsa) is as follows: "I am like a doll made of salt. I went to measure the depth of the ocean full of saline water. I was dissolved completely and became one with the ocean. How can I measure the immeasurable?" Taken out of context, this story is banal. But when it is taken to be a way of depicting the experience that is provided with a metaphysical basis by the Advaita Vedānta's thesis of the merging of the individual consciousness into the all-pervasive Brahman consciousness, it assumes a different and profound significance for the disciples. The IME is a warning against the trivialization of such language of the mystics.

VI

Of the three broad ways used by the mystics of India to "express" the ineffable, one is the use of metaphor or poetic language. This is perhaps the chief one, and the other two may be subordinate to it. A mystic may be a poet, and a poet may also be a mystic. A mystic-poet's language is different from ordinary language. It conveys, as the Indian Dhvani theorists such as Ānandavardhana insist, more than what it says. The boundary of the effable domain is transcended by such poetic language, and the mystics (e.g., the Upanishadic *rsi*, or sages, who were excellent poets, such as Yājñavalkya and Uddālaka) employ such poetic language to "break the barrier" and reach the ineffable. A requirement of the *Rasa-dhvani* theory of Indian poetics is that the poet communicate his message (transmit the aesthetic pleasure to the mind of the reader) adequately, provided the readers are also *sahrdaya* (sensitive) or poetically inclined. Similarly, the language of the mystics can be adequately understood by those who are also mystically inclined. In any case, the poetic quality of the mystical writings of the *Upaniṣads* can hardly be denied.

The second method is the use of contradictory predicates to characterize the experience or what is experienced. The same method is reflected in the formulation of paradoxical statements or near paradoxes in the writings of the mystically inclined philosophers. Besides, there is a well-entrenched philosophical tradition in Jainism where the word *avaktavya* (ineffable, inexpressible) is systematically interpreted as the *simultaneous* application of the contradictory truth-predicates to a metaphysical proposition—saying "yes" and "no," or "it is" and "it is not," at the same time in the same breath in the same sense.[15] (Thus Vidyānanda explains it as "the *joint* and *simultaneous* affirmation and denial" and distinguishes it from "both affirmation and denial."[16]) The idea is that we may affirm a proposition from one point of view or in one sense and deny it from another point of view or in another sense. For example, "John does not drink" can be affirmed when it means that John does not take alcoholic beverages, but denied when it means drinking liquids such as water. This will be, for the Jainas, a combined affirmation and denial. The same point can be illustrated with reference to time. For it may be facetiously noted that

John is in the habit of drinking only after 5:00 P.M. A proposition with indexicals can be true at one time and false at another time, or true in one place and false in another, or even true for one person and false for another. But for the Jainas, the "ineffable" is a separate, unitary, truthlike predicate. It is applied to one that is both true and false at the same time in the same sense from the same point of view; that is, it should be affirmed and denied *in the same breath*. The Jaina logicians argue that since it is impossible to express in language such joint affirmation and denial made in the same breath, they call it "ineffable." It transcends our ordinary mode of speaking. The truth-value here, we may say, can be *shown* but not *said* in the language. The word "ineffable" is only an indicator.

The third way of communicating or presenting what is ordinarily ineffable is to use the *neti neti* method, or what is sometimes called negative dialectics. The simple meaning of *neti* is "No is the answer." The idea is almost implicit in the word "ineffable" itself. Constructing a possible description or assigning a possible predicate to the mystical object, the mystic may then go ahead and negate it, and it is believed that if this is done repeatedly several times with a variety of possible descriptions, the general idea will get across. One may cite a number of Upaniṣadic passages dealing with Brahman as examples of this method. It was Yājñavalkya who for the first time used the nickname *neti neti* for this method, in the concluding part of his spectacular discourse on Soul or Brahman to his wife Maitreyī, in the *Bṛhadāraṇyaka Upaniṣad*.[17] In his commentary on this text, Sankara explains that although the truth or the Universal Soul or Brahman may be determined by hundreds of means, the final determination is through "not this" and "not that" — in other words, through negation of all other possible characterizations. In Yājñavalkya's description, this is an experience where the subject-object duality completely collapses and merges into a unity, and hence it negates all characterizations that are ascribed from the dualist point of view.

The Mādhyamika Buddhist may also endorse this method. In fact, Nāgārjuna had described *tattva* — "that-ness" or truth — in this way: "The characteristic of *tattva* is such that it can not be instructed by others, it is *not* diversified by diversifying speech, devoid of thought-construction, and *non*-dual in meaning."[18] In the beginning of his *Madhyamakaśāstra*, he characterizes the doctrine of dependent origination, the ultimate truth in Mādhyamika, by eight negative adjectives that take account of four contradictory pairs of positive characterization: "(Having) no cessation, no origination, no annihilation, no eternality, no single meaning, no multiple meaning, no arising, and no going out of existence."

VII

This method, of course, brings us back to the previous method, to paradoxes and contradictions. In fact, the notion of negation here creates problems for ordinary logical discourse. For negation of the two opposite alternatives may land us *in* a contradiction, if the law of the excluded middle is seriously entertained. In fact, the notion of negation is one of the fundamental concepts of any conceptual schema, but it is also one of the most controversial and ill-understood notions across a wide philosophical spectrum. The discussion of IME, as well as of paradoxes and multiple-valued logic, brings this problem to the fore. In talking about multiple-valued logic, we obviously pay little attention to the law of the excluded middle. We tend to define contradiction and negation in a different way. If we tolerate paradoxes in a discourse (as the saying "paradoxes we live with" shows), we allow contradiction at some level. The mystics believe in the instrumentalism of paradoxes, which, according to the mystics, help us to look beyond the normal domain of discourse. I have elsewhere argued[19] that the Nāgārjunian "no" may be interpreted as an illocutionary negation (à la Searle)[20] or a simple refutation that is *nonassertive* in the sense that refutation of P is not incompatible with refutation of not-P. This will be possible if refutation, as distinct from classical negation, of P is not equivalent to, or does not even imply, the assertion of not-P. This explanation, I contend, is quite in accord with Nāgārjuna's pronouncement: "I have no [asserted] thesis to defend."[21] I read this assertion as a claim that the statement about the truth of "Emptiness," that any thesis about reality is empty, is itself not an *asserted* statement (for otherwise this statement would itself either be false or face contradiction). A *nonasserted* statement may

Mysticism and Ineffability: Some Issues of Logic and Language 155

be a very peculiar statement indeed, and my suggestion is that it is as good as an *unstated* statement—that is, ineffable. The emptiness of all metaphysical theses can be *shown*, not *stated* in language.

Our initial reaction to the notion of a nonasserted statement may not be very sympathetic. Some may even call it bizarre. For it is like saying something and then adding, "I did not say it." Indeed, what Nāgārjuna does is to make a statement (even a *pratijñā*, statement of a thesis) and then add that he has not made that statement.[22] We may put the matter in another way. Having said or argued or shown that Emptiness is a thesis that refutes all other metaphysical theses, Nāgārjuna adds that that is not a thesis. In a way, this seems unavoidable in such a philosophical argument. Suppose we use the word "impredicable" for "no predicate can be applied to it." A Vedāntin would readily agree: yes, Brahman is impredicable. Now the question arises: Is impredicability a predicate? If it is, it falsifies the Vedāntin's proposition. Or we may say that "impredicability is a predicate" is, if true, false. But it may be false. Then, of course, we can not say "Brahman is impredicable," or if we say it, we have to add "but this is not a predication."

If this account of refutation is accepted, then it would be possible to construct a position (*koṭi*) equivalent to the third "no" of Nāgārjuna's fourfold negation. This "no" rejects a proposition as well as its negation, *both* P and not-P. The fourfold negation is, as is well known, saying "no" to the four alternatives: Is it? Is it not? Is it both? Is it neither? The third position is a *combined* rejection of the first two. But this position is also rejected by the third "no." The fourth, or final, "no" here is, however, more intriguing. The position refuted in the last case may be seen to be equivalent to the third "no," or the third rejection, refutation of both P and not-P. But the result of the third "no" seems again to have been refuted by the fourth "no." I shall call it the *ultimate* negation, which refutes the constructed or given universe of discourse. After the rejection of the combined rejection of "it is" and "it is not," we have here further *rejection* of that very rejection. It is like the mystic's saying, "I do not wish to play this (language) game." Imagine a tennis game where either player tries to send the ball to the opponent's court, but at some point one player (our Mādhyamika friend) says "enough of it" and refuses to send the ball back—in other words, refuses to play. We can thus once again *show* what is ineffable by means of what is effable in the language game that we play. (If we do not wish to play the language game, what else can we play?)

Obviously, there may be other ways to show what is ineffable and thereby vindicate or explain the IME. I have noted that our natural language possesses unexplored powers and contains untried or hitherto unknown devices, and a creative and ingenious author, a mystic-poet, can easily explore such areas and experiment with such devices. He would then be able to successfully communicate or get the message across, and there would be no need to throw one's hands up in despair. Advancing the claim of IME is only a preliminary gambit employed to break open the boundary of effability and a timely reminder that not everything needs to be conveyed *literally* in linguistic expression.

Notes

1. William James, *Varieties of Religious Experience* (1902; reprint, New York, n.d.).

2. Dharmakīrti, *Pramāṇavārttika*, ed. Swami Dwarikadas Sastri (Varanasi, India, 1972).

3. John Searle, *Speech Acts* (Cambridge, Mass., 1969), pp. 19–21; J. J. Katz, "Effability and Translation," in F. Guenthner and M. Guenthner-Reutter, eds., *Meaning and Translation* (New York, 1978), pp. 209–20. Earlier reference can be found in G. Frege, "Compound Thoughts," *Mind* (1963): 1–17, and A. Tarski, "The Semantic Conception of Truth," *Philosophy and Phenomenological Research* (1944).

4. Ludwig Wittgenstein, *Philosophical Investigations*, trans. G. E. M. Anscombe (Oxford, 1958), sec. 243.

5. Saul Kripke, *Wittgenstein on Rules and Private Languages: An Elementary Exposition* (Cambridge, Mass., 1982).

6. Wittgenstein, *Philosophical Investigations*, sec. 302.

7. Bhartṛhari, *Vākyapadīya*, Kāṇḍa I, ed. K. A. Subramania Iyer (Poona, India, 1963); Kāṇḍa III, pt. 1, ed. K. A. Subramania Iyer (Poona, India, 1963).

8. Bhartṛhari, *Vākyapadīya*, I.115.

9. For an elegant version of this issue, see R. Martin, "Are Natural Languages Universal?" *Synthese* 32 (1976): 271–91.

10. Hans Herzberger, "Paradoxes of Grounding in Semantics," *Journal of Philosophy* 67 (1970): 145-67.

11. Martin, "Are Natural Languages Universal?"

12. Paul Henle, "Mysticism and Semantics," *Philosophy and Phenomenological Research* 9 (1949): 416-22.

13. Bimal K. Matilal, "Mysticism and Reality: Ineffability," *Journal of Indian Philosophy* 3 (1975): 217-32.

14. For more on this point see Bimal K. Matilal, *Logical Illumination of Indian Mysticism* (Oxford, 1977).

15. This is how the Jaina writers explain the third "predicate" *avaktavya* (ineffable). This seems to be an admission that a contradiction in the strictest sense cannot be expressed in our natural language. No one can utter "yes" and "no" at the same time to have the same effect!

16. For further discussion of this view, see Bimal K. Matilal, *The Central Philosophy of Jainism (Anekāntavāda)* (Ahmedabad, India, 1981), p. 55.

17. Yājñavalkya, *Bṛhadāraṇyaka Upaniṣad*, IV.5.

18. Nāgārjuna, *Madhyamakaśāstra*, 18.9.

19. Matilal, *Logical Illumination of Indian Mysticism*, pp. 7-16.

20. Searle, *Speech Acts*, pp. 32-33.

21. Nāgārjuna, *Vigrahavyāvartani*, ed. P. L. Vaidya (Darbhanga, 1960), verse 29.

22. Bimal K. Matilal, *Buddhist Logic and Epistemology* (Dordrecht, 1986), pp. 25-29.

7

Fair and Unfair Language Games in Chan/Zen

BERNARD FAURE

As is well known, Chan/Zen emerged in seventh- or eighth-century China as a new form of Buddhist practice based on the teaching of "sudden awakening." But it was first of all a discourse on practice and a discursive practice: in other words, a new "art of speaking." Such discourse often claimed the privilege of being undetermined, spontaneous, absolute. Without rejecting completely its truth claim, it is clear that it was nevertheless submitted to specific epistemological, cultural, and sociopolitical constraints. The fundamental duplicity of such a discourse, in its attempt to merge into a unified vision the two planes—absolute and relative—or reality, with formulas such as "saṃsāra *is* Nirvāṇa" (*shōji soku nehan*) and "passions are awakening" (*bonnō soku bodai*), may be a necessary product or ordinary language that reintroduces the overwhelming presence of everyday life (in which saṃsāra *is not* Nirvāṇa, passions *are not* awakening). The use of language, resulting from the desire to "translate" the insights gained in *samādhi*, implies the impossibility of remaining on the absolute plane of "pure experience." As Peter Berger and Thomas Luckmann point out, "It is important to stress . . . that the reality of everyday life retains its paramount status even as such 'leaps' take place. If nothing else, language makes sure of this."[1]

Buddhists were, of course, acutely aware of the problem and

tried to address it in several ways. The fundamental choice was between trying to reach transparency to oneself and communication with others through a sign system and trying to achieve it precisely through the absence of such a system. The common understanding is that awakening breaks (or should break) with language. However, language itself has an infinite depth; it is, to quote the *Taittiriya Brāhmaṇa*, "endless, beyond all creation, immense."[2] We cannot, therefore, exclude the possibility of an awakening *within* language. We may understand in this way the famous opposition drawn by Dōgen between Linji Yixuan's notion of the "true man without a rank" (*mui shinnin*) and his own advocacy of the "true man with a rank" (*ui shinnin*), the latter having awakened with and within language, the former without.[3] Various compromises adopted by many Chan masters consisted, to use Mallarmé's expression, in "giving a clearer meaning to the words of the tribe," in particular by adding apophatic markers. An alternative solution was, as I will try to show, to use language in an essentially performative way (thus acknowledging the failure of its descriptive function). Hence the breaking of syntax, and by the same token of discursiveness and rationality, in the *kōans*—which, however, as we will see, were soon to turn into a new form of syntax, or at least some kind of semiotic system.

In order to examine the various strategies that characterize Chan discourse, we would have to consider Chan conceptions relative to language, logical thinking, writing, and poetry, and see how these conceptions, when grafted onto Chan discourse, came to give themselves a specific semiotic or ideological role. Some Chan adepts, in the process, may have become grafters. Thus descriptive or prescriptive discourse on awakening may be, depending on the circumstances, heard in a dream or when awake; and it may serve to awaken others or, on the contrary, to put them to sleep. Thus the question is never that of language *in abstracto*, but always that of *legitimate* language and the power it gives access to. We will limit ourselves to the most prevalent conceptions of language held within Chan tradition and try to assess what role these conceptions may have played in fields such as Chan poetry and Chan "encounters," or *kōans*.

Chan is well known for its motto: "No dependence on the written letter, a special transmission outside the Scriptures" (*buli wenzi jiaowai biezhuan*). This motto first appeared toward the eighth century; it was not found as such in the earliest texts, such as the so-called *Treatise of Bodhidharma* (*Damo lun*), though this Chan anthology already made some very similar points.[4] The rejection of writing(s) seems to be the corollary of a fundamental suspicion toward language in general as unable to express reality. Words have been condemned on various grounds, and this attitude may be traced back to the famous opening verse of the *Laozi*, with its pun on Dao[5] and Zhuangzi's well-known comparison of the fishnet.[6] It also reflects the Buddhist *via negativa* stemming from the Mādhyamika tradition. A recurring expression in Chan texts, intended to convey the inexpressibility of awakening, is "The path of language being cut, all mental functions are extinguished."[7] Words can express only conventional truth; they are incapable of expressing ultimate truth. Of course, the common assertion—found, for example, in Zhuangzi's parable of the wheelwright—that Dao, or awakening, cannot be taught verbally may also reflect the reluctance of a spiritual or an artistic elite to disclose the secrets of its science, its attempt to preserve its social distinction and symbolic capital. The apparent difficulty of conveying truth through language does not exclude some bad will from those who have a specific interest in remaining the privileged holders of ultimate truth.

At first glance, the only way out of what Nietzsche called the "prison-house of language" appears to be silence. In Wittgenstein's words, "Whereof we cannot speak, thereof we must remain silent."[8] There are, however, many kinds of silence, as one can find out when one reads Father Dinouart's little book, *The Art of Keeping Silent* (1771). The particular type that Chan adepts tried to emulate is the "thundering silence" of the mythical layman Vimalakīrti. But how could they forget that the praise of silence still takes place within language? And fail to realize the "unacceptable character (the nonsense) of any proposition that attempts to escape toward 'that which cannot be said'"?[9] As Emile Benveniste has shown, "the characteristic of linguistic negation is that it can cancel only that which is uttered, that it must grant explicitly in order to suppress, that a judgment of non-existence has also necessarily the status of a judgment of existence. Thus negation is first of all admission."[10] To avoid this basic difficulty of the *via negativa*, the negation of language had to be attempted in nonlinguistic ways, through "skillful means" (*upāya*) such as blows, shouts, gestures, facial expressions, or some kind of "qualified" silence. According to the founding legend of Chan, Śākyamuni, desiring to transmit the "essence of the True Dharma," held a flower in front of the assembly. Everyone was puzzled, except Mahākāśyapa, who smiled and was therefore designated as the true heir. The problematic aspects of this transmission are well expressed by Wumen Huikai, the author of the famous *kōan* collection *Wumenguan*:

> Yellow-faced Gautama, acting as if there were no one near him, forced good people into slavery, and hanging up a sheep's head, sold dog meat instead. But if at that time everybody had smiled, then how could he have transmitted the treasure of the true dharma eye, or if Mahākāśyapa had not smiled, how could he have transmitted the treasure of the true dharma eye? If he says there is a transmission of the true dharma eye, then that yellow-faced old geezer would be cheating country bumpkins. But if he says there is no transmission, then why did he approve of Mahākāśyapa alone?[11]

In the same vein, the tradition records that when Bodhidharma asked his four main disciples to demonstrate their understanding, three of them came forward with various philosophical explanations. Only one of them, Huike, stood at his place and prostrated himself, thereby becoming the second Chan patriarch. The Japanese monk Kakua (1143–?), asked by the emperor about Zen on his return from China, simply played the flute—and, not surprisingly, his answer was dismissed as irrelevant. The emperor wanted some kind of explanation, not a flute recital. This story may point to a basic problem of the nonverbal approach. Words are still needed if Chan is to make converts. An emperor does not take a nonverbal answer or a verbal non-answer for an answer, and Kakua missed the chance to be the first Japanese patriarch. Thus Bodhidharma's famous reply, "I don't know," to Liang Wudi's question, "Who is standing in front of me?" may be a model of Chan; but if it had actually taken place, would probably have endangered the future of the Chan School. The legend acknowledges this point when it tells us that Bodhidharma was banished to another kingdom, the Northern Wei, where he was ostracized and perhaps eventually murdered. During the Tang dynasty, an imperial edict made it clear that monks could not resort to sitting *dhyāna* when questioned about the Buddhist doctrine; by doing so, they would lose their clerical status.[12]

Thus Chan masters had to use words, however reluctantly, in order to convey their teachings to the powers that be. Language was given a provisional value as a signpost, a "skillful means" (*upāya*), or a "necessary evil." Linji Yixuan (d. 866), the founder of the Linji (Rinzai) School of Chan, when asked by the prefectural governor and other officials to instruct them, accepts in the following terms:

> Today, I, this mountain monk, having no choice in the matter, have perforce yielded to customary etiquette and taken this seat. If I were to demonstrate the Great Matter in strict keeping with the teaching of the Patriarchal School, I simply couldn't open my mouth and there wouldn't be any place for you to find footing. But since I've been so earnestly entreated today by the Counselor Wang, why should I conceal the essential doctrine of our school?[13]

Of course, Linji's first "answers" turn out to be somewhat paradoxical, consisting mainly of shouts and blows, or enigmatic utterances. But very soon he has to obey the rules of the discursive game and give relatively straightforward answers. And he must have been aware that these answers would be recorded. His strategic denial of language is all the more significant, as is his admiration for his acolyte and accomplice Puhua, who, by simulating madness, was able to remain until the end outside the field of discourse of Chan (or on its margins). The following "dialogue" is in this respect typical:

> One day Puhua was eating raw vegetables in front of the Monk's Hall. The Master saw him and said: "Just like an ass!"
> "Heehaw, heehaw!" brayed Puhua.
> "You thief!" said the Master.
> "Thief, thief!" cried Puhua, and went off.[14]

Puhua, like a few other trickster figures who fascinated the Chan tradition, is depicted as a kind of Daoist immortal. The contrast between these two figures is significant and reflects two different approaches to language. Linji's words, aiming at putting an end to all quirks, are eventually reduced to quirks themselves, increasing the grip of discourse on the listeners. But by resorting to a kind of glossolalia, Puhua apparently succeeds in evading the paradox. He avoids becoming a master and taking a position in authorized discourse. Unwilling to accept the legitimacy of a patriarchal seat, he seems to be the "true man without a rank," idealized by Linji. However, even he is not without spiritual posterity and will later be "tamed" by the Zen tradition, which will promote him as the "founder" of the Fuke (Chinese, Puhua) School, a relatively obscure school introduced in Japan by the flute player Kakua and Muhon Kakushin (1207–1298).

According to the French philosopher Vladimir Jankélévitch, "there are at least three ways to elude the obstacle of inexpressibility: the first is the euphemism, the second the apophatic inversion, the third . . . the conversion to the ineffable."[15] Puhua clearly represents the third case, while Linji's position varies from the first (though he uses metaphors rather than euphemisms) to the second. But for Linji, language is not defined primarily by its finitude, its poor capacity to express the unexpressable. It is also, primarily perhaps, a decisive weapon in an agonistic encounter with others. In his dialogues, like in the discursive challenges described by the French anthropologist Jeanne Favret-Saada in her book on witchcraft, "what matters . . . is less to decipher utterances or what is being said — than to understand who speaks, and to whom."[16] In other words, as we will see later, words are strokes or moves in a complex game whose stakes are never clearly stated. In order to play the game, one has to abide by its rules. Of course, one can also choose to remain outside the game and "roam freely," as Zhuangzi would say, outside the closure of language, but this means losing the fun of the game.

The situation just described is not specific to Linji. It reflects an ambiguity already at play in the early Chan tradition, the so-called *Laṅkāvatāra* School. The text on which it relied, the *Laṅkāvatāra-sūtra*, is famous for, among other things, its distinction between *siddhānta-naya* and *deśanā-naya*, the first concept referring to the personal and nondiscursive experience of reality, the second to the realization obtained through an external teaching.[17] While stressing the complementarity of these two approaches (overlapping that of the Twofold Truth in the Mādhyamika tradition), the *Laṅkāvatāra* also constantly underscores the inexpressibility of truth and claims that, during his fifty years of predication, the Buddha "never spoke a single word." His sermons were mere "skillful means," void of any ontological reality, "golden leaves to stop the crying of an infant," empty talk from a "golden mouth." In the biographical notice of one of the main representatives of the *Laṅkāvatāra* tradition, Fachong (587–ca. 665),[18] we find an interesting distinction between Bodhidharma's two main disciples, Huike and Daoyu. While Daoyu, "having received the Dao, practiced it in his mind and abstained from talking about it," Huike apparently did try to express his realization. Incidentally, this contradicts the legend, mentioned earlier, of the transmission between Bodhidharma and Huike.[19] Again, the denial of language or its "homeopathic" use appears to play a rather ambiguous role in sectarian strategies.

Let us now consider another attitude toward language: language as not just an imperfect tool, much less a trap, but as allowing a full expression of reality. One witnesses during the Tang dynasty a gradual shift from apophatic to "kataphatic," or positive, discourse. Many factors, both within and without the Buddhist tradition, led to this change. Among them was probably the widespread feeling that, as Benveniste has stressed, "for the speaking subject, there is between language and reality a complete adequacy: the sign covers and commands reality; better, it *is* this reality."[20] The power of invocations and incantations was well known to the Chinese, and the notion that the name is the thing or at least is, in an almost Cratylian way, intimately related to it had been commonly accepted since Confucius. According to Marcel Granet,[21] Chinese words are emblems rather than signs, and consequently the Saussurian theory concerning the "arbitrary nature of signs" may not apply. As the author of the *Wenxin diaolong* puts it: "The reason why words can arouse the world is that they are the *wen* ("patterns") of the Dao."[22] Esoteric Buddhism, with its stress on *mantras* (translated in Chinese as "true words") and *dhāraṇīs*, provided a further rationale for this tendency to extol words. The traditionally exalted status of poetical language also contributed significantly to this rehabilitation of "true words" in the Japanese context. Tantrism and its theory of language significantly influenced early Chan (and later Japanese Zen).

Another theoretical justification was the Mahāyāna doctrine of nonduality. If everything is a manifestation of Suchness (*tathatā*), if every being, sentient and nonsentient, possesses a Buddha-nature, if the Dao is to be found, as Zhuangzi argued, in every phenomenon, it follows that any utterance, any writing, is liable to express ultimate reality. Thus according to an early Chan chronicle, the second patriarch, Huike, held that "everything affirmed about the true Dharma is reality as such,"[23] and the fourth Chan patriarch, Daoxin (580–651), taught that "if only one word impregnates the vital principle, it remains forever incorruptible."[24] Then Mazu Daoyi (709–788) coined his famous motto—"The ordinary mind is the Dao"—and even words uttered in a deluded frame of mind gained ontological nobility. According to the Chan "historian" Zongmi (780–841), Mazu taught that

> all Dharmas, whether existent or empty, are nothing but the absolute Nature. . . . Things such as language and action, desire and hatred, compassion and patience, good and evil deeds, suffering and enjoyment, all these are the Buddha-nature within yourselves; they are the original Buddha apart from which there is no other Buddha. . . . [All actions such as] the arising of mind, the movements of thought, a snapping of the fingers, a sigh or a cough, or taking up a fan, all are the functionings of the whole substance of Buddha-nature.[25]

The antinomian excesses that seemed to derive from the notion of the immanence of truth within beings and things were criticized within the Chan School itself, but the basic premise—that is, the positive attitude toward language—was shared even by some of its detractors, such as the Japanese Zen master Dōgen. In the chapter "Gabyō" of his *Shōbōgenzō*, Dōgen addresses the question of representation through the old proverb "A painted rice-cake [*gabyō*] does not satisfy hunger."[26] This proverb had been used in early Chan texts to deprecate the oral teachings vis-à-vis sitting meditation. For example, in the *Faju jing*, an apocryphal scripture popular in early Chan, we find the following comment: "If names were reality, one should be able to satisfy the hunger of people by talking to them about food. And if one could satisfy them in this way, all aliments and beverages would be useless. Why? Because he whose hunger can be satisfied by a talk about food is not really hungry."[27] However Dōgen, in his typical fashion, inverts the whole hierarchy between reality and representation, and concludes that "only a painted rice-cake can satisfy hunger," or, to use another of his metaphors, "only a painted dragon can bring rain." A similar idea may already have been expressed by the Northern Chan master Shenxiu (606-706), to whom is attributed the paradoxical statement that "the body may disappear, but not its shadow."[28] By so upending the traditional hierarchy between reality and representation, truth and language, these statements seem to imply a departure from the Buddhist "metaphysics of presence" and its correlative downplaying of words as ancillary to "pure experience."

The very notion of *Shōbōgenzō*, which gives its title to Dōgen's work, implies a radical reinterpretation of the value of language. This "essential repository of the true Dharma" is a linguistic one. Although Śākyamuni, according to the legend often quoted as historical proof by Dōgen, transmitted it silently to Mahākāśyapa, he had to say that he was doing so. The whole thing appears as a performance, both in the Austinian sense of "doing what one says,"[29] and in the theatrical sense of impressing a somewhat gullible audience. This is the way in which the author of the *Wumenguan*, quoted earlier, seems to interpret the story.

Another famous case of transmission is that of Linji, who, shortly before his death, asked his disciple Sansheng to show his understanding of the "True Dharma Eye." Sansheng replied with a shout, for which Linji praised him in the following way: "Who would have thought that my True Dharma Eye would be extinguished upon reaching this blind ass!"[30] Here we already have a few words, but they need to be taken with a grain of salt. Language is still used in a self-deprecating fashion, with apophatic markers. Such is not the case anymore with Dōgen, who asserts the value of words. These are not the words of ordinary language, though, but words vivified by a spiritual realization, words for which Dōgen coins a special term, *dōtoku*.[31]

Another interesting trend of thought surfacing in the *Shōbōgenzō* is the notion of the "preaching of nonsentient beings" (*mujō seppō*). Although this preaching, according to the Chan tradition, cannot be heard in an ordinary way—its sounds must be perceived through the eyes, not through the ears—what matters here is that the whole world becomes a sacred text or discourse, the "sūtra of mountains and rivers." There is nothing, therefore, in the whole world that does not reveal the Buddhist truth. Words and scriptures are no exception. According to Dōgen: "There are nothing but *sūtras* everywhere in time and space. Thus, whatever phenomena we perceive, . . . all are letters of the sūtras, the outer coverings of the sūtras."[32] While in early Mahāyāna only sentient beings had a Buddha-nature, for Sōtō Zen masters everything *is* the Buddha-nature, every word *is* the Dharma. But it takes an enlightened person such as Dōgen to realize this.

In the chapter "*Keisei sanshoku*" ("The Sound of the Valley, the Forms of the Mountains"), Dōgen quotes the following poem written by Su Shi (alias Su Dongpo) on the occasion of a visit to Lushan:

> The sound from the valley stream is from a great tongue,
> The forms of the mountains are the pure body.
> The eighty-four thousand verses heard during the night,
> How to tell them to the people the next day?[33]

Su Dongpo may not be able to convey the truths he has heard, but he still intends to convey a message through his "apophatic inversion." Dōgen is aware of the fact when he says: "By telling this to men, Su Shi leaves them far behind and advances alone."[34] The truth is that truth is inexpressible, and this truth has been expressed. The very obstacle to its expression becomes the channel or instrument of its expression. The fact that the medium is a poem is not insignificant. The instrumental words of prose, as Zhuangzi pointed out, can be forgotten when their meaning is understood. However, the words of poetry are to be remembered and reactualized every time the poem is recited. They have a resonance that cannot be exhausted on one hearing. In Valéry's words, "the poem is a prolonged hesitation between sound and meaning."

This is also true of certain, if not all, words—for example, those uttered by a master. The day before he was enlightened, Su Dongpo had had a conversation with the Chan master Changzong Zhaojue concerning the preaching of nonsentient beings. However, the words of the master had to sink deeply into him before he could understand them. Dōgen offers the following comment:

> Although at the time these words could not cause in him any revulsion, the sound of the valley stream, when he heard it,

seemed like the tide assaulting heaven. But was it the sound of the valley stream that seized him in this way, or the words of Zhaojue flowing into him? One may wonder whether the latter's words on the predication of the non-sentient, which were still resonating, did not secretly merge with the sound from the valley.[35]

Poetic Language in Chan

The problem of resonance, of the repercussion of words within the mind, will lead us to examine briefly the role(s) imparted (or denied) to poetry by Chan adepts. Not surprisingly, we find here some of the ambiguities that appeared in the judgments about the value of language in general. The dominant conception seems to be a deep-rooted prejudice against literary pleasure and a disbelief in the power of a poem to express ultimate reality. Poetry is presented, then, as an ancillary practice, an *upāya*, a mere starting point — and possibly a double-edged tool, a stumbling block for the practitioner who forsakes the goal for the means while indulging in his poetic achievements. Thus two kinds of poetry are distinguished: one that leads toward a higher goal, another that detracts from it. While the latter, purely profane use of poetry is of course dismissed, the status of the former is somewhat floating. The *locus classicus* is to be found in the famous statement of the Chinese poet Bai Juyi (772–846) about "wild words and specious phrases" (Japanese, *kyōgen kigo*): "May the wordly writings of my present life, with all their wild words and specious phrases, serve in future ages as the inspiration of hymns of praise extolling the Buddha's teachings, and turn the Wheel of the Dharma forever."[36] Bai Juyi concludes another of his poems with the lines: "Gradually I have conquered the wine devil, no more getting hopelessly drunk. / But I still go on making mouth karma, not having ceased writing poems."[37]

Like Bai Juyi, Su Dongpo seems at first to consider poetry as a means to an end, a mere stepping stone toward spiritual realization:

> The Qiantang monk Sicong at the age of seven played the lute well. At twelve he gave up the lute and studied calligraphy. After he became skilled in calligraphy, in ten years he gave it up and

studied poetry; in his poems there are extraordinary passages. Then he read the *Huayan sūtra,* and entered into the Realm of Reality and the Sea of Wisdom. . . . I have heard that when one's thoughts are trained so they are reaching close to the Dao, the *Huayan,* the Realm of Reality and the Sea of Wisdom are only way-stations; and this is even more true of calligraphy, poetry, and the lute. No matter how hard he tries, no student of the Dao achieves it if he starts from nothing. . . . If Cong does achieve it, his lute-playing and calligraphy, and above all his poetry, will have had something to do with it. Like water, Cong will be able to reflect all things in one, and his calligraphy will become still more extraordinary. I will keep watch on them, and take them as indications of how profoundly Cong achieves the Dao.[38]

Thus poetry is presented by Su Dongpo as not only a valuable practice, as a possible cause or condition of enlightenment, but also, a posteriori, a legitimate product of the enlightened mind. These two aspects are the two faces of the *upāya*: as a means to reach the absolute from the relative, and as the skillfulness of the Bodhisattva who is able to convey some part of the truth he experiences to people still trapped in the conventional world. This is precisely the way in which Su Dongpo, in the poem quoted by Dōgen, attempts to "translate" the absolute faithfully and to intimate the meaning of the *Dharmakāya,* Buddha's cosmic body, to his fellow men. The "night" might be seen as symbolizing the realm of the absolute; the "next day," that of the relative. A similar device is used by the Tang poet Hanshan, in a poem magistrally analyzed by Iriya Yoshitaka: "My mind is like an autumn moon, / An emerald pool, clear and pure. Nothing will afford comparison . . . / Tell me, how should I explain?"[39]

Su Dongpo provides another justification for poetry, whether preceding or following awakening, as being an expression of what, in man, transcends the limitations of human condition—that is, the irrepressible spontaneity that bears witness to the wonderful workings of nature (Dao, or, in Buddhist terminology, Buddha-nature) within man. Such a naturalness, the ultimate goal (and underlying principle) of Chan or poetic practice, is the hallmark of the true (and gifted) practitioner and dispenses him from following the rules established for common men:

> The excellence of writers of old was not that they could write, but that they could not help writing. Hills and streams have

mists, plants have flowers and fruit, which when full and ripe appear outside—even if they wished not to have them, could they help it? . . . My writing is like a ten-thousand-gallon spring. It can issue from the ground anywhere at all. On smooth ground it rushes swiftly and covers a thousand *li* in a single day without difficulty. When it twists and turns among mountains and rocks, it fits its form to the things it meets: unknowable. What can be known is, it always goes where it must go, always stops where it cannot help stopping—nothing else. More than that even I cannot know.[40]

Thus instead of the notion that words are an attempt, flawed from the start, at *expressing* some inner reality, we have here the idea that poetry is a transcendent speech-act, reality itself in action, the joyful outpouring of a "sportive samadhi." Poetic speech/writing is the intransitive act of *realizing*, while there is actually *nothing* to be realized or expressed.

Su Dongpo makes yet another, possibly more important, claim for poetry when he declares:

> In salty and sour are mixed a host of preferences,
> But in their middle there is a great savour, everlasting.

He is alluding to the theory of the "savour beyond savour" (*wei wai wei*), advocated in the ninth century by Sikong Tu (837–908).[41] According to James Liu, Sikong Tu was the first poet to voice explicitly the concept of poetry as an embodiment of the poet's apprehension of the Dao.[42] He compared the resonance of the poem in the sensitive mind to the subtle taste that a gourmet can find even in spicy aliments, though preferably in apparently insipid ones. This notion apparently stems from Laozi's comments that "the five tastes injure man's palate"[43] and that "music and food will induce the wayfarer to stop, while the Dao in its passage through the mouth is without flavour."[44] Su Dongpo elaborates on Sikong Tu's ideas by distinguishing between the "center" and the edges of a savor:

> According to Buddhists, "it is like when people eat honey; they find that everything is sweet, at the center as well as on the edges." When people taste the five flavours they all distinguish between the bitter and the sweet; but rare are those who, for the same flavour, can distinguish between the center and the edge.[45]

Thus, just like aliments, poetic texts have an aftertaste, a center that may be reached only after a long process of savoring, leaving the edges of words and meanings. The same is true of the *huatou* (literally, "head of speech," the central part of the *kongan* [Japanese, *kōan*, or "public cases"] used in Chan maieutics), which can be approached in two ways (depending on the level of the practitioner): via the meaning—this is usually described as "investigating the dead word"; and through (and beyond) the word itself—this approach to the "live word" being described as "tasteless." In all cases, the savoring amounts to a rejection of all superficial, "peripheral" interpretations elaborated by the intellect. At the center of the tasteless resides an infinite savor; at the core of the word an infinite meaning—Rabelais's "substantifique moelle" or Bodhidharma's "marrow"—reveals itself. The infinite nature of the phenomenal world, well expressed by Dōgen in *Genjōkōan*,[46] is also that of the word or the poem. Dōgen was well aware of the semantic depth of words and of the "two sources," natural and cultural, of poetry. He nevertheless rejected poetry as an idle pastime, an attachment to the world of forms. This did not prevent him from writing poems, and he seems even to have participated in *waka* meetings. The ornate style of his prose is typical of the Chinese literary form known in Japan as *shiroku benrei*. One may, as Valéry did, deem that "no direct thinking is able of such a discourse."

A recurrent theme is that despite the appearances, the words of poetry have a higher status than ordinary language. They are the expression of Chan awakening; the language things speak through man. Thus they are not the language of a deluded subjectivity that would create a hiatus in the natural flow of things. Emanating from and producing reality, they participate actively in ontogenesis. Like the words of the Chan master Xuefeng Yicun (823–909), they leave no traces or track.[47] They are, to use a Chinese poetical cliché, "similar to the antelope hanging itself by its horns to the branches of trees."[48] According to the poet Wu Ke (d. ca. 1174), "dead poetry is a poetry in the language of which there is still language; live poetry is a poetry whose language is no more language."[49] "Live words" can thus become the "preaching of nonsentient beings," the language of the cosmic Buddha, ultimate reality speaking of itself. Spontaneous speech in response to things, as it takes place in Chan or in poetry, becomes the hallmark of awakening. However, as soon as spontaneity itself becomes an ideal, if not from the outset, its nature changes drastically, and it is eventually reappropriated, like the *kōan*, into a larger, performative discourse.

The Performative Nature of the *Kōan*

The analogy between the poem and the *huatou* or the *kōan* is far-reaching. While the *kōans* may be considered to be obstacles to discourse, they are originally part of an unfolding dialogue (Chinese, *wenda*; Japanese, *mondō*),[50] at least in the "classical" tradition.[51] When we consider the proliferation of discourse around *kōans*, such as the famous *Wu* (Japanese, *Mu*; Zhaozhou's "answer" to the question "Has a dog a Buddha-nature?") and their mantric or incantatory use, one may wonder whether they are really "words destined to put an end to words." This raises the question of their actual function in the general economy of Chan spirituality.

I have already mentioned what we may call the "gustatory" interpretation of the *huatou*. The traditional interpretation of the *kōan* as an irrational riddle destined to create in the practitioner a kind of double bind, the so-called great doubt, that will eventually force him to bypass or break through his intellectual screen seems itself too commonsensical for its flavor to persist on the sensitive palate of an authentic practitioner. It was already rejected on various grounds within the Chan tradition itself. The psychological elaboration provided by D. T. Suzuki for well-intentioned psychoanalysts is clearly a further rationalization. It has significantly contributed to the development of a "false consciousness" and some enduring misunderstandings concerning Chan practice.

These various conceptions of the *huatou* and the *kōan* share a hermeneutical premise: the belief that under the surface, behind the apparent non-sense of the words, there is a deep meaning to be retrieved, an insight to be gained. This may have been the case in certain dialogues borrowed from Buddhist scriptures or the "recorded sayings" (*yulu*) of famous Chan masters. But precisely, the "discourse situation" or dialogic context of the *kōans* is most of the time irremediably lost, and so is their contextual meaning. All the more so when the cultural setting has become radically different, as it was in Japanese Zen, where *kōans* became increasingly systematized, ritualized, and routinized. The possibility of some kind of hermeneutical "fusion of horizons" has become a rather dim one. Like any ritual or like poetry, *kōans* sometimes turned into a practice that had its end in itself, and this is why it might be misleading to try to retrieve a meaning at all costs.

Why, then, would the tradition have stressed an interpretation that does not, or at least does not always, explain the actual practice? It might have had some ideological stakes in doing so. I would like to submit a few working hypotheses that suggest the need to take into account the social and historical contexts of the various conceptions of language underlying Chan practice. This does not cancel the truth claim of these conceptions as such, since they may have reflected originally the genuine insights of some practitioners. However, as Zhaozhou Congshen (d. 897) once said in joining the funerary procession for one of his monks: "What a long train of dead bodies follow in the wake of a single person!" Thus when these conceptions became routinized, Chan masters tended to become just another "interest group," and it is on this ideological level that the analysis could legitimately focus. It is, for example, likely that in many cases the rejection of the written letter manifested an elitist tendency, a desire to distinguish oneself by preserving a certain symbolic capital.

But more important is the performative nature of "classical" Chan, and of *kōans* in particular. If Chan dialogues often end with blows (*coups*), it is because they are themselves "coups," strokes or moves in a game.[52] Perhaps they do not intend to express a meaning, but to impress an interlocutor, to gain the upper hand in a contest where all moves are allowed. Like any ritual or language game, they work simultaneously on several levels — the semantic, the syntactic, and, more important, the semiotic or pragmatic levels. They are essentially performative. Their function is, to use Austin's terminology, illocutionary (insofar as they create an "event" and necessitate some kind of social ceremonial) and perlocutionary (insofar as they produce effects that are not always perceived by the interlocutors).[53] They also imply a departure from ontology, from the conception of truth as already there, *ab aeterno*, toward a conception of truth in the process of emerging, in constant actualization. Such is the "actualized *kōan*" (*genjō kōan*) or "enacted truth" advocated by Dōgen, and this truth is never separated from a specific historical situation or sectarian position.[54]

The paradigmatic example of this conception of truth may be the episode in which the Buddha, holding a bird in his (upper) hand, asks his disciples whether the bird is alive or dead. Of course, this turns out to be a losing game for the disciples (and possibly for the bird as well). Truth may thus be the outcome of a will to power, instead of its denial. According to Jean-François Lyotard, "to speak is to fight, in the sense of playing, . . . and language acts belong to a general agonistic."[55] The agonistic or conflictive nature of Chan "encounter dialogues," sometimes called "Dharma battles," has often been pointed out,[56] but it is usually downplayed as a "skillful means" used by the master to test and awaken his disciple. This may be true in the case of a Linji, but cannot simply be taken for granted in the cases of those Chan masters to whom Linji himself referred as "blind shavepates and wild foxes." Quite possibly, many of them, consciously or not, were trying to obtain some symbolic profit from these encounters with novices. What matters here, as in the case of the "deadly words" uttered in the magical encounters analyzed by Favret-Saada, is less what is said than who speaks and to whom. The dialogue produces a winner and a loser, and the gain and the loss, if only symbolic, can be very real and activate quasi-magical forces. According to Favret-Saada, "a force is 'magical' in that it cannot be contained in the system of names; by this very fact, it produces its effects without passing through the ordinary symbolical mediations."[57]

In some cases at least, Chan dialogues turned out to be a deadly serious game. But we may now turn to the opposite interpretation, and see them as a humorous game whose parodic purpose may have been lost on later practitioners. According to Mikhail Bakhtin, "there never was a . . . single type of direct discourse . . . that did not have its own parodying and travestying double, its own comic-ironic *counter-partie*."[58] The following "Dharma battle," borrowed from a somewhat different context, will illustrate the point in a contrapunctal mode. It is quoted from the chapter of Rabelais's *Pantagruel* entitled "How Panurge Confounded the Englishman Who Argued by Signs." Panurge engages in this controversy against the English scholar Thaumaste on behalf of his master, Pantagruel. Unfortunately, I cannot quote the passage in full and in its original language (the savor is considerably diminished by translation). But hopefully, a "savour beyond savour" might still be found in this short excerpt:

> Then, with everyone attending and listening in perfect silence, the Englishman raised his two hands separately high in the air, clenching all the tips of his fingers in the form that is known in the language of Chinon as the hen's arse, and struck the nails of one against the other four times. Then he opened them and struck the one with the flat of the other, making a sharp noise. Next, clenching them again, as before, he struck twice more and, after opening them, yet another four times. Then he joined them afresh and laid them one beside the other, as if offering devout prayers to God.[59]

Panurge answers in a similar way, and the silent dialogue intensifies gradually, leading toward its climax:

> Next [Panurge] put the thumb of his left hand to the corner of his left eye, extending his whole hand like the wing of a bird or the fins of a fish, and flapping it very daintily this way and that, afterwards repeating the action with his right at the corner of his right eye.
> Thaumaste began to tremble and to grow pale, and made him a sign. . . .
> Then Panurge struck one hand against the other and blew in his palm. After which he once more thrust the forefinger of his right hand into the ring made by his left, pushing in it and drawing it out several times. Then he stuck out his chin and looked intently at Thaumaste. . . .
> Thaumaste now began to sweat great drops, and had all the appearance of a man rapt in high contemplation. . . .
> Finally, Thaumaste admits his defeat, telling the by-standers how Panurge has opened to him "the true and encyclopaedic well and abyss of learning."[60]

Finally, Thaumaste cried out, "Ha, my Masters, a great secret!" and admitted his defeat, telling the onlookers how Panurge had resolved his doubts and shown him "the true well, fountain and abyss of the encyclopaedia of learning."

This typically Rabelaisian contest will remind us of certain Chan "encounters." But the parodic intent here is more obvious. The point is that the esoteric signs used by the protagonists have no referent; they are empty. Their "meaning" is not to be found at the semantic or syntactic levels, but at the semiotic or pragmatic levels. In the same way, Thomas Merton explains that "the acts and gestures of a Zen master are no more 'statements' than is the ringing of an alarm clock. . . . Usually the Master is simply 'producing facts' which the disciple either sees or does not see. . . . In so far as the disciple takes the fact to be a sign of something else, he is misled by it." Merton then criticizes the Western tendency to "interpret" everything: "Nothing is allowed just to be and to mean itself: everything has to mysteriously signify something else."[61] However Merton himself, following Suzuki, still "interprets" the master's actions as stemming from his "will to truth," without questioning the various possible strategies in which this "will to truth" might be playing a specific part, thus sometimes becoming a "will to power." To a certain extent, the language of truth may have been replaced by the language of persuasion. The difficulty is to think together these two aspects of language, as simultaneously symbol and function, signifying and performative.

On the contrary, I want to stress the multiplicity of possible scenarios enacted by different actors in different tones and with different stakes through the genre known as "Chan dialogues," or *kōans*. Significant is the fact that what may have been in the beginning spontaneous encounters of "raids on the unspeakable," to use Merton's metaphor, became in due time, precisely, a genre—that is, a highly ritualized type of discourse with a given sociocultural setting and specific role expectations. We have to be aware of this internal differentiation between various "cases" or various uses of the same "case" in order to understand the manifold "sound of one hand clapping."

Despite (or because of) its denial of language, Chan appears first of all as a new "art of speaking." Just as there are many kinds of silence, there are many ways to speak and to avoid speaking. Some of them happen to be genuine, while others may turn out to be mere strategical moves. Many, if not all, are essentially performative, or more precisely perlocutionary, insofar as they serve more distant ends than straightforward communication. It is therefore essential to qualify the Chan denial of language by placing it, whenever possible, in its various sociocultural and historical settings and examining the way it has been reappropriated by various "speakers." To give just an example, the rejection by early Chan masters of "language as absolute" may be seen against the background of their ambivalence toward Tantric speculations on sound and toward Taoist and Confucianist belief systems. If, as Pascal believed, "nature abhors the void," we should keep in mind that the emptiness (*śūnyatā*) underlying Buddhist experience is an elusive reality, too easily reified, and that Chan discourse—not to mention secondary discourse on Chan discourse—always runs the risk of becoming empty talk.

Notes

1. Peter L. Berger and Thomas Luckmann, *The Social Construction of Reality* (New York, 1967), p. 26.

2. *Taittirīya Brāhmaṇa*, II.8, 4-5.

3. Dōgen, *Shōbōgenzō*, in Takakusu Junjirō and Watanabe Kaigyoku, eds., *Taishō shinshu daizōkyō* (*Taishō Edition of the Buddhist Canon*) (Tokyo, 1924-32), vol. 82, 2582, p. 181c (hereafter abbreviated as *T.*; the references give the volume number, the catalog number, and the page and column). See also *Linji lu*, in *T.* 47, 1985, p. 496c, and Ruth F. Sasaki and Iriya Yoshitaka, trans., *The Recorded Sayings of Ch'an Master Lin-chi Hui-chao of Chen Prefecture* (Kyoto, 1975), p. 3.

4. Yanagida Seizan, ed., *Daruma no goroku* (Tōkyō, 1969), p. 32; Bernard Faure, *Le Traité de Bodhidharma* (Paris, 1986), pp. 69, 154.

5. *Laozi*, sec. 1: "The Dao that can be spoken of (*dao*) is not the constant *dao*" (D. C. Lau, trans., *Lao Tzu* [New York, 1963], p. 57).

6. See *Zhuangzi*, chap. 26: "The fish-trap exists because of the fish; once you have gotten the fish, you can forget the trap. The rabbit snare exists because of the rabbit; once you've gotten the rabbit, you can forget the snare. Words exist because of the meaning; once you've gotten the meaning, you can forget the words" (attributed to Zhuang Zhou, commentary by Guo Xiang, *Zhuangzi*, ed. Sibu beiyao [Taibei, 1973], 9.6a; see also Burton Watson, trans., *The Complete Works of Chuang Tzu* [New York, 1968], p. 302). See also Edward T. Ch'ien, "The Conception of Language and the Use of Paradox in Buddhism and Taoism," *Journal of Chinese Philosophy* 11 (1984): 375-99.

7. The *locus classicus* for this expression is the *Da zhidu lun*, chap. 5, attributed to Nāgārjuna (*T.* 25, 1509, p. 96c). See Etienne Lamotte, trans.,

Le Traité de la grande vertu de sagesse de Nāgārjuna (Mahāprajñāpāramitāśāstra) (Louvain, 1944), vol. 1, p. 323.

8. Yet, as Frederic Jameson points out, "the famous sentence, in that it can be spoken at all, carries its own paradox within itself" (*The Prison-House of Language: A Critical Account of Structuralism and Russian Formalism* [Princeton, N.J., 1972], p. 12). The same point has often been made concerning Laozi's apology of silence.

9. Michel de Certeau, *The Practice of Everyday Life*, trans. Steven Randall (Berkeley, 1988), p. 10.

10. Emile Benveniste, *Problèmes de linguistique générale* (Paris, 1974), vol. I, p. 84.

11. Wumen Huikai, *Wumenguan*, in *T.* 48, 2005, p. 293b; J. D. Schmidt, trans., "Ch'an, Illusion and Sudden Enlightenment in the Poetry of Yang Wang-li," *T'oung Pao* 60 (1974): 240.

12. Decree of 20 July 742, in *Tang huiyao* 49, p. 6b, quoted in Paul Demiéville, *Le Concile de Lhasa* (Paris, 1952), p. 113, n. 1.

13. Sasaki and Yoshitaka, *Recorded Sayings of Lin-chi*, p. 1.

14. Sasaki and Yoshitaka, *Recorded Sayings of Lin-chi*, p. 42.

15. Vladimir Jankélévitch, *La Mort* (Paris, 1977), p. 60.

16. Jeanne Favret-Saada, *Les Mots, la mort, les sorts* (Paris, 1977), p. 26.

17. See D. T. Suzuki, *Studies in the Lankavatara Sutra* (1930; Taibei, 1977).

18. See Daoxuan, *Continued Biographies of Eminent Monks* [*Xu Gaoseng zhuan*], in *T.* 50, 2060, p. 666.

19. Huike's disciples again divided in two groups: those (Sengcan, Sengna, etc.) who "expounded the principle orally and did not produce any writing," and those who wrote commentaries on the *Laṅkāvatāra*. Fachong himself, when asked by his disciples to explain the deep meaning of the *sūtra*, declared: "The meaning is no other than the principle. Oral explanations are already too summary, how then could it be written down!" But, the chronicle continues, "despite his reticence, he eventually wrote a five scroll commentary, titled *Personal notes*, which is nowadays very popular (Daoxuan, *Biographies of Eminent Monks*, p. 666b).

20. Benveniste, *Problèmes de linguistique générale*, p. 52.

21. Marcel Granet, *La Pensée chinoise* (Paris, 1968), p. 42.

22. Quoted in François Jullien, "L'Oeuvre et l'univers: imitation ou déploiement," *Extrême-Orient, Extrême-Occident* 3 (1983): 86.

23. *Lengjie shiziji*, in *T.* 85, 2837, p. 1286a.

24. *Lengjie shiziji*, p. 1289a.

25. Zongmi, *Chanyuan zhuguanji duxu*, in *T.* 48, 2015, p. 402c; Jan Yün-hua, trans., "Tsung-mi: His Analysis of Ch'an Buddhism," *T'oung Pao* 58 (1972): 39.

26. Dōgen, *Shōbōgenzō Dōtoku*, in *T.* 82, 2582, pp. 165a–167a.
27. *Faju jing*, in *T.* 85, 2901, p. 1432b.
28. *Lengjie shiziji*, in *T.* 85, 2837, p. 1290c.
29. J. L. Austin, *How to Do Things with Words* (Cambridge, Mass., 1975).
30. Sasaki and Yoshitaka, *Recorded Sayings of Lin-chi*, p. 62.
31. Dōgen, *Shōbōgenzō Dōtoku*, in *T.* 82, 2582, pp. 163a–165a.
32. Dōgen, *Shōbōgenzō Dōtoku*, p. 194b.
33. Dōgen, *Shōbōgenzō Dōtoku*, p. 38c.
34. Dōgen, *Shōbōgenzō Dōtoku*, p. 41b.
35. Dōgen, *Shōbōgenzō Dōtoku*, p. 39a.
36. Quoted in Herbert Eugen Plutschow, "Is Poetry a Sin?: *Honjisuijaku* and Buddhism versus Poetry," *Oriens Extremus* 25 (1978): 208. On *kyōgen kigo*, see William LaFleur, *The Karma of Words: Buddhism and the Literary Arts in Japan* (Berkeley, 1986), p. 8, and Margaret Childs, "Kyōgen-kigo: Love Stories as Buddhist Sermons," *Japanese Journal of Religious Studies* 12 (1980): 91–103.
37. Quoted in Burton Watson, "Zen Poetry," in Kenneth Kraft, ed., *Zen: Tradition and Transition* (New York, 1988), p. 114.
38. Andrew L. March, "Self and Landscape in Su Shih," *Journal of the American Oriental Society* 86 (1966): 387.
39. Quoted in Iriya Yoshitaka, "Chinese Poetry and Zen," trans. Norman Waddell, *Eastern Buddhist* 6 (1973): 57.
40. March, "Self and Landscape in the Su Shih," p. 385.
41. Concerning this notion, see François Jullien, "Le Plaisir du texte: l'expérience chinoise de la saveur littéraire," *Extrême-Orient, Extrême-Occident* 1 (1982): 73–119.
42. James J. Y. Liu, *Chinese Theories of Literature* (Chicago, 1975), p. 35.
43. *Laozi*, sec. 12 (Lau, *Lao Tzu*, p. 68).
44. *Laozi*, sec. 35 (Lau, *Lao Tzu*, p. 94).
45. Quoted in Jullien, "L'Oeuvre et l'univers," p. 88.
46. Dōgen, *Genjōkōan*, in *T.* 52, 2582, p. 24b.
47. *Laozi*, sec. 27: "One who excels in travelling leaves no wheel tracks; one who excels in speech makes no slips" (Lau, *Lao Tzu*, p. 84).
48. See also Han Yu: "What is called 'not touching the path of reason (*li*) nor falling into the trammel of words' is the best. . . . The poets of the High T'ang relied only on inspired feelings (*hsing-chü*), like the antelope that hangs by its horns, leaving no traces to be found. Therefore, the miraculousness of their poetry lies in its transparent luminosity, which cannot be pieced together; it is like sound in the air, color in appearances, or an image in the mirror; it has limited words but unlimited meaning" (quoted in Liu, *Chinese Theories of Literature*, p. 39).

49. Quoted in Paul Demiéville, "Langue et littérature chinoises," in *Annuaire du Collège de France* (Paris, 1962), p. 330.

50. Strictly speaking, *mondō* and *kōan* should be distinguished as two different genres, but for a first approximation, we can consider them together.

51. Notice the difference between the "progressive," linear dialogues of early Chan and the "disruptive" dialogues of "classical" Chan.

52. Concerning this notion, see François Lyotard and Jean-Loup Thébaud, *Just Gaming* (Minneapolis, 1985).

53. On this question, see Austin, *How to Do Things with Words*. See also "Performative Utterances," in Paul Edwards, ed., *The Encyclopedia of Philosophy* (New York, 1967), vol. 5-6, pp. 90-91; Jacques Derrida, "Signature, événement, contexte," in *Marges de la philosophie* (Paris, 1972), pp. 382-84; and Paul de Man, *Allegories of Reading* (New Haven, Conn., 1979), pp. 119-32. Notice, however, that, contrary to Austin's definition, Chan "speech-acts" are polysemic, irreducible to a single meaning, and do not imply a self-controlled intentionality.

54. See Bernard Faure, *La Vision immédiate* (Paris, 1987), pp. 30-54.

55. Jean-François Lyotard, *La Condition postmoderne* (Paris, 1979), p. 23.

56. In a round-table discussion on Chan, Nishitani Keiji stated, for example, that these encounters, "different from the dialogues that take place in schools or elsewhere, . . . were direct body attacks," while his interlocutor, Shibayama Zenkei, compared their protagonists to "two swordsmen fighting with real swords" (*Eastern Buddhist* 8 [1975]: 70).

57. Favret-Saada, *Les Mots, la mort, les sorts*, p. 261.

58. Mikhail M. Bakhtin, *The Dialogic Imagination*, trans. Caryl Emerson and Michael Holquist (Austin, 1981), p. 52.

59. Francis Rabelais, *The Histories of Gargantua and Pantagruel*, trans. J. M. Cohen (City, 1955), p. 234.

60. Rabelais, *Histories of Gargantua and Pantagruel*, pp. 235-36, 237, 238.

61. Thomas Merton, *Zen and the Birds of Appetite* (New York, 1968), p. 50.

8

Mystical Language and the Teaching Context in the Early Lexicons of Sufism

CARL W. ERNST

How does mystical language differ from other types of language? If one wishes to answer this question without relying on a priori definitions of mysticism, it would seem desirable to inquire how mystics have described their attitude toward language in general, and how they distinguish the characteristics of the special terminology and modes of discourse used in mystical writing. The literature of Islamic mysticism features a subgenre that is particularly appropriate for such an inquiry: lexicons of the technical terminology of the Sufis. The Sufi lexicons have the appearance of the standard academic dictionaries that proliferated in all the fields of Arab-Islamic scholarship, yet the Sufis distinguished themselves from other lexicographers by consistently referring their technical terms to a manifold range of mystical experiences. Most of the early Sufi lexicons, written between the tenth and thirteenth centuries C.E., are designed for novices in the Sufi path, and amount to maps of the internal topography of Sufism. The mystical language of the Sufi lexicons expresses a wide range of experiences, not propositions, and it presupposes the authority of the master–disciple relationship as the basis for the intended experiences of transcendence.

It is the special context of this teaching relationship that gives these Sufi lexicons importance for the concept of mystical language.

The construction of dictionaries was an activity that scholars of the Arab-Islamic world pursued diligently, to a degree rivaled perhaps only by the Chinese before modern times.[1] As an independent discipline, lexicography emerged slowly from the study of the Qur'ān, as an attempt to deepen the understanding of the sacred book.[2] Arabic philological scholarship proceeded along the lines of the science of *ḥadīth*, which studies the sayings and deeds of the Prophet Muhammad; transmitters of definitions, like *ḥadīth*-transmitters, had to pass scrutiny of their ethical and religious character to gain full acceptance. Dictionaries were arranged in a number of ways, sometimes by subject or by a variety of alphabetical orders.[3] A general dictionary such as the famous *Mafātīḥ al-'Ulūm* (*Keys of the Sciences*) of al-Khwārazmī (ca. 977) attempted to cover the terminology of both the traditional Islamic sciences and the intellectual sciences inherited from the Hellenistic world; this eclectic reference work was perfectly suited to the literary *adab*-culture of government secretaries in the late 'Abbasid period.[4] The vast multivolume Arabic dictionaries of Ibn Manẓūr (d. 1311) and al-Zabīdī (d. 1791) were models of literary scholarship, and used abundant specimens of pre-Islamic Arabic poetry as testimonies (*shawāhid*) to the usage of various words. While the study of the Arabic language thus enlarged its scope by absorbing secular literature, philology was never entirely separate from religious concerns; doctrinal considerations often precluded the conclusions that literary scholarship might have reached on its own, since the Qur'ān could never be considered on the level of ordinary writings.[5]

Sufi dictionaries first appeared as appendixes to the Arabic treatises on Sufism written in the tenth and eleventh centuries. Abū Naṣr al-Sarrāj (d. 988) included a chapter with definitions of 155 terms in his *Kitāb al-Luma' fī 't-taṣawwuf* (*Book of Glimmerings on Sufism*).[6] Substantially the same list of terms, with significant development of the definitions, appeared two centuries later in the Persian work of Rūzbihān Baqlī (d. 1209), the *Sharḥ-i Shaṭḥiyyāt* (*Commentary on Ecstatic Sayings*).[7] Briefer lexicons were included in the *Risālah* (*Epistle*) of Abū al-Qāsim al-Qushayrī (d. 1074) and the Persian *Kashf al-Maḥjūb* (*Revelation of the Veiled*) of 'Alī al-Hujwīrī (d. 1072).[8] Of special interest are two dictionaries by the great Sufi master Muḥyī al-Dīn Ibn 'Arabī (d. 1240), one a separate treatise written in 1218 and the other a section in his encyclopedic *al-Futūḥāt al-Makkiyyah* (*Spiritual Conquests of Mecca*).[9] These texts are some of the most significant early Sufi lexical works.[10] Later works, such as the compendious Sufi dictionary of 'Abd al-Razzāq al-Kāshānī (discussed below), adopted a different focus and arrangement to reach a wider audience, but in the process they departed from the original orientation toward Sufi novices. In more recent times, the publication of broadly aimed dictionaries with significant amounts of Sufi terminology has continued, particularly in Persian.[11]

European scholars have devoted relatively little attention to the Sufi lexicons, though two of the earliest works of nineteenth-century scholarship on Sufism highlighted this genre. Tholuck cited excerpts from Kāshānī's dictionary in 1828, and Aloys Sprenger published Kāshānī's complete text in 1845.[12] Ibn 'Arabī's separate lexicon, the *Iṣṭilāḥ al-Ṣūfiyyah*, was the first of his writings to be published in Europe, appearing in 1845 in an edition by Gustavus Flügel along with the general dictionary of Islamic subjects by Jurjānī (d. 1329).[13] These early efforts, however, did not inspire much further interest in the vocabulary and semantics of Sufism. Indeed, Sprenger called Sufi mysticism a "monomania" and a "disease" characteristic of civilizational decadence, though he conceded the importance of Sufism in poetry, "because the noblest feelings of man are morbidly exalted in this disease."[14] Reinhold Dozy, author of the *Supplément aux dictionnaires arabes*, spoke contemptuously of the recondite language of Sufism, observing, "I think that I would lose my mind if I submerged myself in the study of certain types of these words, in the alembical terminology of the Sufis, for example. This is a task that I voluntarily leave to others."[15] The principal work on Sufism that might have been expected to deal with the Sufi lexicons was the epochal study by Louis Massignon, *Essai sur les origines due lexique technique de la mystique musulmane*. Massignon, despite his wide-ranging comments in this work, intended it to be specifically a study of the vocabulary of al-Ḥallāj, the Sufi martyr who exerted a consuming fascination over Massignon's studies. The early lexicons of Sufism, he observed, could be profitably compared with the terms used by al-Hallāj, but Massignon also left this inquiry to others.[16] This essay is a brief survey of the early Sufi lexicons, with special reference to their explicit presentation of language as the expression of mystical experiences.

What was the purpose of a Sufi lexicon? As the authors of these texts explain, a lexicon is only necessary for a subject when a specialized technical vocabulary comes into existence, which only experts in that field properly understand. Unlike Khwārazmī's dictionary, however, the Sufi lexicons were not typically designed to assist outsiders to comprehend their vocabulary. On the contrary, the special terminology of Sufism was partially designed to conceal meanings from outsiders who were not qualified to understand them. The Sufi authors expound on this exclusive aspect of their terminology in the prefatory remarks to the lexicons. Qushayrī observes,

> Know, regarding the sciences, that every group among the scholars has words they employ on matters they share, by which they are distinguished from others, and they agree in this for the sake of their common goals: increasing understanding for those who discuss, or facilitating for the people of this art the comprehension of their meanings without restriction. This group [i.e., the Sufis] employs words on matters they share, through which they intend to reveal their meanings to themselves, and to summarize and conceal from those who oppose them in their path [*tariqah*], so that the meanings of their words may be obscure to outsiders, out of jealousy toward them for their secrets. Thus they form a party against those who are unworthy. . . . By the commentary on these words we wish to facilitate the understanding of those among the wayfarers of these paths and the followers of their example [*sunnah*] who wish to comprehend their meanings.[17]

So the vocabulary of Sufism is designed both to facilitate understanding among Sufis and to frustrate it for outsiders. It should not be surprising that some Muslim scholars, such as the Ḥanbalī jurist Ibn al-Jawzī, therefore severely criticized Qushayrī's Sufi terminology as a reprehensible innovation.[18] Hujwīrī is equally firm in maintaining the two functions of the mystical vocabulary, though he underlines the utility of the Sufi terminology as being more for novices than adepts:

> Know (may God make you happy) that the people of every art and the masters of every activity have expressions with each other in the issuing of their secrets, and words the meaning of which none knows but themselves. The purpose of setting up expressions is twofold: one is better instruction and simplification of intricacies to approximate the understanding of the aspirant, and the other is concealing the secret from those who are not worthy of that knowledge. The proofs of that are clear, for the philologists are distinguished by their own set expressions, such as "past tense," "future," "correct," [etc.; examples are given from jurists, ḥadīth scholars, and theologians] . . . Now this group also has set words to conceal and display their speech, so that they may act accordingly in their path; they show what they wish and hide what they wish.[19]

The terms of Sufism, then, are explicitly intended both to conceal and to display, to show and to hide. It might be supposed that secretive "jealousy" of the Sufis (in Qushayrī's phrase) is not altogether different from the professional egotism that leads to jargon in every field. The Sufis have a different reasoning, however; their theory of meaning insists that the mystical language is esoteric in its essence, as we shall see.

It may not be easy to draw the line between novices who can benefit from having technical terms defined and outsiders who should be prevented from learning the Sufi vocabulary. The difference between Ibn 'Arabī's two lexicons illustrates this difficulty; the lexicon in the *Futūḥāt* occurs in the middle of an esoteric discussion of different types of divine knowledge, and it is aimed at the reader who has a deep acquaintance with Sufi teachings. This lexicon has the unusual feature, moreover, of chaining all the terms together so that the conclusion of each definition includes the next term, in this way introducing the next term's definition. This linkage of terms is certainly no accident; it suggests that they share an essential relationship beyond their purely lexical connotations.[20] The ingenious structuring of Ibn 'Arabī's lexicon is based on the simultaneously experiential and transcendental nature of the Sufi vocabulary, as discussed below. It is, in addition, expressed in a teaching formula ("If you say . . . then we say") characteristic of the Islamic religious sciences. Ibn 'Arabī's lexicon by these formal characteristics perfectly illustrates the intentionality of mystical language in the teaching relationship. Ibn 'Arabī noticed the difficulty of the Sufi vocabulary for "conventional scholars" when he replied to the request of the unnamed friend who inspired the separate lexicon:

> You asked us to explain the words that the Sufi mystics, God's people, circulate among themselves, when you saw many of the conventional scholars ask us about the meaning of our writings, and the writings of the people of our path, despite their lack of knowledge about the words which we have agreed upon, by which we understand one another. Just so is the custom of the people of every art among the sciences. So I answered you on that . . .[21]

It appears that Ibn 'Arabī's response to his friend's request is not really destined for a conventional audience, but for the friend, whom Ibn 'Arabī calls a trusted intimate. Nonetheless, the separate lexicon is somewhat simpler than the excerpt in the *Futūḥāt*, though both contain substantially the same terms (in precisely the reverse order), and it seems to be aimed more at the Sufi novice.[22] The situation is different with Kāshānī, who in introducing his lengthy dictionary (516 terms in 167 pages) states that he wrote it for "the scholars of the traditional and intellectual sciences [who] did not recognize" the technical terms of Sufism.[23] As James Morris has pointed out, Kāshānī wrote on Sufism principally for mystically inclined intellectuals and scholars trained in the Avicennian philosophical tradition.[24] By adopting a philosophical approach, Kāshānī made his dictionary an intellectual commentary on Sufi vocabulary for non-Sufis.

What are the sources of the terms in the Sufi lexicons? The studies of Massignon and, more recently, Paul Nwyia have shown the fundamental importance of the Qur'ān in the formulation of the Sufi vocabulary.[25] This point should not be overstressed, however. Massignon's establishment of the Qur'ānic and Islamic sources of Sufi language served the purpose of refuting the early Orientalist theories that sought extra-Islamic origins (Christian, Greek, or Indian) for Sufism. The Sufis' reliance on the Qur'ān is unquestionably the beginning point for understanding the language of Sufism, but the controversies over novel and un-Qur'ānic terms in Sufism are sufficient indication that the Sufis went outside Qur'anic language to formulate their insights.[26] Massignon himself pointed out three other sources of Sufi terminology: Arabic grammar and the Islamic religious sciences, the early schools of Islamic theology, and the vocabulary of the Hellenistic sciences.[27] Many of the terms that occur in the early Sufi lexicons are not to be found in the Qur'ān at all; since our concern here is not linguistic but hermeneutic, for the moment it will suffice to make this general observation. Academic inquiries about literary sources (*Quellenforschungen*) are in any case inclined to fasten on minutiae to the neglect of authors' intentions. The Sufi authors are unanimous in agreeing that the real source of their terminology is mystical experience, a point that is examined more fully below. As far as the definitions themselves are concerned, poetic testimonies and quotations from authoritative Sufis appear frequently, particularly in the works of Sarrāj and Qushayrī. Occasionally, verses from the Qur'ān are cited as illustrations.[28] There is sometimes a wide variation in the definitions themselves, from one author to another; each one seems to have felt a considerable freedom to add to or subtract from the received definitions, in accordance with personal experience or the authoritative pronouncement of a teacher.

The loose arrangement of terms in the Sufi lexicons suggests, moreover, that small groupings of related but discrete mystical experiences form the basic units of terms that are defined. Most of the definitions are psychological, in terms of the soul's experience of different aspects of God; this is true even of poetic phrases and metaphysical terms usually given objectified and philosophical meanings in non-Sufi contexts.[29] Overall, there is no discernable order to the terms in these dictionaries, alphabetical or otherwise (here, again, Kāshānī breaks the pattern of the early dictionaries by adopting a standard alphabetical arrangement). The lexicons instead group words into sets of two, three, or four, based on similarity of derivation (from a single root), semantic clusters, rhyme, grammatical form, semantic polarity, or parallel phraseology.[30] Comparison of the sequence of terms in the different lexicons shows a number of sections of terms that are repeated in roughly the same order, but with some variation. It is possible that a core list of Sufi mystical terms was widely used in oral teaching, and later became the basis for the similarity of sequence in the different texts; the similarities are not so great, though, as to suggest literary dependence in every case.

All the Sufi authors agree that their special terms designate mystical experiences, variously designated by such names as "realities" (*ḥaqā'iq*), "meanings" (*ma'ānī*), "states" (*aḥwāl*), "stations" (*maqāmāt*), and "unveiling" (*kashf*). Qushayrī, in his discussion of the esoteric nature of Sufi terminology, points out that mystical states are the result not of effort but divine grace: "Their [the Sufis'] realities are not collected by any sort of effort nor are gained by any kind of action; rather, they are meanings that God has promised to the hearts of a people, and by the realities of which he selects the consciences of a people."[31] Sufi esotericism, jealously guarding the secrets, is therefore designed to prevent wild misunderstandings on the part of people who have no access to the underlying experiences of encounter with God. Rūzbihān becomes rhapsodic in describing the mystical sources of Sufi language:

> Because there are certain words that are vessels for secrets and charged with lights, a subtle commentary will be spoken on that, God willing, so that the listener may recognize the understanding of the folk's expressions [*'ibārat*], and know their indication [*ishārah*]. Those words hold the cyphers [*rumūz*] of the treasures of subtleties of [divine] commands, the stopping-places of the secrets of [mystical] states, the annunciations of [divine] commands, the desires of gnosis, and the radiance of the lights of unveilings, which are disclosed to the beginners in love in the journeying of spirits and consciences, from the revelation of the manifestation of eternity, the eternal speech, the unique [divine] actions, and the realities of the manifestation of the [divine] attributes. Since with one taste of the drink of the spirits' fonts,[32] in the unique and marvellous subtleties of the hidden world, they become masters of their momentary state [*waqt*], they make an indication of that sweetness with these words.[33]

The rushing torrent of words does not immediately reveal a pattern of interpretation, but on closer examination the sources expressed by mystical terms can be discerned again; the "expressions," "indication," and "cyphers" derive from the divine commands, mystical states, gnosis, and unveilings. Rūzbihān also gives a theological content to these experiences, consisting of eternity, the speech of God, and the divine actions and attributes (all terms familiar to Islamic dialectical theology). He insists, further, that mystical terminology has a firm relationship with states that are fully known to the adepts: "Every cypher is connected to a station, every indication is the description of a state, and every expression is the discovery of an unveiling. None knows save the master of stations and the adept of indications. I shall repeat these points and names from the marvel of their states, so that you may know how sweet and subtle is the elegance of their motions."[34] In most of the entries of his dictionary, Rūzbihān therefore begins with the definition of Sarrāj or another clear description, and then follows with a characterization of the experiential basis of the term, which he introduces with the phrase "Its reality is . . ." Kāshānī also agrees with the experiential grounding of Sufi terminology, though he puts it in a typically intellectualist and systematic way: "I have indicated that the principles mentioned in the book are from the stations of the folk, which ramify into a thousand stations. I have pointed out the quality of their ramification and that which distinguishes the quality of their ramifications according to their type."[35] Whether poetic like Rūzbihān or systematic like Kāshānī, the Sufis maintain that the essence of mystical terminology is the experience.

The experiential nature of the Sufi vocabulary is particularly evident in the terms from grammatical categories. Even the terms for "word" and "name" have reference to mystical experience. To give some parallel examples: Sarrāj begins his definition of "name" (*ism*) prosaically, as "words put to give information about the named by a naming, to affirm the named; if the words fail, its meaning is not separated from the named."[36] In his view of language, meaning transcends the name. Rūzbihān partially translates and expands on this definition in a more overtly mystical way: "certain words by which they give information about the named. The name in reality is the attribute of the named. Know that the names [of God] manifest in the hearts of the faithful so that their certainty may increase."[37] In this definition, it becomes clear that in speaking of "name" and "the named," Sufis tend naturally to think of the names of God (the ninety-nine names derived from the Qur'ān) and how they experience God through those names, which are theologically the divine attributes. Since the names of God form a staple of Sufi meditation, it is scarcely surprising that the divine names are assumed to be the main referents for the term "name." For Ibn 'Arabī, names other than the names of God are not even included in the definition; he defines "name" as "that one of the divine names that governs the state of the devotee during his momentary state."[38] Likewise, Ibn 'Arabī defines "word" (*harf*) as "that expression by which God addresses you."[39] In the Sufi lexicon, all words and names function in the relationship of intimacy between the human soul and God.

The semantic categories of mystical language have an obviously experiential dimension, but their meaning is so transcendent that it is sometimes very difficult to pin down. Rūzbihān likes to use the word "cypher" (*ramz*), a term that occurs once in the Qur'ān (3.41) to describe the signs by which the silent Zachariah communicated to his people. As Rūzbihān defines it, "cypher is the inner meaning [*ma'nā*] hidden beneath the external speech, which no one can grasp except those who are worthy of it. The cypher of the hidden realities pronounced by the tongue in the subtleties of knowledge is the secret in inverted letters."[40] The inner secret is so far beyond the outer speech that the letters of the word are described as "inverted" in comparison. An Arabic verse quoted by Sarrāj may have assumed silent Zachariah as the model of esoteric symbolism: "When they speak, may the goal of their cyphers incapacitate you, and when they are silent, how far you are from joining Him!"[41] Another favorite semantic category is "indication" (*ishārah*), which almost means "gesture" and implies a communication of so subtle a nature that it can scarcely be verbalized. As Sarrāj describes it, "The indication is that which is hidden from the speaker's revelation of it by verbal expression, because of the subtlety of its meaning. Abū 'Alī al-Rūdhbārī said, 'This knowledge of ours is an indication which, when it becomes an expression, is hidden.'"[42] Verbalization conceals reality; esotericism is inevitable. For Rūzbihān, "indication" is primarily the inner communication with God, and only derivatively is it the mystic's account of the experience to others:

> The reality of indication is the shining of the light of hidden subtle speech with God in the clothing of consciousness during the onslaught of finding God [*wujūd*] in the heart. The gnostic alludes to that from the mine of union with the tongue of reality for the people of the presence, so that he may thereby make an indication of that which is unveiled to him in the expansiveness of "the spirit of the spirit," which is present, witnessing, and speaking from God to God.[43]

The essence of mystical language is, again, the mystical experience, which the word attempts to convey; this is above all true of the controversial "ecstatic expressions" (*shaṭḥiyyāt*) of Sufism, which burst all conventional bounds in their intensity.[44]

What are the implications of the Sufi lexicons for the general concept of mystical language? The "contextual" studies of mysticism in the 1978 and 1983 volumes edited by Steven Katz have stressed how mystical experiences are preconditioned by traditional concepts and metaphysical structures. Katz observes that "there is a clear causal connection between the religious and social structure one brings to experience and the nature of one's actual experience."[45] Without denying the importance of religious and social background as a background for mystical experience, I would not wish to reduce this complex phenomenon to pure immanence through psychologism; to state that mystical experience is a mediated, configured outcome of epistemological activity, as does Katz, might be interpreted as a one-sided relationship between language and experience, in which the built-in expectations of language have a "self-fulling prophetic aspect" for the experiential outcome.[46] Let us see how a broad contextual understanding of mystical language might apply to Sufism, and whether there are adequate reasons for resisting sociological and psychologistic reductionism. Sufis certainly use the theological and legal language of the Islamic tradition. Their special mystical teachings, too, constitute a tradition of consolidated wisdom and experience. Mystical teaching presupposes that there are certain goals that the teacher communicates to the student, toward which the student is guided; the student's attempts at understanding are corrected, shaped, and stimulated in the proper direction. Sufis were thus aware of the intentional function of language, above all as used in teaching, and this intentional function of mystical language is the basis of the Sufi lexicons. The terms used to indicate the master–disciple relationship put intentionality at the heart of this personal connection: the disciple is the *murid*, or seeker (aspirant), and the master is the *murād*, or object of search (that which is desired). Words are useful in the teaching to help shape the categories by which the student will approach experience, but since the Sufi terminology opens up unsuspected new possibilities of experience, the effect of absorbing them is broadening rather than narrowing. Yet the study of Sufi materials is not intended to be a solitary activity. The teaching is an interpersonal process, not an abstract doctrine. If it is correct to assume that the Sufi lexicons are an outgrowth of oral teaching, that suggests even more strongly the importance of the personal teaching factor. In Sufism, as in the *ḥadīth*-based religious sciences generally, the focus on the personal source of the teaching is an essential part of the disciple's ability to remember the teacher's words, to preserve them for himself and others.[47] The intentional language as used in the teaching relationship has two implications: first, it is language addressed to a specific audience for the sake of creating the conditions for the desired experience and understanding, not an independent body of philosophical propositions; and second, this language is a process implying the polar relationship of transcendence, in which the master and disciple occupy roles analogous to those of divinity and humanity.[48] Each of those implications needs to be addressed separately.

The intentionality of mystical language in Sufism as a teaching points at certain experiential sources, but this is an enterprise that is distinct from instruction in abstract philosophical positions. Sufism needs to be understood in this kind of "contextual" fashion, for the master–disciple relationship decisively shapes the interpretive tradition. The views of W. T. Stace on mysticism, which have been so trenchantly criticized in the previous volumes of this series, would not in fact advance our understanding of Sufism appreciably.[49] The abstract monism of Stace, it has been rightly observed, destroys the meaning of the traditional religious language of mysticism, regarding it as mere camouflage retained to satisfy the orthodox and provide conventional means of communication. Such an approach would have been familiar to the Sufis, being reminiscent of the views of the Arab–Islamic philosophers like Ibn Sīnā (Avicenna, d. 1037), who regarded religion as an imitation of philosophy through the imagination. Although there was some overlap in the aims, epistemologies, and terminology of philosophy and Sufism, the intellectualism of the Aristotelian philosophers was fundamentally in contrast with the Sufis' insistence on attaining a state beyond reason.[50] Thus when the Andalusian philosopher Ibn Rushd (Averroes, d. 1198) asked Ibn 'Arabī if the truths known to the philosophers and the Sufis were the same, the answer was "yes . . . and no."[51] The vital element of personal verification by experience (*taḥaqquq*) has for some philosophers given way to abstraction. Even so, let us remember that consistency for its own sake was not a goal of philosophy either, to the degree that it also was a teaching tradition. The Jewish philosopher Maimonides spoke for the Arab-Islamic intellectual tradition as well when he pointed to the need to adapt knowledge to the capacities of particular audiences as one of the principal causes of authorial inconsistency.[52] This principle of esotericism in philosophical teaching is entirely parallel to that of Hujwīrī for Sufi teaching, which is "better instruction and simplification of intricacies to approximately the understanding of the aspirant."[53] Abstract propositions, whether those of Stace about "mysticism" or those of rationalist philosophers in general, are not the subject of Sufi teaching. The priority of teaching over reason received a comparable stress in Shi'ism. The Isma'ili theorist Ḥasan-i Sabbāḥ underlined the essential importance of the imam's teaching authority by pointing out that reason alone cannot be a guide; if one refutes another's position by reason, one is acting as a teacher.[54] Even the doctrines of Islamic theology are not the subject of Sufi teaching, though it is impossible to separate the language of Sufism from its theological environment. Therefore, to reduce Sufi teaching to the terms of its theology or "ontological structure" can be another form of de-contextualizing.[55]

The intentionality of mystical language in Sufism assumes the master-disciple relationship, as mentioned earlier, and within this language each term implies transcendence as both structure and experience. The role of the guide (whether master, Prophet, or God) is to act as a check on individual self-will and to open up the soul to what the Sufis call the "realities," "stations," and "names." The technical terminology of Sufism, properly understood, has the same function. An example is Rūzbihān's definition of a "visitation" (*wārid*): "The source of 'visitation' is the unveiling of the gnostic's object [*murād*], which enters spontaneously [*bi-qaṣd*], increasing his longing."[56] The intentionality of the "visitation" as the unveiling of the "object" coincides with the intentionality of focusing on the master; as we have seen, both the unveiling and the master are the "object" (*murād*). As Sarrāj defines the term, "the *murād* is the gnostic in whom there remains no seeking [*irāda*], who has attained the goals, and who has expressed the states, stations, aims, and seekings, for he is the sought object [*murād*] by which is sought that which is sought."[57] The one who has attained the goals, and who can express them, is not to be distinguished from them. The expression of the goals in the form of teaching indicates the transcendent experience to the student through a term or concept, just as the teaching personally mediates the attained experience. And just as transcendence is built into the teaching relationship, the Sufi sources agree that the language of Sufism has been articulated to express experiences that are transcendental. Although known and intended as object, the experience comes unasked, without reference to the aspirant's volition and beyond one's conscious control. It is for this reason that the Sufi authors define even semantic categories like "word" and "name" in terms of an experience of divine–human interaction. At the risk of repetition, let me stress that the Sufi vocabulary does not objectify the transcendent as a separate "object," but constitutes it as transcendent in consciousness. The transcendent is indicated by the various experiential modes that the Sufi tradition has defined.

If the experiential and transcendental orientation just outlined fairly corresponds to the self-understanding of the Sufis, can we generalize from this case to speak about mystical language more generally? If we call the Sufi tradition mystical, then mysticism is not a particular doctrine or even a particular experience, and the term should not be used in an objectified way; it can, however, be useful as a term to describe the tendency to return to the experiential sources of philosophical and theological symbols. The very origin of the concept of experience in Western thought attests to a tension with rationalism, whether religious, philosophical, or scientific; it is experience that enlarges the field of thought.[58] In religion, it was primarily the Protestant reformers who invoked religious experience against the authority and doctrine of the Catholic church, and this nondoctrinal usage continued down to William James's use of the term in his classic study.[59] In the scientific field, along with Baconianism, alchemy was another source of our concept of experience in its struggle against Aristotelian orthodoxy; alchemy, of course, had religious implications as well. Here I would like to invoke an image from a seventeenth-century alchemical text, which allegorically depicts Experience as the Queen of Heaven, before whom Philosophy bows down and worships. The poem concludes,

There with arose Phylosophy as one filled with grace,
Whose looks did shew that she had byne in some Heavenly place;
For oft she wipt her Eyes,
And oft she bowd her knees.
And oft she kist the Steps with dread,
Whereon Experience did tread;
And oft she cast her Head on high
And oft full low she cast her Eye
Experience for to espy.[60]

So, with apologies to Philo, I would like to suggest that we think of philosophy (and by extension language) as the handmaiden of experience. This is not to suggest that language and prior conceptual formation have no role in mystical experience; their role is very real and significant, but it remains secondary to the experience itself.

It cannot be denied that mystical language is inextricably connected to religious and social contexts. Yet to assert that these religious and social contexts have a dominant causal relationship to mystical experience and its interpretation is, in my view, unjustified, and it contradicts the very structure of mystical language as discussed above. If mysticism always has a religious and social aspect, then perhaps religion and society always have a mystical aspect. Here Ibn 'Arabī might fundamentally agree with Nagarjuna, that there is no *nirvāna* without *samsara*; transcendence and immanence are relational poles, not hypostatic entities.[61] Eric Voegelin, in his illuminating studies of the experiential sources of Western civilization, has convincingly argued that the interpretive symbol, the experience of reality, and consciousness itself are inseparable aspects of a participatory whole: "A vision is not a dogma but an event in metaleptic reality. . . . There is no 'object' of the vision other than the vision as received; and there is no 'subject' of the vision other than the response in a man's soul to divine presence."[62] Voegelin has also given an incisive analysis of the deformations that occur when philosophical propositions and theological doctrines are separated from the experiences to which they were originally tied.[63] The vocabulary of Sufism is one kind of source that can help us avoid this error; if we are right in generalizing about this mystical tendency, then mystical vocabularies in other religious traditions will have a similar experiential thrust.

The mystical language of Sufism as found in the Sufi lexicons is an expression of experiences of transcendence formulated according to the inner structure of the master-disciple relationship. In this sense, there is no point in arguing that mystical experience is unmediated or "pure" experience. To the contrary, the teaching tradition is a powerful mediation that enables the individual to have symbolic access to experiences that might otherwise never be imagined. Yet the fundamentally transcendental orientation of the symbols and terms of mystical teaching is liberating rather than limiting. The model suggested by the Sufi lexicons condenses mystical experiences in terms designed to reveal the experiential possibilities to those who are prepared for them. At the same time, these terms tend to shut out those who are not participants in the teaching process. Outsiders will naturally tend to analyze mystical terms by their externals, but mystical language retains the ability to indicate the transcendent by its own reverberation in the soul.

Notes

1. John A. Haywood, *Arabic Lexicography: Its History, and Its Place in the General History of Lexicography*, 2nd ed. (Leiden, 1965), p. 1; Fuat Sezgin, *Geschichte des arabischen Schrifftums*, vol. 8: *Lexikographie* (Leiden, 1982), p. 15, citing A. Fischer.

2. Frithiof Rundgren, "La Lexicographie arabe," in Pelio Fronzaroli, ed., *Studies on Semitic Lexicography*, Quaderni de Semitistica, no. 2 (Florence, 1973), pp. 145-59.

3. For details of dictionary arrangements, see Haywood, *Arabic Lexicography*, and Sezgin, *Geschichte des arabischen Schrifftums*, pp. 7-16.

4. Abu Abdallah Mohammed ibn Ahmed ibn Jusof al-Katib al-Khowarezmi, *Liber Mafatih al-Olum*, ed. G. Van Vloten (Leiden, 1895; reprint, Leiden, 1968), pp. 3-4. For a list of translations of the different sections of this dictionary, see A. I. Sabra, "al-Khwārazmī, Abū 'Abd Allāh," *Encyclopedia of Islam*, new ed.

5. Lother Kopf, "Religious Influences on Medieval Arabic Philology," in Kopf, *Studies in Arabic and Hebrew Lexicography*, ed. M. H. Goshen-Gottstein, with the assistance of S. Assif (Jerusalem, 1976), pp. 19-45.

6. Abú Naṣr 'Abdallah B. 'Alí al-Sarrāj al-Ṭúsí, *Kitāb al-Lumaʿ fi 't-taṣawwuf*, ed. Reynold Alleyne Nicholson, E. J. W. Gibb Memorial series, vol. 22 (London, 1914; reprint, London, 1963), pp. 333-75, listed on pp. 86-99 of the English summary; I count separately terms that Nicholson left grouped together to arrive at his total of 143 terms.

7. Ruzbehan Baqli Shirazi, *Commentaire sur les paradoxes des Soufis (Sharh-e Shathîyât)*, ed. Henry Corbin, Bibliothéque Iranienne, no. 12 (Tehran, 1966), pp. 545–80, 613–32, giving 159 terms, plus a brief glossary of 47 additional terms on pp. 632–35. The *Sharh-i Shathiyyāt* was Rūzbihān's own Persian translation of his earlier Arabic work *Mantiq al-Asrār*; in the dictionary section, the Persian text drops most of the specimens of Arabic Sufi poetry (originally given by Sarrāj' and adds elaborations from Rūzbihān's own experience.

8. Abū al-Qāsim 'Abd al-Karīm al-Qushayrī, *al-Risālah al-Qushayriyyah*, ed. 'Abd al-Halīm Mahmūd and Mahmūd ibn al-Sharīf, 2 vols. (Cairo, 1972–74), pp. 200–74, with forty-nine terms in the dictionary proper, followed by fifty-one chapters on various states; Abū al-Hasan 'Alī ibn 'Uthmān al-Jullābī al-Hujwīrī al-Ghaznawī al-Lāhawrī, *Kashf al-Mahjūb*, ed. 'Alī Qawīm (Islamabad, 1398/1978), pp. 320–37, with ninety-two terms in four sections; cf. the English translation by Reynold A. Nicholson, *The Kashf al-Mahjúb, The Oldest Persian Treatise on Sufiism*, E. J. W. Gibb Memorial series, vol. 17 (London, 1936; reprint, London, 1976), pp. 367–92.

9. Muhyī al-Dīn Abī 'Abd Allāh Muhammad ibn 'Alī ibn-'Arabī, *Kitāb Istilāh al-Sūfiyyah*, in *Rasā'il* (Hyderabad, 1367/1948), with 198 terms; Ibn 'Arabī, *al-Futūhāt al-Makkiyyah* (Beirut, n.d.), vol. 2, pp. 127–34. I am indebted to Professor William Chittick for calling the latter text to my attention.

10. Other early Sufi writings, such as Ansārī's *Manāzil al-Sā'irin* and Abū Tālib al-Makkī's *Qūt al-Qulūb*, are relevant to the development of mystical language in Sufism, but cannot be considered here for reasons of space.

11. Much material from Kāshānī's lexicon appears in that of Jurjānī, and Kāshānī's work received a commentary by Shams al-Dīn Ghaffārī (d. 1430) as well as an abridgement by the Shi'i scholar Haydar Āmulī (d. 1385). See Hājjī Khalīfah, *Kashf al-Zunūn*, ed. Gustavus Flügel, *Lexicon Bibliographicum et Encyclopædicum a Mustafa ben Abdallah Katib Jelebi Dicto et Nomine Haji Khalfa Celebrato Compositum* (London, 1845). The lengthy Arabic dictionary of the Indian scholar Muhammad al-T'hānawī (ca. 1745), *Kashshāf Istilāhāt al-Funūn*, Bibliotheca Indica, no. 17 (Calcutta, 1853–62; reprint, Beirut, 1966), added to the main entries a number of mystical definitions in Persian. Su'ād al-Hakīm's *al-Mu'jam al-Sūfi: at-Hikmah fi Hudūd al-Kalimah* (Beirut, 1981) is a comprehensive guide to Ibn 'Arabī's terminology. Ja'far Sajjādī's Persian dictionary of technical terms, *Farhang-i Mustalahāt-i 'Urafā wa Mutasawwifah* (Tehran, 1339/1960), includes many excerpts from Sufi sources. Dr. Javad Nurbakhsh, the Ni'matullahi Sufi leader, is currently publishing a multivolume *Farhang-i Nurbakhsh* on Sufi terminology in Persian. The Pakistani

Chishti leader Dhawqi Shah also compiled an excellent Urdu lexicon of Sufism, *Sirr-i Dilbarān* (Karachi, 1405/1985), with many quotations from Arabic and Persian authorities.

12. Tholuck, *Die Speculative Trinitätslehre des Späteren Orients* (1828), pp. 7, 11, 18, 26, 73, cited in D. B. MacDonald, "'Abd al-Razzāk al-Kāshānī," *Encyclopedia of Islam*, vol. 1, pp. 88–89; 'Abd al-Razzāq Kāshānī, *'Abdu-r-Razzāq's Dictionary of the Technical Terms of the Sufies*, ed. Aloys Sprenger (Calcutta, 1845).

13. 'Ali Ben Mohammed Dschordschani, *Definitiones*, ed. Gustavus Flügel (Leipzig, 1845). Two translations of Ibn 'Arabī's lexicon exist: A. Regnier, "La Terminologie mystique des Ibn 'Arabī," *La Museon* 48 (1935): 145–62; Rabia Terri Harris, "Sufi Terminology: Ibn 'Arabī's *Al-Iṣṭilāḥāt al-Ṣūfiyyah*," *Journal of the Muhyiddin Ibn 'Arabi Society* 3 (1984): 27–54.

14. Kāshānī, *'Abdu-r-Razzāq's Dictionary*, pp. v–vi.

15. Quoted in Louis Massignon, *Essai sur les origines du lexique technique de la mystique musulmane*, 2nd ed. (Paris, 1968), p. 12.

16. Massignon, *Essai sur les origines du lexique technique*, pp. 19–20; the index of Hallajian terms is on pp. 19–36.

17. Qushayrī, *al-Risālah al-Qushayriyyah*, p. 200.

18. Abū al-Faraj 'Abd al-Raḥmān ibn 'Alī ibn al-Jawzī, *Talbis Iblīs*, ed. Khayr al-Dīn 'Alī (Beirut, n.d. [1970]), p. 185.

19. Hujwīrī, *Kashf al-Maḥjūb*, p. 320.

20. Each definition concludes with a term (X), followed by the phrase "And if you say, 'What is X?' then we say, 'X is . . .'" Ibn 'Arabī traces this "strange method" (*ṭariqah gharibah*) of chaining to the early Sufi Ibrāhīm ibn Adham (ca. 765) (*Futūḥāt*, vol. 2, p. 134).

21. Ibn 'Arabī, *Iṣṭilāḥ*, p. 1.

22. The lexicon in the *Rasā'il* contains mostly briefer versions of the definitions in the *Futūḥāt* lexicon, and it lacks the additional parts of the definitions that chain the terms one to another in the *Futūḥāt*. Thus in the *Rasā'il*, Ibn 'Arabī avoids, on the surface, the complex problem of the interrelationship of the technical terms of Sufism.

23. Kāshānī, *'Abdu-r-Razzāq's Dictionary*, p. 3; he states particularly that he wrote his lexicon to assist the comprehension of his commentaries on Anṣārī's *Manāzil al-Sā'irin*, Ibn 'Arabī's *Fuṣūṣ al-Ḥikam*, and the Qur'ān.

24. James Winston Morris, "Ibn 'Arabī and His Interpreters, Part II (Conclusion): Influences and Interpretations," *Journal of the American Oriental Society* 107 (1987): 101–06. Many of the later Sufi dictionaries share more or less in Kāshānī's systematic tendencies.

25. Massignon cites twenty-four terms taken directly from the Qur'ān and an equal number derived from the roots occurring in the Qur'ān (*Essai*

sur les origines du lexique technique, pp. 45-47). Paul Nwyia, in *Exégèse coranique et langage mystique, nouvel essai sur le lexique technique des mystiques musulmans* (Beirut, 1970), has analyzed a series of early Sufi texts that illustrate the development of mystical exegesis of the Qur'ān in Sufism.

26. On the problem of non-Qur'ānic language in the heresy trials of Sufis, see in addition to the critical remarks of Ibn al-Jawzī, Carl W. Ernst, *Words of Ecstasy in Sufism* (Albany, N.Y., 1985), pp. 97-98, 112.

27. Massignon, *Essai sur les origines du lexique technique*, pp. 49-52.

28. I count fourteen Qur'ānic citations of terms in Sarrāj's dictionary (*ḥaqq, mushāhadah, shuhūd, qabḍ, basṭ, ru'yah, 'aqd, maḥw, ṭamas, bādī, baḥr, istinā', istifā'*, and *talbis*); and in the *Sharḥ-i Shaṭḥiyyāt* Rūzbihān cites only ten terms in Qur'ānic contexts (*maqām, qabḍ, basṭ, faṣl, hamm, athar, bādī, istinā', istifā'*, and *rūḥ*).

29. The difference between Sufi definitions and philosophical definitions may be quickly verified by comparing terms such as *ḥāl, ḥaqiqah, fanā', faṣl, ishtibāh,* and *rūḥ* in the Sufi lexicons and in Aristotelian usage. See Soheil M. Afnan, *A Philosophical Lexicon in Persian and Arabic* (Beirut, 1968), s.vv.

30. Examples of lexical order taken from Sarrāj: root (*ḥaqq, ḥuqūq, taḥqīq, taḥaqquq, ḥaqīqah*); semantic clusters (*ḥāl, maqām, makān*); rhyme (*kawn, bawn*); form (*lawā'iḥ, lawāmi'*); polarity (*qabḍ−basṭ, saḥw−sukr*); parallel phraseology (*anā bi-lā anā, naḥnu bi-lā naḥnu*).

31. Qushayrī, *al-Risālah al-Qushayriyyah*, p. 200.

32. The phrase "spirits' fonts" (*mashārib al-arwāḥ*) recalls the title of Rūzbihān's treatise "The Spirits' Font," or *Mashrab al-Arwāḥ, wa huwa Mashhūr bi-Hazār u Yak Maqām*, ed. Naẓif Muḥarram Khwājah (Istanbul, 1973), a work that describes the 1,001 stations (*maqāmāt*) of the spiritual path from the creation of the universe to its end. Although the term *mashrab* has become conventionalized to mean "sect," for Rūzbihān it still holds something of the root meaning of "source of water" (or font); as his book on 1,001 stations shows, the sources he has in mind are spiritual experiences.

33. Rūzbihān, *Sharḥ-i Shaṭḥiyyāt*, pp. 544-45.

34. Rūzbihān, *Sharḥ-i Shaṭḥiyyāt*, p. 545.

35. Kāshānī, *'Abdu-r-Razzāq's Dictionary*, p. 3.

36. Sarrāj, *Kitāb al-Luma' fi 't-taṣawwuf*, p. 350.

37. Rūzbihān, *Sharḥ-i Shaṭḥiyyāt*, p. 570.

38. Ibn 'Arabī, *Rasā'il*, p. 12. The topic of the different types of gnosis of the divine names introduces Ibn 'Arabī's lexicon in the *Futūḥāt*.

39. Ibn 'Arabī, *Futūḥāt*, vol. 2, p. 130.

40. Rūzbihān, *Sharḥ-i Shaṭḥiyyāt*, p. 561.

41. Sarrāj, *Kitāb al-Luma' fi 't-taṣawwuf*, p. 338, quoting Qannād.

42. Sarrāj, *Kitāb al-Luma' fī 't-taṣawwuf*, p. 337.
43. Rūzbihān, *Sharḥ-i Shaṭhiyyāt*, p. 560.
44. On *shaṭhiyyāt*, see Ernst, *Words of Ecstasy*, esp. chap. 1.
45. Steven T. Katz, "Language, Epistemology, and Mysticism," in Steven T. Katz, ed., *Mysticism and Philosophical Analysis* (New York, 1978), p. 40.
46. Katz, "Language, Epistemology, and Mysticism," p. 59. [Katz is also aware of this trap and seeks to avoid it (see pp. 64–65)–Ed.]
47. See Carl W. Ernst, "The Textual Formation of Oral Teachings in the Early Chishtī Sufism," in Jeffrey Timm, ed., *Texts and Contexts: Traditional Hermeneutics in South Asia* (Albany, N.Y., 1991), pp. 271–97.
48. The Sufi master is not technically divinized, but there is a parallelism between the role of the master and that of God, reflected in the progression of mystical experience implicit in the formula, "annihilation in the master" (*fanā' fī al-shaykh*), "annihilation in the Prophet" (*fanā' fī al-rasūl*), "annihilation in God" (*fanā' fī allāh*).
49. For these criticisms, see Katz, *Mysticism and Philosophical Analysis*, index, s.n. "Stace, W. T."
50. This is the position of 'Ayn al-Quḍāt al-Hamadānī. See Ernst, *Words of Ecstasy*, p. 112.
51. Henry Corbin, *Creative Imagination in the Sufism of Ibn 'Arabī*, trans. Ralph Manheim, Bollingen Series, no. 91 (Princeton, N.J., 1969), pp. 41–42. The issue of the relationship between Islamic philosophy and Sufism is highly complex, and can only be touched on here; readers should refer to the studies of Corbin, S. H. Nasr, Fazlur Rahman, James Morris, and Parviz Morewedge (among others) for further details.
52. Moses Maimonides, Introduction of *Guide for the Perplexed*, trans. Schlomo Pines, in *A Maimonides Reader*, ed. Isadore Twersky (New York, 1972), pp. 244–45.
53. Hujwīrī, *Kashf al-Mahjūb*, p. 320. On esotericism as a principle of knowledge in the Islamic world, see Marshall G. S. Hodgson, *The Venture of Islam, Conscience and History in World Civilization*, vol. 2: *The Expansion of Islam in the Middle Periods* (Chicago, 1974), pp. 195–200, and Carl W. Ernst, "Esoteric and Mystical Aspects of Religious Knowledge in Sufism," *Journal of Religious Studies* 12 (1984): 93–100.
54. Ḥasan-i Sabbāḥ, "Four Chapters," cited in Marshall Hodgson, *The Order of Assassins* (New York, 1978), pp. 325–28.
55. For a discussion of the "ontological schemata which shape the configuration of the [mystical] quest and its goal," see Steven T. Katz, "The 'Conservative' Character of Mystical Experience," in Steven T. Katz, ed., *Mysticism and Religious Traditions* (New York, 1983), esp. pp. 32–43.

A critique of doctrinal reductionism is found in Sallie B. King, "Two Epistemological Models for the Interpretation of Mysticism," *Journal of the American Academy of Religion* 61 (1988): 257-79. [Katz has replied to King in "On Mysticism," *Journal of the American Academy of Religion* 56 (1989): 751-57-Ed.]

56. Rūzbihān, *Sharḥ-i Shaṭḥiyyāt*, p. 549. Likewise, the Sufi Najm al-Dīn Kubrā (d. 1220), when asked by the philosopher Fakhr al-Dīn Rāzī (d. 1209) how the Sufis know God, replied, "By certain visitations [*wāridāt*] that occur in the heart, and which the soul is incapable of falsifying" (Ibrāhīm Shaṭṭārī, *Ā'inah-i Ḥaqā'iq-numā, Sharḥ-i Jām-i Jahān-numā* [Hyderabad, 1313/1895-6], pp. 7-8).

57. Sarrāj, *Kitāb al-Luma' fī 't-taṣawwuf*, p. 342. Ibn 'Arabī defines the *murād* as "an expression for the one who is ravished of his seeking while his affairs remain in readiness; he has passed all the customs and the stations without effort" (*Rasā'il*, p. 2).

58. André Lalande, *Vocabulaire technique et critique de la philosophie*, 5th ed. (Paris, 1947), s.v. "experience," pp. 309-11.

59. H. Pinard, "La Théorie de l'expérience religieuse. Son évolution, de Luther à W. James," *Revue d'histoire ecclesiastique* 17 (1921): 63-83, 306-48, 547-74.

60. "Experience and Philosophy," quoted in Elias Ashmole, *Theatrum Chemicum Britannicum* (London, 1652; reprint, Hildesheim, 1968), p. 341.

61. Frederick J. Streng, "Language and Mystical Awareness," in Katz, *Mysticism and Philosophical Analysis*, pp. 141-69.

62. Eric Voegelin, *Order and History*, vol. 4: *The Ecumenic Age* (Baton Rouge, La., 1974), p. 243, discussing "The Pauline Vision of the Resurrected"; see also Voegelin, *Anamnesis*, trans. Gerhart Niemeyer (Notre Dame, Ind., 1978), esp. pt. 3.

63. Voegelin, *Ecumenic Age*, pp. 1-57.

9

The Language of Love in Christian and Jewish Mysticism

BERNARD McGINN

Dedicated to Jean Leclercq, OSB, master of both the love of learning and the desire for God.

Georges Bataille's book *Death and Sensuality* begins with the following provocative statement: "The human spirit is prey to the most astounding impulses. Man goes constantly in fear of himself. His erotic urges terrify him. The saint turns from the voluptuary in alarm, she does not know that his unspeakable passions and her own are really one."[1] I start with Bataille's statement not because I agree with his philosophy of eroticism, though he stands out among twentieth-century thinkers in the serious attention he gives to the relation between eroticism and mysticism, but because his stark formula, at least at first glance, suggests a view that many both before and after Freud have shared: the notion that descriptions of the heights of mystical experience are really nothing more than sublimated expressions of libidinal urges.

The Christian mystics seem to provide a good deal of evidence for this case, not only in their unconscious use of sexual symbolism (witness the frequent descriptions of the mystic path as mounting a ladder to reach the state of union), but especially in the way in which they resort to explicitly erotic language and images, both scriptural and nonscriptural, to describe their experiences. Let me cite some examples from different mystics of different centuries making use of different images.

Bernard of Clairvaux might be called the premier theologian

of the kiss in the history of Christian mysticism.² His great and unfinished *Sermons on the Song of Songs* are replete with kisses and analyses of kisses, especially the "kiss of the mouth" (Song 1:1), which he identifies with the gift of the Holy Spirit that Christ the Bridegroom bestows on his Bride, the soul. Although the Cistercian makes use of a wide range of erotic images from the Song, the kiss is the center of his concerns insofar as it signifies the union between God and the soul that Bernard understood as a loving union of wills, the *unus spiritus* of a famous Pauline text (1 Cor. 6:17) that the abbot loved to cite. The Bridge conceives through the kiss that fills her breasts with the milk of effective preaching. A passage in Sermon 9 puts it thus:

> While the Bride is conversing about the Bridegroom, he, as I have said, suddenly appears, yields to her desire by giving her a kiss, and so brings to fulfillment those words of the Psalm: "You have granted him his heart's desire, not denied him what his lips entreated" (Ps. 20:3). The filling up of her breasts is a proof of this. For so great is the potency of that holy kiss, that no sooner has the Bride received it than she conceives and her breasts grow rounded with the fruitfulness of conception, bearing witness as it were with this milky abundance. Men with an urge to frequent prayer will have experience of what I say.³

Bernard's accounts of the exchange of kisses between the human and divine lovers generally appear in the third person. A text found in the writings of his older contemporary Rupert of Deutz (ca. 1075-1129) is more direct. In commenting on the Gospel of Matthew in his great work, *The Victory of the Word of God*, the abbot describes a dream vision he had of the living Christ crucified on the altar. This vision of the Divine Lover causes Rupert to break out into scriptural expressions of praise and thanksgiving: "But this was not enough for me without grasping him with my hands and kissing him. But what could I do? The altar was too high to come near him." Christ himself responds to Rupert's fervent desire by inviting the abbot to draw near by entering the altar: "When I quickly entered, I took hold of him whom my soul loved. I held him, I embraced him, I kissed him for a long time. I felt how deeply he appreciated this sign of love when in the midst of the kiss he opened his mouth so that I could kiss more deeply."⁴

The great Beguine mystics of the thirteenth century, such as the Dutch Hadewijch (ca. 1250) and the German Mechthild of Magdeburg (ca. 1210-1297), know much of the kisses between the Bride and Bridegroom, but they also speak more directly of marital union between the divine and human lovers. Chapter 44 of the first book of Mechthild's *The Flowing Light of Godhead* is a love drama in which the Soul, her handmaidens the Five Senses, God the Holy Spirit, and the beautiful youth who is Christ converse in alternating prose and poetry. The highly charged erotic interchanges culminate with the following passage:

> Then the Most-Beloved goes in the Most-Beautiful in the hidden chamber of the immaculate Godhead. There she finds love's bed and love's embrace ready for God and human.
> Then Our Lord said: "Stand, Dame Soul."
> "What do you command, Lord?"
> "You must be free of self."
> "Lord, what shall happen to me?"
> "Dame Soul, you are already so much mine by nature that there can be nothing at all between us. . . .
> Soul speaks,
> > "Lord, now I am a naked soul
> > And you in yourself All-Glorious God.
> > Our mutual intercourse
> > Is eternal life without end."
>
> Now comes a holy silence
> That both them will.
> He gives himself to her and she to him.[5] (cf. Song 2:16, 6:2)

Accounts of a marriage ceremony between God and the soul are fairly frequent in late medieval mysticism,[6] though the actual consummation of the marriage has rarely been so exquisitely described.[7]

In the year 1559 Teresa of Avila, the celebrated Carmelite mystic, experienced her "transverberation," a vision so famous that in 1726 it was even accorded its own feast day by Pope Benedict XIII. In chapter 29 of her *Life*, the saint tells us that a short and very beautiful angel appeared at her left side:

> I saw in his hands a large golden dart and at the end of the iron tip there appeared to be a little fire. It seemed to me that this angel plunged the dart several times into my heart and that it

reached deep within me. When he drew it out, I thought that he was carrying off with him the deepest part of me; and he left me all on fire with a great love of God. The pain was so great that it made me moan, and the sweetness this greatest pain caused me was so superabundant that there is no desire capable of taking it away; nor is the soul content with less than God. The pain is not bodily but spiritual, although the body doesn't fail to share in some of it, and even a great deal.[8]

The image of the "wound of love," a term found in Song of Songs 2:5, had a long history before Teresa's vision;[9] but the Spanish mystic's description is unique for its erotic potency, a dimension magnificently brought out in Bernini's famous rendering of the scene.[10]

Images like Bernini's swooning saint and the erotic language of Bernard, Mechthild, Teresa, and other mystics have appeared scandalous to some—and not just since Freud. The study of Christian mysticism shows that we should be scandalized not so much by the presence of such erotic elements as by their absence. Still, even earlier ages were aware of the ambiguities and dangers involved in the relation of mysticism and eroticism,[11] and the question has become more insistent in our own time. We are in need of both more detailed historical studies and more nuanced theoretical frameworks to investigate this important dimension of comparative mysticism.

In the Hebrew Scriptures, God is described as the unfailing lover of his people Israel, while in the New Testament, God, the Father of Jesus, not only is loving, but is identified with Love itself (1 Jn. 4:8). Both Christianity and Judaism, then, conceive of God not just as some impersonal Highest Good, but as the transcendentally personal Creator and Goal of human beings. It is scarcely surprising that both religions describe the relation between God and the human person in terms of love. There are, to be sure, many forms of love—love of parents, love of friends, love of those we call lovers. All three types have provided metaphors for expressing the relation between God and the believer; but the intensity of erotic love, as well as aspects of the revelation shared by Jews and Christians, gives to the last of these if not pride of place at least some pride of power.

The characterization of the divine–human relation as a love affair or marriage is not part of the Torah itself, though it appears to be hinted at in the equation of apostasy with prostitution (e.g., Ex. 34:15; Num. 15:39). Such a view becomes explicit in the prophets, as the witness of Hosea (1:2–3:5), Isaiah (1:21, 50:1, 54:4–10, 62:4–5), Jeremiah (2:2, 3:1–13), and Ezekiel (16:1–63, 23:1–49) shows.[12] In the prophets this relationship is not between Yahweh and an individual, but between Him and Israel or Zion, the faithless Bride ever whoring after strange gods, but always welcome back into the loving arms of divine mercy. It is in the Song of Songs, however, that the Hebrew Bible offers its richest, most direct, and, to some, scandalous erotic imagery. In light of the highly personalized language used in the Song, the conviction of later interpreters that the text is to be applied not only to the relation of God and his people, but also to that of God and the individual, is not unwarranted. Gershom Scholem, the great student of Jewish mysticism, has suggested that through the use of the Song of Songs in Jewish and Christian mysticism, the ancient symbol of the *hieros gamos*, the sacred marriage between a god and a human, took on remarkable new life.[13] In both the Jewish and the Christian traditions, the Song's place in the scriptural canon allowed it to function as a paradigmatic expression, a divine warrant, for what some might have seen as the illegitimate use of explicitly erotic language to understand the relation between God and the human person.

The Song of Songs remains as much of a mystery to modern scholars as to ancient ones. Our forebears, Jewish and Christian, thought that the mystery of the Song was in the subject matter — that is, in how physical love could serve as a mirror to understand the human relation to God. They resisted any merely erotic reading of the book. In 1651 the Westminster Assembly's *Annotations upon all the Books of the Old and New Testament*, in introducing the Song, noted that "there were some that had lower conceptions of it, and received it as an hot carnall pamphlet, formed by some loose Apollo or Cupid, rather than the holy inspiration of the true God. But this blasphemy hath perished with the authors of it."[14] Contemporary historical-critical exegetes, many of whom seem to prefer to restrict themselves to the search for the origins of texts to the neglect of their historical use, place the mystery of the book in more mundane questions, such as the debate over whether these love poems reflect anything of the Near Eastern fertility cults that were anathematized in most of the Hebrew Scriptures.[15] The Song's sizzling language and suspect origins have put it on the margin of most modern Old Testament theology. (To anyone who doubts this, I suggest a glance at the indexes of such noted Old Testament theologies as those of Walther Eichrodt and Gerhard von Rad.)[16] Such marginality would have been surprising to Jews and Christians of an earlier era. Rabbi Akiva ben Joseph's defense of the inclusion of the Song in the Hebrew canon is well known: "The whole world is not worthy of the day the Song of Songs was given to Israel, for all of Scripture is holy, but the Song of Songs is the Holy of Holies."[17] Not less is the testimony of Origen, the greatest exegete of early Christianity:

> Rightly, then is this Song to be preferred to all songs. The other songs that the Law and the Prophets sang were sung to the Bride while she was still a little child and had not yet attained maturity. But this Song is sung to her now that she is grownup, and very strong, and ready for a husband's power and the perfect mystery.[18]

Marital symbolism, if not erotic imagery, is found in the New Testament, as in the Old. The parables ascribed to Jesus picture the eschatological kingdom as a marriage feast (Mt. 22:2-10), and the Apocalypse speaks of the marriage supper of the Lamb (Apoc. 19:7-9). The most famous New Testament reference to marriage is that found in Ephesians 5:23-32, which speaks of the mystery of the marriage of Christ and the Church (cf. 2 Cor. 11:12).

The relation of the New Testament and other early Christian documents to erotic symbolism, and even erotic practices, is an area that needs further investigation. Some have argued that Jesus' willingness to depart from Jewish law, as well as the debates evident in the New Testament epistles, bears witness to a "libertine" tradition in early Christianity that has not yet been fully appreciated.[19] From the second century on, the Romans accused the Christians of both sexual excess and ritual cannibalism. Orthodox Christians said the same, and worse, about the Gnostics.

Truth is not easy to come by in this controverted area. Both the New Testament and other early writings give witness to the prominent place taken by the kiss in early Christian life and liturgy.[20] It has been suggested that the prevalence of kissing in early Christianity can be interpreted as a special transposition of the ancient *hieros gamos* tradition of a divine–human conjunction, but this seems farfetched.[21] What is sure, however, on the basis of texts dating from the second through the fourth centuries, is that early Christian kissing sometimes went too far. In his *Paedagogue*, Clement of Alexandria attacks "those that do nothing but make the churches resound with a kiss not having love itself [i.e., Christian *agape*] within. For this very thing, the shameless use of a kiss, which ought to be mystic, occasions foul suspicions and evil reports."[22]

While the evidence of sexual excess in orthodox Christian communities is slim, the "cosmologizing" of sexuality among the Gnostics (i.e., the description of cosmogony in terms of male–female relations and sexual intercourse) may well have given a handle to their opponents' charges of promiscuity. Irenaeus, writing toward the end of the second century, condemned the Gnostics for acting out the mystery of the sacred conjugation of the heavenly male and female principles here on earth,[23] and Clement of Alexandria excoriated the Carpocratians for treating "carnal and sexual intercourse as a sacred religious mystery."[24] A more detailed and frankly pornographic picture of orgiastic practices, infanticide, and cannibalism is found in Epiphanius's description of the Gnostic Phibionites, written in 375.[25]

Exactly how far we can trust the accounts of the heresy-hunters is not easy to say. Was ritualized sexual activity given a religious and perhaps even mystical meaning in some Gnostic groups? The textual evidence is ambiguous at this point. The Coptic Gospel of Philip, which probably embodies a form of Valentinian Gnosticism, teaches a fivefold sacramental system consisting of baptism, eucharist, chrism, redemption, and the bridal chamber. "The Holy of Holies is the bridal chamber. Baptism includes the resurrection and redemption; the redemption [takes place] in the bridal chamber. But the bridal chamber is in that which is superior to [it and the others, because] you will not find [anything like] it."[26] The ritual of the bridal chamber is contrasted with "marriage in the world" or "marriage of defilement."[27] Authorities disagree whether the bridal-chamber rite was a spiritual marriage involving cohabitation without sex or a true sexual union between Gnostics whose superior wisdom allowed the use of sex without defilement.[28] The insistence that conception takes place only through the kiss, "conceiving by means of the grace that is in one another,"[29] seems to argue for the former option, as is clearly the case in other Gnostic texts, such as the Acts of Thomas.[30] Even orthodox Christian texts, such as the Shepherd of Hermas, bear witness to the spiritual-marriage theme. In the ninth Similitude, Hermas gets to spend the night with the twelve beautiful maidens who have helped build the tower representing the Church. He is embraced and kissed by them all, but they insist, "You shall sleep with us as a brother and not as a husband."[31]

The invocation of erotic language and the possible use of ritualized erotic activity by early Christians and Gnostic Christians was in conflict with those elements in the new religion that saw abstention from sexual activity for the sake of the Kingdom of God as an important value (e.g., Mt. 19:12; 1 Cor. 7:1-9, 32-34) and that pointed to Christianity's high standards of sexual morality as proof of its superiority over paganism. This tension between the use of erotic language, on the one hand, and the ideal of virginity, on the other, has been a recurring theme in the history of Christian mysticism.

It is not my purpose either to defend or to attack the ascription of spiritual superiority to the life of sexual abstention that so many Christians have accepted as self-evident for so many centuries. Nor is it feasible to think of giving an account of the historical and cultural roots and development of this preference, many aspects of which are still obscure.[32] This essay is primarily directed to an analysis of the ways in which some Christian mystics sought to deal with the tension between profane and sacred love imagery, and what their efforts have to tell us about the special nature of Christian attitudes toward eroticism as compared with those of Judaism, or at least of Spanish Kabbalah. These brief comparisons are also meant to cast some light on the more general issue with which we began: Is erotic talk about God merely a disguised sexual urge?

In the first volume of his study *The Nature of Love*, Irving Singer observes that in the Orient sex tends to be either rejected (if desire is seen as something harmful) or divinized in its full physiological reality. Western notions of both religious and romantic love, on the contrary, tend to create "erotic idealizations that remove one from the reality of desire at the same time as it becomes the basis of philosophical and literary glorification."[33] The issue is exactly where "the reality of desire" is to be found. For Christian mystics, the archetype of desire exists on a higher level than that usually experienced in this life, and hence for them "transformation" in the sense of elevation to this higher level, rather than mere "idealization," would be a more accurate term for the change involved.

It is important to point out that what is involved here is not so much the disguising of erotic language (what has made the mystics so shocking to more timid believers is exactly how direct their use of the language of love has been) as the full and direct use of certain forms of erotic expression for a different purpose—the transformation of all human desire in terms of what the mystic believes to be its true source. Transformation, then, can be conceived of as the gradual conscious conversion of all forms of human energy into the divine love that is its source and goal. The mystics contend that divine love is at the heart of all reality, and hence, in loving God, the mystic can come to recognize this divine love in an experiential way and can even eventually be able, at least in some way, to love as God loves—that is, to synthesize all the forms of love (whether conceived of as desire, possession, or overflowing bounty) into a single transcendental act of loving.

To the nonmystic, and especially to the nonbeliever, this claim will doubtless look like a personal delusion. The issue at stake is that of the perspective used to interpret the ultimate meaning of physical desire and its fulfillment. What is a suspect "sublimation" or an ambiguous "idealization" from the nonmystical perspective is judged to be a higher "transformation" from that of the mystic or of the believer convinced of the reality of mystical claims. My purpose is not so much to try to adjudicate between the perspectives—a formidable task—as to try to be as clear as possible about their distinction. From the transformation point of view, which is that of the mystics themselves, human sexual desire is always an image of the true, not merely "idealized," eros. For these religious interpreters, the most sublime function of human eros and the language that represents it is to serve as a privileged symbol, a way of revealing this hidden higher reality. Let us look at two examples of this process of the transformation of eros in detail.

Origen, the earliest surviving Christian commentator on the Song of Songs, allowed for an individual as well as a communal interpretation of the book.[34] He worked out rules for one form of the transformation of desire that were an important source for much that followed, not only in the mystical exegesis of the Song, as in the cases of Gregory of Nyssa in the East or Bernard in the West, but also in the wider mystical tradition.

Origen's reading is founded on a Platonic interpretation of the Pauline distinction between the inner and outer person (e.g., 2 Cor. 4:16). For him, only the inner spiritual person can profit from the Song; one who still lives on the level of the flesh will find it so conducive to carnal desire that he advises anyone who is not yet rid of the vexations of the flesh to stay clear of the book—advice that, had it been literally followed, would have left the Song perilously few readers. Why risk the danger? Here Origen's argument becomes more interesting because he refuses to leave love and desire to the enemy, either to philosophers like Plato who said much that was true about the power of spiritual love, or to those who perverted the philosophers' message to serve carnal ends. The true reality of love, even the yearning "erotic" love of the best philosophers, is the proper heritage of the Christian, as is shown by Scripture, which, although it usually uses the terms *caritas/dilectio* (*agape*) to describe love in condescension to our weakness, also is willing to use *amor/cupido* (*eros*), a word Origen found in the Septuagint (e.g., Prov. 4:6, 8; Wis. 8:2). "You must take whatever Scripture says about charity as if it had been said in reference to passionate love," he claims, "taking no notice of the difference in terms; for the same meaning is conveyed by both."[35] This passionate love that is the same as charity "is implanted in the soul by the Creator's kindness."[36] Directed to the goods of the outer person, such as money, glory, sexual gratification, or even the higher goods of human skills and sciences, it will always end in perversion. Only when aimed at God and other persons through God is it rightly used.

Origen's distinction between the inner and outer person seems to suggest an almost unbridgeable gap, but another hermeneutical principle serves to qualify this great divide. The Alexandrian exegete insists that "the Divine Scriptures make use of homonyms, that is to say, they use identical terms for describing different things . . . so you will find the names of the members of the body transferred to those of the soul; or rather the faculties and powers of the soul are to be called its members."[37] This is the source for the noted doctrine of the "spiritual senses" of the soul, which holds that the inner person possesses "senses" directed to the divine realm analogous to those of smell, taste, hearing, sight, and touch, which the outer person has in relation to the material world.[38] Thus any form of sensuous description found in the scriptures can be read as a message about supersensible experience. The language of love, especially as found in the Song of Songs, becomes a way to read the inner text of the soul in relation to God.[39]

Origen's prologue to his *Commentary on the Song of Songs* is a foundational document for the utilization of erotic imagery in Christian mysticism. Although it deals explicitly with the Song, its principles could be extended to other texts and descriptions of sexual experience. In Latin Christianity we find individualized applications of the imagery of the Song to describe the relation between the virgin soul and God developed as early as the fourth century, as witnessed by Jerome's letter to Eustochium, written in 384.[40]

Origen's Platonic contrast between the inner and outer person was not the only basis for Christian appropriation of the language of love. The mystics of the twelfth century, whom the impartial observer might almost accuse of obsession with erotic language, were particularly creative in working out new paradigms for the use of the language of love in the service of the mystical path to God. Among the most intriguing of these is that found in Richard of St. Victor's *The Four Degrees of Violent Charity*, a text based not directly on the Song or on the Platonic notion of eros, but on a new erotic experience that found its clearest expression in the theory of courtly love.

We usually do not think of "charity" as violent. For Richard, if charity was to be the archetype for all forms of love, it needed to be as impulsive, as violent, even as insane, as the most passionate of human loves. The madness of love was not a new discovery: witness Lucretius's picture of how lovers try to devour each other in the act of love,[41] or Abelard's portrayal of his affair with Heloise in *The History of My Calamities*.[42] No previous Christian mystic, however, devoted as much energy as Richard did to proving that the love of God was the true paradigm of erotic insanity.[43]

Richard's analysis is built on four degrees or stages of erotic love—that is, "the burning and ardent love which pierces the heart and enkindles the affective power."[44] Love "wounds," "binds," "languishes" (i.e, "makes ill"), and "causes to faint away."[45] It is important to note that this is a division of love as violent, and not of love as sacred or profane. Like William Butler Yeats's picture of the double gyre in *A Vision*—two inverted cones spinning back and forth in different directions—Richard views sacred and profane love as contrasting but isomorphic manifestations of these four stages of erotic violence.

The emotional tone of each stage of love is the same whether found on the sacred or the profane level. *Amor vulnerans*, or wounding love, pierces the soul so that it burns with intermittent fever for the object of its desire. *Amor ligans* binds the soul so that it continually thinks of the beloved. In the third degree, *amor languens*, "nothing can give any satisfaction but the one thing and nothing is known but that one,"[46] so that constant desire absorbs every other human concern and becomes a state of tyranny. Finally, in the fourth grade "nothing at all is able to satisfy the desire of the soul on fire . . . because it can always find something more to long for."[47] Richard illustrates this stage by some astute observations on lovers' quarrels in which love and hate feed on each other so that the couple are caught between fire and ice.[48] In nice Scholastic fashion, the Victorine summarizes his degrees as *insuperabilis, inseparabilis, singularis,* and *insatiabilis*.[49]

If the emotional flavor of each level is the same whether directed to a divine or to a human lover, the dynamic implications are diametrically opposed. "In spiritual desires the greater the degree of desire the better; in fleshly desires the greater the worse."[50] Only the first degree, *amor insuperabilis*, which Richard identifies with marriage, is licit in carnal love. This is the love that binds two persons to each other in a sexual bond (*in nuptiali toro*) surpassing any other love between humans. If any form of sexual love, inside or outside of marriage, takes on the characteristics of the three higher stages—that is, if human erotic love becomes *inseparabilis, singularis,* or *insatiabilis*—Richard is sure that it will wind up divinizing the creature and destroying love itself. Inseparable love addressed to creatures prevents us from taking up the other responsibilities we are called to on the human level; singular love goes further in becoming annoyed over not being able to enjoy the beloved as much as we would like; and insatiable love turns this unsatisfied bitterness back on the beloved into the destructive madness in which lovers may psychologically or even literally destroy each other. One may not necessarily agree with the whole of Richard's analysis to appreciate its psychological accuracy.

When the Loved One is God, the logic of desire reverses itself. "Insuperable" love of God is good, but the other stages are better. Richard illustrates the progression in sacred love by a series of erotic images, especially those drawn from marriage considered as a succession of legal or physical facts: betrothal, the marriage ceremony, sexual consummation (*copula*), and the bearing of children.[51] Divine betrothal involves a turning away from carnal pleasures through a grace that enkindles the affections without yet illuminating the intellect.[52] The second degree is primarily an illuminative one in which the soul flies to the second heaven to see what no eye has seen.[53] The third degree, that of consummation, features the most erotic language, for it is in this stage that the soul is ecstatically united to God in a complete identity of will and desire. Richard's prime analogy here is one of liquifying fire, but he also cites the Song of Songs (e.g., 5:6, 2:5).[54] Like the majority of Christian mystics, Richard insists that the analogy between divine and human love does not end with ecstasy, at least in this life, but that it proceeds to childbirth — that is, a stage in which the soul overcomes the ecstasy of spiritual death (another highly erotic image) to be reborn with Christ and to continue his work of fruitful love in the world. The goal, then, is not the marriage bed, as pleasant as that may be, but the busy household in which the mother cares for her children despite distractions and difficulties. Richard insists that this, too, is an "insane" love, since it abandons ecstatic union to return to service to others, even to the extent of being willing to be separated from the love of Christ for the sake of one's fellows (citing Rom. 9:3; Ex. 33:32; and Gen. 18:25).[55]

I have spoken of the background to Richard's treatise as courtly, not because he explicitly makes use of the theme of adulterous passion as the paradigm of profane erotic love, but because his analysis of the progress of passion seems to me to be colored by the theme of yearning desire that was central to the courtly tradition. How far this element in his thought comes from the courtly poets themselves and how far it was a discovery of the mystics of the time is still a disputed question.[56]

While Richard's evaluation of the place of sexual love in marriage is a more positive one than Origen's, the way in which he compares human and divine eros still insists on the necessity of radical transformation of the human analogue. The fundamental principle on which the Victorine constructs his transformation is a different one, however; no longer the difference between the inner and the outer person, as in Origen, but the transcendent difference between loving an Infinite and a finite subject.

Richard's treatise is a good example of a new stage in the eroticization of mystical language evident from the twelfth century on. Broadly speaking, this could be described as a change in the relation between the role of the scriptural text and the text of the mystic's experience. Richard, and other contemporary mystics like Bernard of Clairvaux, were far more willing than Origen or Gregory of Nyssa had been to invoke the erotic experiences, remembered or imagined, of their hearers and readers.[57] The Song of Songs is never forgotten by these authors or their successors; but anyone who has read Hadewijch or Mechthild, Suso or Ruusbroec, Teresa or John of the Cross, will sense how much more freely they also use appeals to what we may call "existential" eros as the base text for their transformative task.

Did the Christian mystics always insist that real progress on the path to the experience of divine love is not possible in this fallen world until human eros, even in its legitimate marital form, is abandoned? However much allowable for the sake of procreation, is married love incompatible with the delights of the divine variety?

The orthodox Christian tradition, of course, had never insisted that the life of virginity was necessary for salvation, and many of the twelfth-century mystical authors had a deep appreciation of marriage, as Jean Leclercq has shown.[58] Still, it is easy to find texts that affirm or at least strongly suggest that it is difficult, if not impossible, for a married person to enjoy the experience of divine love in this life in the same way that a virgin can.

Nevertheless, there are some elements in the classic medieval mystical tradition that suggest that the exercise of married love is not incompatible with erotic union with the Divine Lover. Even Augustine, whose views on marital intercourse have been more often attacked than understood, described the delights of marital embrace (*conjugales amplexus*) as licit pleasures,[59] though he could scarcely have been expected to try to relate them to the experience of "touching" God in this life. The life of at least one female saint of the early Middle Ages goes out of its way to point out how she was able to combine love of her husband with love of the Divine Bridegroom, even within intercourse itself. The tenth-century *Life of Ida of Herfeld*, written by the monk Uffing, says of the sanctity of Ida and her husband, Count Egbert: "What expresses this more perfectly than at the time of their being two in one flesh there is one undivided operation of the Holy Spirit in them which internally enflamed them with a more burning love of heavenly things while they were externally joined by the law of matrimony."[60] In the context of the Cathar attack on marriage in the late twelfth century, Cardinal Lothario Segni, the future Pope Innocent III, wrote a treatise, *The Fourfold Form of Marriage*, on "the likenesses [*similitudines*] that exist between spiritual marriage and physical marriage" in which he showed how "marriage becomes a means of sharing in the love of God in Christ."[61] Finally, there are a number of late medieval mystics such as Meister Eckhart and Julian of Norwich who insist that mystical perfection is independent of any form of life and external practice and who therefore imply that physical virginity is a matter of indifference. Margery Kempe, the eccentric early-fifteenth-century English mystic, was much comforted when Jesus told her, "Yea, daughter, trow thou right well that I love wives also."[62]

What we do not find in classical expositions of Christian mysticism is anything similar to the insistence of some Jewish mystics that marital intercourse plays a necessary role in the mystical life.[63] To put it in other words, we might say that for Christian mystics human sexual language is used as a way of describing—or, better, suggesting—the ultimate erotic encounter with God. For some Jewish mystics, as we shall see, the exercise of marital sexuality itself is an essential activity in the mystical path. Christian mystics use sexual language to describe something that lies beyond it; some kabbalists also go further to consecrate sexual activity in order to restore the integrity of both the divine and human realms.[64]

The use of the language of love in Jewish mysticism is very rich; only a few comparative dimensions can be suggested here.[65] Among the many intimate bonds between Jewish and Christian mystical traditions none is more important than the fact that both found in the Song of Songs the mystical text par excellence. For Jews and Christians, the Song was not some excuse for the surreptitious use of forbidden themes, but was the authorized model that guided their personal appropriation of the divine–human encounter.

The rabbinic Midrashes on the Song had insisted that the proper way to read the book was in light of the prophetic passages about the love of God for Israel; but the Jewish tradition, like the Christian, came to admit a variety of readings. Elisha Gallico, a Safed kabbalist of the sixteenth century, speaks of four: a Midrashic reading in which "the community of Israel longs for and seeks out her lover and He responds in kind"; one in which the Song speaks of "the desire of students to attain Torah, both hidden and revealed"; an Aristotelian reading in which intellect and matter are lovers; and a Neoplatonic interpretation in which "the soul, drawn from beneath the throne of God, longs to return to the spiritual delights of her master's home, in which she delighted before her descent into the world."[66] The individual, or mystical, interpretation of the erotic language of the Song of Songs appears to be the creation of medieval Judaism.[67] We find examples of it in many Jewish mystical movements, such as the German pietists of the twelfth and thirteenth centuries,[68] as well as in Safed kabbalists like Elijah de Vidas.[69] I will restrict my examples to Spanish kabbalism of the thirteenth century, that intensely creative phase in Jewish spiritual life that Gershom Scholem saw as a "remythologizing" of the Jewish religion.[70]

Individualizing interpretations of erotic imagery are widespread among the Spanish kabbalists, especially in the commentators on the Song of Songs, such as Rabbi Ezra ben Solomon of Gerona, who wrote in the mid-thirteenth century, and Isaac ibn Sahula, who wrote a commentary in the 1280s. Both writers understood the "kiss of the mouth" as the perfected soul's striving to cleave to God,[71] something that reminds us of Christian authors, like Bernard of Clairvaux. The individualizing interpretation of the Song is found in both branches of Spanish Kabbalah, but with a difference. In the ecstatic or prophetic Kabbalah of Abraham Abulafia and his followers, the mystic sage, like the Christian saint, is conceived of as female in relation to the Divine Lover, the Active Intellect symbolized as the male. While these mystics see no incompatibility between married life and ecstatic erotic union with the Divine Mind, they do not give marriage a central ritual role in the mystic path in the way that the theosophical or theurgical Kabbalah does.[72]

Theosophical Kabbalah, best represented by the *Zohar* written by Moses de Leon from about 1275 to 1286, went beyond Christian use of erotic language in two important ways: first, in projecting the marital relationship into the divine realm itself; and second, in establishing a necessary bond between marital union in this world and the divine conjugations. This also involves a significant gender switch (or better, nonswitch), in that the human lover retains his male character while the Divine Beloved, the *Shekhinah*, is female.[73] However, the love affair between the kabbalist and the *Shekhinah* in this life is more of a pursuit than a conquest. Moses alone is said to have been called to abandon his earthly wife in order to be directly united to the *Shekhinah*.[74] The best that seems to be held out for anyone else, like Rabbi Shimon ben Yohai, the pseudonymous author of the *Zohar*, is to be able to celebrate one's death as a wedding, the time of the passage to union with God.[75]

The root of Spanish kabbalism's unique transformation of erotic imagery is found in its teaching regarding the *Sefirot*, the ten emanations or manifestations of *Eyn Sof*, the hidden God. The *Sefirot*, which bear interesting analogies to the Gnostic systems of divine emanations, introduced a remarkable dynamism into traditional Jewish conceptions of God and opened up a whole new world to Jewish mysticism.

The kabbalists treated the mysterious *Sefirot* under myriad images, symbols, and disguises. Any brief description or diagram is bound to flatten out the complexity and richness of the system.[76] The ten *Sefirot* proceed from *Eyn Sof*, the hidden God, in the pattern of an inverted cosmic tree connecting the divine and created worlds, or according to the model of the primordial androgynous human, Adam Kadmon. *Keter* (Crown) is the first *Sefirah*, the eternal undifferentiated source of the other emanations. From *Keter* on the right, or male, side comes *Hokhmah* (Wisdom) and then on the left, or female, side, *Binah* (Intelligence), which is the

Womb or Divine Mother that receives *Hokhmah*'s seed in order to give birth to the seven other *Sefirot*. These three form the head of the divine body. *Binah* first bears *Hesed* (Love) and *Gevurah* or *Din* (Judgment), the right and left arms of God, which must be kept in harmony if the world is to function properly. Their balance is symbolized in *Tiferet* or *Rahamin* (Beauty), the son of *Hokhmah* and *Binah* who forms the trunk of the body. There follow *Nezah* (Endurance) and *Hod* (Majesty), the right and left legs connected with the gift of prophecy, and then *Yesod* (Foundation), representing the male sex organ or the *axis mundi* of the universe.[77] It is through *Yesod* that *Binah* produces the final *Sefirah*, her daughter *Shekhinah* (Divine Presence), also called *Malkhut* (Kingdom), who is identified with the *Kenneset Yisrael*, the Community of Israel. The marriage of *Shekhinah* and *Tiferet* is the main focus of the kabbalistic sexualization of the divine world.

In the *Sefer ha-Bahir*, the earliest work of the Provençal kabbalism that preceded the Spanish variety, the Bride of the Song of Songs is already identified with the "Field" or "Vessel"—that is, the *Shekhinah* into which the other *Sefirot* enter;[78] but it is in the *Zohar* that the theme reaches its full expansion. According to the *Zohar*, the divine marriage takes place on several levels in the Sefirotic world: first between *Hokhmah* and *Binah*, then between *Hesed* and *Din*, and finally between *Tiferet* and *Shekhinah*.[79] Sexual symbolism taken from the Song of Songs is frequently invoked to describe the lowest divine union:

> When the Holy King [*Tiferet*] begins to yearn for the Queen [*Shekhinah*] and for Israel
> He climbs up on roofs, runs down stairs, scales walls;
> He peers through the holes in walls just to see them!
> When he catches a glimpse of them he starts to cry.
> As it is written:
> "My beloved is like a gazelle, like a young deer," jumping from wall to roof, from roof to wall.[80] (Song 2:9)

For the *Zohar*, Solomon's Song is the highest of all biblical songs because "there had been no man since the creation of Adam, who had brought about love and affection through words of coupling alone, until King Solomon."[81]

The daring and complexity of the *Zohar*'s teaching on the female aspect of God and the divine marriages involves a darker side. Spanish kabbalism explains the origin of evil through an appeal to "the other side of God," a sort of breakdown in the Sefirotic emanations involving an unholy union between the evil female figure *Lilith* and the angel *Samael*.[82] Theosophical kabbalism is not unlike Gnosticism in both its explanation of evil and the way in which it sexualizes cosmogony.

The ways in which the *Zohar* and other kabbalistic texts establish the connections between marriage above and marriage below is the second original aspect to the use of erotic language and practice in Spanish Kabbalah. The Sefirotic world of emanation is the source of three lower worlds: the world of creation (i.e., the realm of the celestial throne and chariot); the angelic world of formation; and the sublunar, human world of making. There are intimate structural resemblances among the worlds, as well as spatial connections and special affinities between each world and individual *Sefirah*.[83] Our world has a special connection with the *Shekhinah*, so that not only is the *Shekhinah* the "Heavenly Woman" or "Eternal Feminine," the ground for everything female in the world,[84] but the marriage of *Shekhinah* and *Tiferet* above and man and woman below actually partake of the same reality. "Everything above and below comes about through male and female," as the *Zohar* puts it.[85] Thus marriage becomes the most holy of all the *misvot*, or commandments of the Torah. When performed according to the prescriptions of the Law, the sexual union of husband and wife not only mirrors the divine conjugation, but also facilitates the harmonization of the Sefirotic world and the reintegration of the divine and human realms. In theosophical Kabbalah, although sexuality descends from above, so that intercourse in this world is patterned on the couplings of the higher realm, the correct performance of the *misvot*, of which pure sexual relations and procreation are the most important, reverses the flow and makes the reintegration of the upper world depend on the lower. As Moshe Idel puts it, "The correlation between the various levels of reality permitted the Kabbalists to regard sexual union as an *imitatio Dei* from one side and as a theurgical act intended to induce a harmonious state in the supernal entities on the other."[86]

Sex still retains an ambivalence or, better, danger for the author of the *Zohar*, because its illicit use is definitely a source of destruction.[87] Human illicit passions participate in the evil couplings of *Lilith* and *Samael* in the Sefirotic world as surely as the Sabbath eve union of the kabbalist and his wife partake of the union of *Shekhinah* and *Tiferet*.[88] But as far as the holiness of proper marital union is concerned, there is no doubt that Moses de Leon was in full agreement with his younger contemporary Rabbi David ben Yehudah in his *Sefer Marot*, who insisted: "This garment [the reward given to the faithful in heaven] is prepared only for him who is perfected below and has maintained the Image of the Chain of Being in this world by engendering new life."[89]

Another kabbalistic text, the *'Iggeret ha-Kodesh* (*Holy Letter*), is a systematic defense of the sanctity and mystical meaning of marriage against the Maimonidean depreciation of sex as unfitting for the enlightened philosopher. The *'Iggeret* not only emphasizes the proper time, diet, and techniques for the beneficent and fruitful marital act, but also teaches how the intentions of the partners toward each other serve to put them in harmony with the coupling in the divine realm. The goal of the act is at once mystical — "sexual union can be a means of spiritual elevation when it is properly practiced"[90] — as well as creative — "through the act they become partners with God in the act of creation."[91] Through the correct conjunction of the male and the female, the kabbalist's intention, when fused with the *Shekhinah* in a true mystical union, brings the divine power down on the *semen virile* to ensure a good conception. This reverses the use of sexual techniques found in Indian Tantrism, where incomplete intercourse serves to heighten mystical consciousness, by paradoxically insisting that mystical union is in the service of the *misvot* of procreation.[92] The *'Iggeret*'s position is closer to the sexual mysticism of the late classical Hermetic text the *Asclepius*, in which the act of intercourse allows the couple to partake of the divinity sowed in the opposite sex and thus briefly regain the unity of the androgynous Creator.[93] It is also interesting to note that both the Jewish mystic and Christian mystics like Richard of St. Victor insist that transformed desire must become fruitful, though in far different ways.

The contrasts between the language of love is the embodied mysticism of Spanish Kabbalah and what we have seen in some selected Christian mystics is evident.[94] Despite the fact that the Holy Spirit, understood as the bond of love uniting the Father and the Son in the Trinity, was sometimes spoken of as a "Kiss,"[95] and in some early Christian traditions was symbolized as female,[96] Christianity generally resisted attempts to introduce sexual language and images, especially those of intercourse, into the inner life of God.[97] As noted earlier, there is also nothing in traditional Western Christian mysticism that would give marital intercourse a privileged place in the mystic path. There is, however, at least one interesting Christian analogue to Spanish kabbalism's incorporation of the feminine into God.

Christian mystics usually spoke of God as masculine and the soul as feminine. But there are texts where the reverse is the case. Just as recent study has shown that the traditional Christian language of God as Father has often been complemented by speaking of God or Christ as Mother,[98] there are also examples in the history of Christian mysticism where the Divine Lover is conceived of as feminine.

These occur, for example, in the pillar of orthodoxy, Augustine of Hippo. The sapiential books of the Old Testament viewed *Sophia* (*Hokhmah*) as a female emanation from God whom Solomon pursues and weds (Wis. 8:22). Following this lead, Augustine spoke of Christ as Divine Wisdom (*Sapientia*, a female figure) in a decidedly erotic way in some texts.[99] Another example of the same way of speaking occurs in a less respectable figure, Giovanni Pico della Mirandola, the Renaissance Platonist who was one of the first Christians to take an interest in the Kabbalah. In the *Commentary* he wrote on his friend Girolamo Benivieni's "Canzone d'Amore," he appears to have been influenced by both Platonic and kabbalistic traditions in identifying the Celestial Venus with the Christian God whom the ardent lover pursues to be granted the supreme reward of the kiss:

> As a result of the soul's first "death," which is the separation only of the soul from the body (and not the opposite) the lover can see the beloved heavenly Venus, and talking with her face to face, can happily feed his purified eyes on her divine image. But anyone who wishes to possess her more intrinsically, who is not content merely to see and hear her, but wishes to be deemed worthy of her intimate embraces and panting kisses, must be separated from his body through the second "death," that is through total separation.[100]

The materials briefly presented here are by no means adequate to answer all the questions implied by the use of erotic language in Jewish and Christian mysticism. My remarks are only a series of soundings in a vast and turbulent ocean, "the ocean of love," as the Spanish mystic Ramon Lull called it.[101] Even these few soundings, though, are sufficient to raise anew the question I began with. Are the passions of the voluptuary and the saint really one and the same?

There are many ways in which this vague rhetorical question could be made more precise. For instance, love of God and love of a human lover could be said to be one because they are both manifestations of a single source of psychic energy. Were we to call this force *affectus* many medieval Christian authors would agree, though it is hard to think that they would if we were to call it *libido*. Alternatively, the passions of saint and voluptuary could be said to be the same because they have the same goal in mind, or because they follow a structurally similar logic. Again, agreement and disagreement would demand a more detailed analysis than can be given here. The saint would claim that the voluptuary is looking for the right thing, but in the wrong place; some modern psychologists think that the saint is finding the same thing as the voluptuary, only calling it by the wrong name.

Georges Bataille insisted that physical, emotional, and religious eroticism are all obedient to the same motivating force, "the concern to substitute for the individual isolated discontinuity a feeling of profound continuity."[102] But he also affirmed a "gulf separating religious mysticism and eroticism" insofar as the mystical experience remains within the domain of inner awareness, eschewing any intentional physical activity and external object.[103] Although Bataille was critical of Christianity's attempts to outlaw taboo and impurity within religion,[104] in *Death and Sensuality* at least he appears to leave open the question of whether the mystic and the voluptuary overcome discontinuity by achieving different goals — that is, whether God might be a real possibility or whether the only ultimate is death, conceived of as the goal of all eroticism because it is the final cancellation of the yearning of the discontinuous self. It is no wonder, then, that Bataille distanced himself from those psychologists who tried to give a purely sexual reading of mystical experience.[105]

One of the psychologists Bataille criticized was James Leuba, the author of a number of early studies on the relation between mysticism and psychology collected under the title *The Psychology of Religious Mysticism* (1925). For Leuba the highest experiences of the mystics are not the outcome of the transformation of libido, but of its reassertion. Quoting Freud and others, he says: "The thesis which we shall maintain is that the delights said by our great mystics to transcend everything which the world and the senses can procure, involve some activity of the sexual organs."[106] At least part of this untoward activity is to be blamed on the use of sexual imagery. "Is the flesh likely to remain unmoved when continence is combined . . . with indulgence in the imagery dear to the libertine?" he asks rhetorically.[107] But even if all mystical experiences could somehow be proved to be accompanied by genital movements, what exactly would that prove? To someone convinced that the source of all human activity is in the energy of the libido, all striving must by definition follow the dynamics of libidinal expression and can only aim at its satisfaction. (Concrete "proof" of genital movements among the mystics would seem not only difficult to ascertain but also largely superfluous.) But to someone who is convinced that sexual arousal is one expression of a broad range of human appetites (medieval mystics would call this range *affectus*), that different objects specify different modes of *affectus* all subtly linked in the unity of the human personality, and that physical desire does not exhaust the meaning of love, genital movements accompanying mystical experiences would mean something quite different, perhaps a sign of some imbalance in the *ordo affectus* of greater or lesser moment. The debate is not about sexual language or sexual arousal as such, but about sex's place in human nature.

Irving Singer, in his criticism of Freud in *The Nature of Love*, makes the point that the mystic uses erotic symbols knowing full well that they are erotic in the human sense, but on the basis of a religious commitment that "everything physical represents something nonphysical, transcendent, spiritual." We may want to question that commitment and its basis, but we can learn nothing from it if we merely dismiss it. For Freud it was enough to show how various symbols consciously or unconsciously symbolize sexual intercourse; the mystic, as Singer recognizes, asks "But what does sexual intercourse symbolize?"[108]

In her *Notebooks*, Simone Weil goes deeper when she says: "To reproach mystics with loving God by means of the faculty of sexual love is as though one were to reproach a painter with making pictures by means of colors composed of material substances. We haven't anything else with which to love."[109] More recently, Italo Calvino, in his essay "Definitions of Territories: Eroticism," hints that there may be more to libido than even the libidinous intend when he claims that explicitly erotic writers make use of "the symbols of sex to give voice to something else, and this something else, after a series of definitions that tend to take shape in philosophical and religious terms, may in the last instance be redefined as another and ultimate Eros, fundamental, mythical, unattainable."[110] I cite these authors not to argue that they hold the same position on the meaning of the transformation of eroticism, but only to indicate that a convergence of approaches suggests that there is more to the use of erotic language in mystical texts than simple sublimation.

Jewish and Christian mystics felt no embarrassment in using rich sexual symbolism that has frequently made more timid believers nervous and that has alternately scandalized and titillated nonbelievers. They did this not only because such language was found in the Scriptures, notably in the Song of Songs, but also because sexual language offered them a unique set of symbols to present experiences that were, at least according to the mystics themselves, incapable of being fully circumscribed by language.

The interpretation of the oft-repeated claims of mystical texts concerning the ineffability of the experience of God and the need to use paradoxical—that is, at least seemingly contradictory—language to describe both God and the encounter with God is a complex and much debated area. The employment of erotic language as a tool for exploring how the divine–human encounter is both ultimately indescribable and yet indirectly capable of presentation through human language is a major chapter in this crucial issue in the study of mysticism. Mystics from the time of Augustine have reflected on the peculiarity of the situation in which anyone who attempts to speak of the ineffable finds him- or herself:

> Have we spoken or announced anything worthy of God? Rather I feel that I have done nothing but wish to speak. . . . Whence do I know this, except because God is ineffable? If what I said were ineffable, it would not be said. And for this reason God

should not be said to be ineffable, for when this is said something is said. And a contradiction in terms is created, since if that is ineffable which cannot be spoken, then that is not ineffable which can be called ineffable.[111]

Augustine's discussion goes on to indicate that language about an ineffable God is always more "transformative"—that is, more intended to reveal an attitude, or effect a change, in the believer than to describe what God is or what the believer has experienced.[112] The same may be said for the use of the language of love in mystical presentations of the encounter between the divine and human subjects—its fundamental role is in the transformation of the mystic.

Erotic language forms a test case for studying the complex relations between common human experience—that is, sexual desire and consummation as mediated through language—and forms of human consciousness (also mediated through language) that claim more. It is obvious that erotic language could not be useful (indeed, no form of language could be useful) if the attempt to present the experience of God was absolutely ineffable (*wholly* wholly Other), but it is equally clear that the mystics want to insist that any attempts to construe the God they have come to love according to the usual categories of knowing and loving are quite inadequate. A fuller investigation of the categories of ineffability and paradox lie outside the scope of this essay, which seeks only to cast some light on how one form of language—the language of love—can be used as a tool in the delicate game of creating strategies for allowing us to speak of what lies outside the normal canons of speech.

Over the centuries, both Jewish and Christian mystics were involved in adopting sexual imagery to facilitate the transformation of desire—that is, the preparation for a new kind of erotic encounter: that between finite and Infinite Subject, between embodied and Absolute Spirit. The transformation of eros was realized by Jewish and Christian authors in diverse, though overlapping ways. Jewish mystics were more successful in drawing out the positive aspects of the human sexual relationship in itself. For the Spanish kabbalists, as we have seen, procreative sexuality was both a symbol and a performative act, though like the Christian mystics, they insisted that to make sex a part of the mystical path involved a religious transformation of its meaning and practice. Both Judaism and Christianity also insisted that eroticism and fertility were intimately linked in the mystical life. The ultimate goal of the mystic in this life is to bring forth offspring—the progeny of good works, and for the Jewish mystics, physical progeny as well.

It must be noted, however, that while Spanish Kabbalah was more positive about the role of marriage in mysticism, it was more gender-exclusive than classical Christian mysticism. There are no Mechthilds or Teresas in the history of Jewish mysticism. Christian mystics, both male and female, in their concentration on the dynamics of the encounter between the divine and human lovers, which they developed with unequaled power, neglected the positive role that marital love might play in understanding and facilitating this encounter. Christianity today still wrestles with this exclusivity.

Both Judaism and Christianity continue to try to understand the special role of erotic love as a favored enabling symbol to express union with God. Each religion must work at this vital task primarily in conversation with its own tradition and heritage, but I believe this process of reinterpretation can profit from greater awareness of how these two related traditions have understood what the *'Iggeret ha-Kodesh* means when it says, "In the mystery of man and woman, there is God."[113]

Notes

The original version of this paper was presented as the Rabbi Julian Feibelman Memorial Lecture at Tulane University in February 1985. I am grateful to the Feibelman family and to the Reverend Val A. McInnes, O.P., for the invitation and especially for their generous hospitality. Subsequent versions have been delivered to audiences at Dumbarton Oaks Center, Washington, D.C.; St. John's University, Collegeville; John Carroll University, Cleveland; New York University; the University of Dallas; Harvard Divinity School; and the University of Virginia; and to my colleagues of the Divinity School of the University of Chicago. On each of these occasions, I have received helpful comments from friends too numerous to mention. Special thanks are due to Arthur Green, Karen Guberman, Moshe Idel, Jon Levenson, Steven T. Katz, Arthur Droge, Wendy Doniger, and Jean Leclercq.

1. Georges Bataille, *Death and Sensuality: A Study of Eroticism and the Taboo* (Salem, Mass., 1984), p. 7.

2. For Bernard's use of erotic language, see "St. Bernard and the

Metaphor of Love," in Jean Leclercq, *Monks on Marriage: A Twelfth-Century View* (New York, 1982), pp. 73–86, and Jacques Blanpain, "Langage mystique, expression du désir dans les Sermons sur le Cantique des cantiques de Bernard de Clairvaux," *Collectanea Cisterciensia* 36 (1974): 45–68, 226–47. On the kiss in history, see Nicholas J. Perella, *The Kiss Sacred and Profane* (Berkeley, 1969), pp. 52–57.

3. Bernard of Clairvaux, *On the Song of Songs I* (Spencer, Mass., 1969), Sermon 9.V.7, p. 58. In the *Sermons on the Song*, the marriage is always between the Word and the soul, but in the early *Steps of Humility and Pride* (7.21) the marriage is between the soul and the Father. Other translations, unless noted, are my own.

4. Rupert of Deutz, *Commentary on Matthew*, book 12 of *The Victory of the Word of God*, in J.-P. Migne, ed., *Patrologia Latina* (Paris, 1844–64), vol. 168, col. 1601. On the importance of this text, see Peter Dinzelbacher, "Über die Entdeckung der Liebe im Hochmittelalter," *Saeculum* 32 (1981): 197.

5. Mechthild of Magdeburg, *Offenbarungen der Schwester Mechtilde von Magdeburg oder Das Fliessende Licht der Gotheit*, ed. P. Gall Morel (Regensburg, 1869; reprint, Darmstadt, 1963), I.44, p. 22.

6. P. Adnès, "Mariage spirituel," *Dictionnaire de spiritualité* (Paris: Beauchesne, 1980), vol. 10, cols. 388–408.

7. See, for example, visions 6 and 7 in *Hadewijch: The Complete Works*, trans. and intro. by Mother Columba Hart (New York, 1980), pp. 278–82. For other examples of erotic images among the female mystics of the later Middle Ages, see Caroline Walker Bynum, *Holy Feast and Holy Fast: The Religious Significance of Food to Medieval Women* (Berkeley, 1987), pp. 246–50.

8. Teresa of Avila, *Life*, in *The Collected Works of St. Teresa of Avila: Volume One*, trans. Kieran Kavanaugh and Otilio Rodriguez (Washington, D.C., 1976), pp. 193–94.

9. See A. Cabassut, "Blessure d'amour," *Dictionnaire de spiritualité* (Paris, 1937), vol. 1, cols. 1724–29.

10. For some insightful, if incomplete, observations on the relation of Bernini's work to the mystical tradition, see Irving Lavin, *Bernini and the Unity of the Visual Arts* (New York, 1980), vol. 1, pp. 77–140.

11. See, for instance, the case of the false mystic Benedetta Carlini, described in Judith Brown, *Immodest Acts: The Life of a Lesbian Nun in Renaissance Italy* (New York, 1986), esp. p. 107.

12. My thanks to my colleague Jon Levenson for suggestions on the relation of the Torah and the prophets on marital love. For an opposing view, see W. L. Moran, "The Ancient Near Eastern Background of the Love of God in Deuteronomy," *Catholic Biblical Quarterly* 25 (1963): 77–87.

13. Gershom Scholem, "Schechina; das passiv-weibliche Moment in der Gottheit," in *Von der mystischen Gestalt der Gottheit: Studien zu Grundbegriffe der Kabbala* (Frankfort, 1973), p. 142.

14. Quoted in H. H. Rowley, "The Interpretation of the Song of Songs," in *The Servant of the Lord and Other Essays on the Old Testament* (London, 1952), p. 233, n.3.

15. For an example of a modern lack of sympathy with mystical interpretations, see Marvin Pope, *Song of Songs: A New Translation with Introduction and Commentary* (Garden City, N.Y., 1977), pp. 112-32. Some students of mysticism have been even less sympathetic to the influence of the Song—witness W. R. Inge, who remarks: "As to the Song of Solomon, its influence upon Christian Mysticism has been simply deplorable" (*Christian Mysticism* [London, 1899], p. 43).

16. Walther Eichrodt, *Theology of the Old Testament* (Philadelphia, 1961), has six citations, while Gerhard von Rad, *Theology of the Old Testament* (New York, 1965), manages only one mention in two volumes of almost 1,000 pages!

17. Rabbi Akiva's saying is found in the Tosefta, Sanhedrin XII, 10. For a fuller discussion, see Pope, *Song of Songs*, p. 19.

18. Origen's *Commentary* survives in partial fashion in a reworked Latin version made by Rufinus. The text may be found in volume 8 of the edition of Origen's works by W. Baehrens, in *Die griechischen christlichen Schriftsteller der ersten drei Jahrhunderten* (Leipzig, 1925), vol. 33. I will cite the work here from the excellent annotated translation of R. P. Lawson, *Origen: The Song of Songs Commentary and Homilies* (Westminster, Md., 1957). On the relation of Origen to earlier Jewish exegesis, see Ephraim E. Urbach, "The Homiletical Interpretations of the Sages and the Expositions of Origen on Canticles, and the Jewish-Christian Disputation," *Scripta Hierosolymitana* 22 (1971): 247-75.

19. Morton Smith, *Clement of Alexandria and a Secret Gospel of Mark* (Cambridge, Mass., 1973), pp. 254-63.

20. The most complete study is that of Klaus Thraede, "Ursprünge und Formen des 'Heiligen Kusses' im frühen Christentum," *Jahrbuch für Antike und Christentum* 11-12 (1968-69): 124-80. For some introductory remarks, see Perella, *Kiss Sacred and Profane*, pp. 12-18.

21. See Stephen Benko, *Pagan Rome and the Early Christians* (Bloomington, Ind., 1986), pp. 79-102.

22. Clement of Alexandria, *Paedagogue* 3.11, vol. 2 of *Ante-Nicene Fathers*, p. 291. Cf. Athenagoras, *Plea* 32.

23. Irenaeus, *Against Heresies* 1.6.3-4, and also the attack on Marcus in 1.13.3-6.

24. Clement of Alexandria, *Miscellanies* 3.2.5-10, 3.4.27-28, 3.6.54.

25. Epiphanius of Salamis, *Panarion* 26. See the account in Benko,

Pagan Rome and the Early Christians, pp. 65-73, based on his earlier article, "The Libertine Gnostic Sect of the Phibionites according to Epiphanius," *Vigiliae Christianae* 21 (1967): 103-19. See also Mircea Eliade, *Occultism, Witchcraft and Cultural Fashions* (Chicago, 1976), pp. 102, 109-13.

26. Gospel of Philip 69.24-29, trans. Wesley W. Isenberg, in James M. Robinson, gen. ed., *The Nag Hammadi Library* (San Francisco, 1977), p. 142.

27. Gospel of Philip 81.34-82.25, in Robinson, *Nag Hammadi Library*, p. 149.

28. The spiritual marriage interpretation has been argued by Michael A. Williams, "Uses of Gender Imagery in Ancient Gnostic Texts," in Caroline Walker Bynum, Stevan Harrell, and Paula Richman, eds., *Gender and Religion: On the Complexity of Symbols* (Boston, 1986), pp. 205-11. Other studies conclude to a real marriage: for example, Robert M. Grant, "The Mystery of Marriage in the Gospel of Philip," *Vigiliae Christianae* 15 (1961): 129-40, and Elaine Pagels, "Adam and Eve, Christ and the Church: A Survey of Second Century Controversies Concerning Marriage," in A. H. B. Logan and A. J. M. Wedderburn, eds., *The New Testament and Gnosis: Essays in Honour of Robert McL. Wilson* (Edinburgh, 1984), pp. 166-70.

29. Gospel of Philip 59.6, in Robinson, *Nag Hammadi Library*, p. 135.

30. Acts of Thomas 1.11-15.

31. Shepherd of Hermas, Sim. IX.11.

32. In the vast literature devoted to this topic, I mention only two useful introductory works: for the basis in scripture, Lucien Legrand, *The Biblical Doctrine of Virginity* (New York, 1963); and for the developments in the early church, Peter Brown, "The Notion of Virginity in the Early Church," in Bernard McGinn and John Meyendorff, eds. (in collaboration with Jean Leclercq), *Christian Spirituality: Origins to the Twelfth Century*, vol. 16 of *World Spirituality: An Encyclopedic History of the Religious Quest* (New York, 1986), pp. 427-43.

33. Irving Singer, *The Nature of Love*, vol. 1: *Plato to Luther*, 2nd ed. (Chicago, 1984), p. 151.

34. Origen, *Commentary*, Prologue 2 (Lawson, *Origen*, pp. 21, 38-39, 58, 84, 181).

35. Origen, *Commentary*, Prologue 2 (Lawson, *Origen*, p. 34).

36. Origen, *Commentary*, Prologue 2 (Lawson, *Origen*, p. 36).

37. Origen, *Commentary*, Prologue 2 (Lawson, *Origen*, pp. 26-27).

38. For example, Origen, *Commentary* 1.4, 2.9, 3.14 (Lawson, *Origen*, pp. 80-81, 162, 240). The most insightful studies of this important theme are two early essays by Karl Rahner, "The 'Spiritual Senses' According to

Origen" and "The Doctrine of the Spiritual Senses in the Middle Ages," available in simplified fashion in English in Rahner, *Theological Investigations* (New York, 1979), vol. 16, pp. 81–134.

39. On how the text itself transforms the reader, see Patricia Cox Miller, "'Pleasure of the Text, Text of Pleasure': Eros and Language in Origen's *Commentary on the Song of Songs*," *Journal of the American Academy of Religion* 54 (1986): 241–53.

40. Jerome, Letter XXII, in *St. Jerome: Select Letters*, Loeb Classical Library (Cambridge, Mass., 1980), pp. 54–56, 86, 88, 94, 108–10, 112, 156, 158. On this letter, see the discussion in J. N. D. Kelley, *Jerome* (New York, 1975), pp. 100–03.

41. Lucretius, *On Nature* 4: 1073–1120.

42. Abelard, *Historia calamitatum*, ed. J. Monfrin (Paris, 1967), pp. 71–75. Debate over the authenticity of this letter and the related correspondence continues.

43. Bernard of Clairvaux also believed that true *amor* was necessarily vehement and violent. See Bernard, *Sermons on the Song of Songs* 79.1.

44. G. Dumeige, *Ives. Epitre à Severin sur la charité. Richard de Saint-Victor. Les quatre degrés de la violent charité* (Paris, 1955), p. 127, lines 12–13. My translations and all citations from Richard of St. Victor are from this critical edition of his work. Among the critical studies, see especially G. Dumeige, *Richard de Saint-Victor et l'idée chrétienne de l'amour* (Paris, 1952), and Leclercq, *Monks on Marriage*, pp. 28–32.

45. Dumeige, *Richard de Saint-Victor*, p. 129, lines 10–12.

46. Dumeige, *Richard de Saint-Victor*, p. 130, lines 22–23.

47. Dumeige, *Richard de Saint-Victor*, p. 139, lines 25–29.

48. Dumeige, *Richard de Saint-Victor*, p. 143, lines 16–19.

49. Dumeige, *Richard de Saint-Victor*, p. 143, line 27; p. 145, line 5.

50. Dumeige, *Richard de Saint-Victor*, p. 145, lines 14–18.

51. Dumeige, *Richard de Saint-Victor*, p. 153, lines 20–29.

52. Dumeige, *Richard de Saint-Victor*, p. 159, lines 7–9: "Prius necesse est egyptiacos cibos deficere et carnales voluptates in abominationem vertere quam experiri liceat que sint ille interne et eterne delicie." This implies that Richard shared Origen's view that the first stage in the pursuit of spiritual eros is the abandonment of the carnal variety, even in its legitimate first degree. It is true that Richard does not state this explicitly, but this would seem to be the case if we can equate the "carnales voluptates" of this passage with the "carnalia desideria" of the description of the first degree of carnal love (p. 145, lines 12–20).

53. Dumeige, *Richard de Saint-Victor*, pp. 161–67, for the treatment of the second degree.

54. Dumeige, *Richard de Saint-Victor*, pp. 167–71.

55. Dumeige, *Richard de Saint-Victor*, pp. 171-75.

56. Etienne Gilson argued against any connection between twelfth-century mystics, especially Bernard, and courtly love traditions in *The Mystical Theology of St. Bernard* (New York, 1955), pp. 170-97. Recent studies have questioned this. See, for example, Jean Deroy, "Thèmes et termes de la fin'amour dans les *Sermons super Cantica Canticorum* de Saint Bernard de Clairvaux," in *Actes du XIIIe Congres International de Linguistique et Philologie romanes* (Quebec, 1976), pp. 853-67.

57. For some useful comments on the historical circumstances that helped Bernard to incorporate this new dimension, see Jean Leclercq, *Monks and Love in Twelfth-Century France* (Oxford, 1979), chap. 2.

58. Leclercq, *Monks on Marriage*.

59. Augustine, Sermon 159.2, in Migne, *Patrologia Latina*, vol. 38, col. 868.

60. Uffing, *De sancta Ida vidua* 1.6: "Quid super hoc convenientius profertur, quam duobus in carne una unam inesse Spiritus sancti indiscissam operationem, quae illos deforis connubiali iure connexos ardentiori caelestium intus inflammavit amore" (*Acta Sanctorum*, Sept. II, p. 262). On this and similar texts, see Leclercq, *Monks on Marriage*, pp. 48-52.

61. Leclercq, *Monks on Marriage*, p. 37. Lothario Segni, *De quadripertita specie nuptiarum*, in Migne, *Patrologia Latina*, vol. 219, cols. 921-68.

62. *The Book of Margery Kempe. A Modern Version by W. Butler-Bowden* (New York, 1944), I.21, p. 39.

63. The first Christian writer who reversed the polarities by using the language of spiritual love to highlight the primacy of sexual love was John Donne, according to Irving Singer, *The Nature of Love*, vol. 2: *Courtly and Romantic* (Chicago, 1984), pp. 195-205. On Donne's religious use of the language of sexual union, see also Robert S. Jackson, *John Donne's Christian Vocation* (Evanston, Ill., 1970), esp. chap. 6.

64. For clarifications on the distinction between using sexual language as a metaphor for the divine encounter and employing sexual activity itself for religious and mystical purposes, I am thankful to my colleague Wendy Doniger.

65. For the remarks that follow, I am indebted to Arthur Green for the use of his unpublished paper, "The Song of Songs in Jewish Mysticism." Among other works, see especially Moshe Idel, "Métaphores et pratiques sexuelles dans la Cabale," in *Lettre sur la Sainteté*, trans. and commentaries by Charles Mopsik (Paris, 1986), pp. 327-58.

66. Quoted in Green, "Song of Songs in Jewish Mysticism," pp. 7-8.

67. Idel, "Métaphores et pratiques sexuelles dans la Cabale," p. 332.

68. See Gershom Scholem, *Major Trends in Jewish Mysticism* (New York, 1961), pp. 95-96.

69. See Lawrence Fine, "Kabbalistic Texts," in Barry W. Holtz, ed., *Back to the Sources: Reading Classic Jewish Texts* (New York, 1984), pp. 350-51, and Arthur Green, "Religion and Mysticism: The Case of Judaism," in Jacob Neusner, ed., *Take Judaism, For Example* (Chicago, 1983), pp. 79-82.

70. Scholem, "Schechina," pp. 152-56.

71. On these authors, see Green, "Song of Songs in Jewish Mysticism," pp. 11-15, and Georges Vajda, *L'Amour de Dieu dans la théologie juive du moyen âge* (Paris, 1957), pp. 195-97, 233-36.

72. Idel, "Métaphores et pratiques sexuelles dans la Cabale," pp. 330, 333-35.

73. Idel notes that the human male lover stands between two females, his wife and the *Shekhinah*, while the *Shekhinah* stands between the male *Sefirah* and the male Kabbalist ("Métaphores et pratiques sexuelles dans la Cabale," p. 346).

74. For example, *Zohar* 2:147a, trans. Daniel Matt, *Zohar: The Book of Enlightenment*, The Classics of Western Spirituality Series (New York, 1983), p. 130. The most complete, though still partial, translation of the *Zohar* into English is that of Harry Sperling and Maurice Simon, *The Zohar*, 2nd ed. (London, 1984).

75. See the selections from the Idra Zutra section (3:287b-288a, 291a-b, 296b) (Matt, *Zohar*, pp. 182-89).

76. For accounts of the Sefirotic system, begin with the Sixth Lecture in Scholem, *Major Trends in Jewish Mysticism*; more recent helpful studies are to be found in Matt, *Zohar*, pp. 33-37, and Arthur Green, "The Zohar: Jewish Mysticism in Medieval Spain," in Paul Szarmach, ed., *An Introduction to the Medieval Mystics of Europe* (Albany, N.Y., 1984), pp. 115-23.

77. On phallic symbolism associated with *Yesod*, see, for example, *Zohar* 1:162a, 2:128ab, 3:5ab, 26a.

78. Scholem, "Schechina," pp. 157-65. The sexual symbolism of the *Bahir* is restrained in comparison with the Spanish texts.

79. On these marriages, see especially Scholem, *Major Trends in Jewish Mysticism*, pp. 225-31, and Green, "Zohar," pp. 117-26.

80. *Zohar* 3:114b (Matt, *Zohar*, p. 157). See also 1:162ab.

81. *Zohar* 2:245a (Green, "Zohar," p. 124).

82. See, for example, *Zohar* 1:148ab (Matt, *Zohar*, pp. 77-78). For more on this, see Scholem, "Schechina," pp. 183-86, and Green, "Zohar," p. 125.

83. I am dependent here on an unpublished essay by Karen Guberman, "'To walk in all his ways' (Deut. 11:22): A Kabbalistic Sexual Ethic," pp. 7-8.

84. For example, *Zohar* 2:54b; cf. 1:228b, 2:101a, 3:124a.
85. *Zohar* 2:15 (Green, "Zohar," p. 108).
86. Idel, "Métaphores et pratiques sexuelles dans la Cabale," p. 352.
87. See Green, "Zohar," pp. 125, 128-29. This distances the *Zohar*, I think, from Oriental forms of the use of eroticism in spiritual programs, especially in devotional Hinduism where extramarital, or "lawless," love becomes the model for the divine–human encounter. See Wendy Doniger O'Flaherty, "Sexual Doubles and Sexual Masquerades: The Structure of Sex Symbols," University Lecture in Religion at Arizona State University (April 10, 1986), p. 10, and Mircea Eliade, *Yoga* (Princeton, N.J., 1973), pp. 264-65.
88. For example, *Zohar*, 3:44b.
89. On this early-fourteenth-century text, see Daniel Matt, "David ben Yehudah Hehasid and His Book of Mirrors," in *Hebrew Union College Annual* (Cincinnati, 1980), pp. 129-72; the quotation is on p. 171. For a comparable text in the *Zohar*, see 3:7a.
90. I will see the edition and translation of Seymour J. Cohen, *The Holy Letter: A Study in Medieval Jewish Sexual Morality Ascribed to Nahmanides* (New York, 1976); the quotation is on p. 48.
91. Cohen, *Holy Letter*, p. 60.
92. Idel, "Métaphores et pratiques sexuelles dans la Cabale," p. 344.
93. *Asclepius* 21: "si enim illud extremum temporis, quo ex crebro adtritu pervenimus, ut utraque in utramque fundat natura progeniem, animadvertas, ut altera avide alterius rapiat venerem interiusque recondat, denique eo tempore ex commixtione communi et virtutem feminae marum adipiscuntur et mares femineo torpore lassescunt" (A. D. Nock, ed., in *Corpus Hermeticum* [Paris, 1960], vol. 2, pp. 322-23).
94. For a succinct formulation of the differences, see Scholem, *Major Trends in Jewish Mysticism*, p. 235.
95. On the Holy Spirit as the Kiss, see the texts gathered in Perella, *Kiss Sacred and Profane*, pp. 253-59, and Bertrand de Margerie, *The Christian Trinity in History* (Still River, Mass., 1982), pp. 26-31.
96. The Holy Spirit was usually viewed as female in early Syriac Christianity. See, for example, Robert Murray, *Symbols of Church and Kingdom: A Study in Early Syriac Tradition* (Cambridge, 1975), pp. 143-44.
97. Hildegard of Bingen may form an exception with her visions of the divine figure of *Sapientia* as God's Bride: for example, *Scivias* III.9.25; *Liber vitae meritorum* I.46, III.8, IV.38; and *Epistola* 142.
98. See Carolyn Walker Bynum, *Jesus as Mother: Studies in the Spirituality of the High Middle Ages* (Berkeley, 1982), esp. chap. 4.
99. Some texts from Augustine are translated and discussed in Perella, *Kiss Sacred and Profane*, pp. 47-48. To these can be added a number of

passages from the bishop's *Ennarationes in Psalmos*: for example, *In Ps.* 32., En. II.7; *In Ps.* 33., En. II.6; *In Ps.* 35.5 (Migne, *Patrologia Latina*, vol. 38, col. 282, 310-11, 344).

100. Giovanni Pico della Mirandola, *Commento* on Stanza 4, in Eugenio Garin, ed., *G. Pico della Mirandola. De hominis dignitate, etc.* (Florence, 1942), p. 557. I have used the translation by Sears Jayne, *Commentary on a Canzone of Benivieni* (New York, 1984), p. 150.

101. Ramon Lull, *The Book of the Lover and Beloved*, trans. E. Allison Peers (New York, 1978), p. 73.

102. Bataille, *Death and Sensuality*, p. 15; cf. p. 248.

103. Bataille, *Death and Sensuality*, pp. 22-23, 245-49.

104. Bataille, *Death and Sensuality*, pp. 89-90, 118-26.

105. Bataille, *Death and Sensuality*, pp. 224-26. Bataille writes: "With this in mind we might say that sensuality is to mysticism as a clumsy try is to a perfect achievement, and no doubt we ought to ignore what is after all a wrong turning on the spirit's road to sovereignty" (p. 249).

106. James Leuba, *The Psychology of Religious Mysticism* (1925; reprint, London, 1972), p. 138.

107. Leuba, *Psychology of Religious Mysticism*, p. 144.

108. Singer, *Nature of Love*, vol. 1, pp. 182-83. See also L. Beinaert, "La Signification du symbolisme conjugal dans la vie mystique," in Beinaert, *Experience chrétienne et psychologie* (Paris, 1964), p. 427.

109. Simone Weil, *The Notebooks of Simone Weil*, trans. Arthur Wills (London, 1976), vol. 2, p. 472.

110. Italo Calvino, *The Uses of Literature: Essays* (New York, 1986), p. 66.

111. Augustine, *On Christian Doctrine*, trans., with an introduction, by D. W. Robertson, Jr. (Indianapolis, 1958). I.6, pp. 10-11.

112. On the transformative and descriptive functions of mystical language, see Frederick J. Streng, "Language and Mystical Awareness," in Steven T. Katz, ed., *Mysticism and Philosophical Analysis* (New York, 1978), pp. 141-69. Several other papers in this collection take up the question of the ineffability of mystical language, notably Steven T. Katz, "Language, Epistemology, and Mysticism," pp. 54-56; Peter Moore, "Mystical Experience, Mystical Doctrine, Mystical Technique," pp. 102-6; and Renford Bambrough, "Intuition and the Inexpressible," pp. 206-8.

113. Cohen, *Holy Letter*, p. 50. See also the midrash on Genesis 4:1 attributed to Rabbi Akiva in Ber. Rab. 22:2: "There is no man without woman, and no woman without man, and no pair of them without the *Shekhinah*."

10
Bonaventure's Mysticism of Language
EWERT H. COUSINS

Mysticism stands in a paradoxical relation to language. The very term "mysticism," in its etymological meaning, suggests the limits of language, derived as it is from the Indo-European root *mu* (imitative of inarticulate sounds). From this root are derived the Latin *mutus* (mute, dumb, silent) and the Greek verb *myein* (to close the eyes or lips), from which come the nouns *mysterion* (mystery) and *mystes* (one initiated into the mysteries) as well as the adjective/substantive *mystikos* (mystical, mystic). These terms have their cultural context in ancient Greece in what have been called the mystery religions. When aspirants were initiated into these secret rites, such as the Eleusinian mysteries, they incurred a grave obligation to seal their lips forever on what was enacted there and what they had experienced. In fact, so effective was this taboo that, although countless Greek and Roman citizens over a period of more than six centuries were initiated into the Eleusinian mysteries, with few exceptions they revealed nothing of the secrets, thus leaving the nature of the Eleusinian rites and the personal experience of the initiates largely to scholarly conjecture.[1]

In Christianity, the gap between mysticism and language was widened by the treatise of the Pseudo-Dionysius entitled *The Mystical Theology*. Written in the fifth or sixth century, this text has exercised a major influence on the subsequent history of spirituality in the Christian East and West. The author provided a mystical ascent to God by means of the systematic negation of language—of all sense impressions, images, words, and concepts. The Pseudo-Dionysius thus charted what became the classical version of the apophatic way, whose technical designation is derived from the Greek *phasis* (speech) and *apo* (away from). Thus the apophatic way is the path of the negation of language, of nonspeech or nonlanguage. This contrasted with the kataphatic way spelled out in the earlier treatise of the Pseudo-Dionysius, *On the Divine Names*. In this context "kataphatic" means the way of affirmation, from *phasis* (speech) and *kata* (according to). The Pseudo-Dionysius—and with him much of the subsequent tradition—favored the apophatic rather than the kataphatic way. Thus the original meaning of "mystical" as hidden or secret became associated with the spiritual technique of the negation of language.

In the Middle Ages in western Europe, the Latin adjective *mysticus* (mystical) took on a specialized meaning in relation to the interpretation of the Christian Scriptures. In the writings of theologians, it came to refer to the spiritual, symbolic, or allegorical meaning of a sacred text, as contrasted with its literal meaning. Thus the medieval Latin term echoed its original Greek root in that it referred to a level of meaning that is secret—lying hidden beneath the more obvious literal meaning of the text.

In their evolution, the English adjectives "mystic" and "mystical" carried the medieval Latin meaning, as the early examples in the *Oxford English Dictionary* attest.[2] However, this meaning waned with the decline of the allegorical interpretation of Scripture and shifted to the realm of extraordinary religious experience, as was the case in the emergence of the term "mysticism," whose earliest example is listed in the *Oxford English Dictionary* under 1736 from a text by H. Coventry entitled *Philemon*: "How much nobler a Field of Exercise . . . are the seraphic Entertainments of Mysticism and Extasy than the mean and ordinary Practice of a more earthly and Common Virtue!"[3]

Although the focus of the English term "mysticism" has shifted from its Greek etymological source, the original ambivalence toward language perdures. For in focusing on extraordinary ecstatic experience, it has highlighted the gap between mysticism and language. Thus we can view the Eleusinian mysteries not only as a stage in the development of the term "mysticism," but also as a symbol of the negative relation that has existed between mysticism and language from the earliest times. This has led to the common attitude that concerning mystical experience one should *not* speak. Those who have been initiated into mystical experience should bind their tongue and close their lips. They must not break the taboo, for what they have experienced is holy and should not be desecrated by the profane words of everyday speech. Furthermore, between ecstasy and language there opens an infinite abyss. To speak would be futile. Besides, even if language were commensurate with the experience, it would be meaningless and even deceptive for hearers who themselves have not been initiated into the experience. Far better to remain silent. If one does speak, he or she should use the language of negation, apophatic language, the language of nonspeech.

Mysticism of Language

In the light of the Eleusinian taboo, it may seem sacrilegious to speak of the mysticism *of* language, as the title of this essay states. If one should not speak at all about mystical experience, how can there be a mysticism in and through language? Is not language merely an inadequate instrument to express an ineffable mystical experience? If language shapes mystical experience, can it penetrate into its very core? Can one have an ecstatic mystical experience of language itself?

In approaching these questions, we must realize that the Eleusinian mysteries do not tell the whole story. Throughout the centuries, not all mystics have kept the tight-lipped code of Eleusis. Quite the contrary! Mystics simply have not been silent. Many have spoken without restraint, and others have written voluminously. The genre of mystical literature is not only quantitatively vast, but linguistically luxuriant. In mystical discourse, language runs riot: it leaps, it vaults, it sings. It speaks in prose and poetry; it gives objective descriptions of experience and flies on the wings of ecstasy; it guides neophytes with gentle care and cuts through illusion with razor-sharp arguments. Mystical language can be kataphatic in the extreme, chanting the ninety-nine beautiful names of Allah, or evoking the images of the "three-million" gods and goddesses of the Hindu pantheon. No genre of writing can rival it for complexity, subtlety, and linguistic virtuosity. Furthermore, certain mystics have had their mystical experiences in and through language. By this I mean not only that language evokes and shapes the experience, but that the linguistic forms participate in and reveal the transcendent realm. In this sense, there can be a mysticism *of* language. In fact, for certain Christian mystics language is the key to the inner life of God — so much so that the mystic who experiences this divine life can say that expressive language constitutes the very inner reality of God.

One of the major exponents of this type of linguistic mysticism was Bonaventure, the thirteenth-century Franciscan theologian and spiritual writer who holds a position of eminence in the history of Christian spirituality. He is the chief interpreter of the mysticism of Francis of Assisi and one of the most systematic writers on mysticism in the Middle Ages. His treatise *The Soul's Journey into God*, which is an acknowledged classic in its own right, also presents the closest thing we have to a medieval *summa* of Christian mysticism. Of special interest for our concerns is the fact that he has an elaborated theory of the relation of language and mysticism. This theory is not merely peripheral to his thought, but stands at the very center of his philosophy, theology, and spirituality.

Although I am presenting Bonaventure as a case study, he is not an isolated instance. On the contrary, he is one of the most eloquent spokesmen of the Neoplatonic tradition in the history of Christianity. From the time of Augustine until the Reformation and even beyond, Christian Neoplatonism was the mainstream philosophical-theological tradition in the spirituality of Western Christianity. Hence in viewing Bonaventure, we are observing the tradition that in one way or another touched the majority of Western Christian mystics — at least those in the learned stratum of culture — during more than a millennium of Christian history, and that continues to be a living force into the present. In addition to its historical importance, I believe that the Christian Neoplatonic tradition, as expounded by Bonaventure, contains philosophical and theological resources that are relevant to the present academic exploration of the relation between language and mysticism.

During the recent decades in the West, the academic community has attempted to come to grips with a changing context for its study of mysticism. The vast amount of data gathered from the history of religions has produced a pendulum swing from a focus on the unity of mystical experience to its varieties. At the same time in the Anglo-Saxon world, attention has been directed to the philosophical analysis of language. Originally stimulated by the role of language in the empirical sciences, philosophers have extended their investigations into the relation of language and mysticism. The recent linguistic turn in the academic study of mysticism has proved fruitful in clarifying issues and in stimulating discussion, but it runs the risk of operating within a narrow horizon. It would, I believe, yield its most significant fruit if it were situated within the history of the discussion, which has continued for centuries in the world's religions, on the paradoxical relation of language and mysticism. In this paper, I will attempt to enlarge the present horizon of investigation by giving Bonaventure's position on the mysticism of language.

I will begin by presenting Bonaventure's doctrine of the Trinity, which is the ground of his philosophical, theological, and mystical treatment of language. Then, I will show how he specifically links creation, as God's language, and human language to the Trinity. In conclusion, I will show the bearing of Bonaventure's position on the current academic discussion of language and mysticism.

The Son as the Father's Language

For Bonaventure, the Trinity provides the foundation of the worldview within which he sees language related to mysticism. The Trinity is primarily the mystery of the divine self-expression, the divine speech uttered from all eternity in the Word. Hence the divinity is dynamic and expressive; from all eternity the fecundity of the divinity wells up in the person of the Father and expresses itself in its perfect Image and Word, who is the Son, and who is joined to the Father in the love of the Holy Spirit. Thus we can say that the Son is the linguistic expression of the Father—the Language of the Father. Because of this, human language is not merely functional— an instrument or a tool for operating in society. Rather, it has its grounding in the most intimate life of the divinity. One can say that at its very apex and center — on the level of the Absolute — reality is linguistic. Note — and this is crucial for our study — that language is expressive of the ultimate mystery: the abyss of fecundity that is the Father. This relation of the Son as Word, Image, Language expressing the Father as ultimate abyss of mystery is the basis of Bonaventure's treatment of human language and mysticism.

Bonaventure's doctrine of the Trinity follows that of the Greek Fathers in focusing on the Father as the ground of unity in the Trinity and the dynamic source of the processions. This is in contrast with the approach of Augustine, and later Thomas Aquinas, which focuses on the common divine nature as the ground of the unity of the persons. In the latter tradition, the persons are seen as mutual relations, whose differentiation contrasts with the unity of the divine nature. In the Augustinian approach, attention is directed to the Trinity as the mystery of unity and difference in an abstract and static fashion. This is contrasted with the Greek Fathers' emphasis on the dynamism of the Father as the fountain source of the Trinitarian processions that in Bonaventure becomes especially focused as the linguistic expression of the Father.

Thoroughly developed, even in his early writings, this theme permeates the corpus of Bonaventure's works. One of the finest summaries of his position is found in his last work, *Collations on the Six Days of Creation*, delivered in April 1273, the year before his death. In the first of this series of lectures, Bonaventure says: "The Father generated one similar to himself, namely the Word, co-eternal with himself; and he expressed his own likeness and as a consequence expressed all the things that he could make."[4] In Bonaventure's early work, *Commentary on the Sentences of Peter Lombard*, he developed the dynamism of the Father to express himself, basing his position on the Neoplatonic principle of the fecundity of primacy. He writes of primacy:

> ... but the more primary a thing is, the more it is fecund and the principle of others. Therefore just as the divine essence, because it is first, is the principle of other essences, so the person of the Father, since he is the first, because from no one, is the principle and has fecundity in regard to persons.[5]

In the same book of his *Commentary on the Sentences*, he draws from the Neoplatonic *Liber de causis* to establish his notion of the

Father as fountain-fulness (*fontalis plenitudo*). Although Bonaventure erroneously attributes the *Liber de causis* to Aristotle, it became clear in the thirteenth century that the work was not by Aristotle, but by an Arabian philosopher familiar with Proculus's *Elements of Theology*. Bonaventure writes:

> A further reason for this opinion is found in the dictum of the Philosopher which states that the more primary causes are, the greater power they have, and that the first cause has greater influence and that the cause that is absolutely first has an influence in every respect. Therefore if we see in the order of causes, among which is the order of essence, that primacy involves in a cause the highest influence and a greater influence according to essence; in a similar way, where there is an order of person, primacy in the first person is the reason for the production of other persons. And since innascibility signifies primacy, it follows that it signifies fountain-fulness [*fontalem plenitudinem*] in relation to the production of persons.[6]

Later, in *The Soul's Journey into God*, Bonaventure bases the dynamism of the Father on the self-diffusiveness of the Good. By contemplating the Good as self-diffusive, one can arrive at the Trinity: "For the good is said to be self-diffusive; therefore the highest good must be most self-diffusive." In a tightly reasoned passage, Bonaventure concludes that the absolute self-diffusiveness of the Father must culminate in the generation of the Son and the spiration of the Holy Spirit. It would be impossible, Bonaventure observes, for creation to activate the fulness of the divine capacity for self-diffusion: "The diffusion in time in creation is no more than a center or point in relation to the immensity of the divine goodness."[7]

If we grant that the inner life of God is characterized by the fountain-fulness of fecundity and the fulness of the self-diffusion of the Good, does this warrant our seeing this as a kind of divine language? Note that Bonaventure does not see this as merely any kind of fecundity or self-diffusion. It is precisely the dynamism of the divinity to express itself. Hence the Son is the Image, the Word or Logos of the Father. In metaphysical terms, the Word is the determinate pole of the divinity that completely expresses the two basic aspects of the Father: the divine abyss and the divine power of self-expression. The Son is the perfect expression of the Father;

hence there are not many divine words, in the Trinitarian sense, but one divine Word. In the case of God we have the perfect language, for one Word, since it is infinite and perfect, is sufficient to express the fulness of the divine fecundity. We can say, then, that only in the Trinity does one find the perfect Language.

The Language of Creation

The Word in the Trinity—the perfect language of the Father—is the ground of all finite language in creation. When from all eternity the Father expresses his boundless fecundity in his Word, he expresses also the eternal ideas or forms of all that he can create in space and time. As Bonaventure says: "From all eternity the Father generated a Son similar to himself and expressed himself and his likeness similar to himself and with this his entire capacity. He expressed what he could make, and especially what he wished to make, and he expressed everything in him, that is, in his Son or in that center as in his Art."[8] Within the Logos, then, the Father generated the *logoi*, or eternal forms, which are simultaneously the reflection of the Father's fecundity and the metaphysical foundation of all creatures. These eternal forms are the Platonic ideas—the divine intelligible structures—which since the time of Augustine, Christian theologians in the West situated in the mind of God.

According to Bonaventure, the Word contains the ideas not only of universals but also of singulars: "Because the divine wisdom is most perfect, it knows most distinctly universal and singular things and represents all these things most distinctly and perfectly. Hence it is said to have the forms and ideas of singular things as the most perfectly expressive likenesses of things."[9] Creatures not only exist in their exemplars in the divine Word, but have their greatest reality there. Hence we will know them most truly when we know them in the Word. Since these eternal ideas represent God preeminently, Bonaventure can say, "I will see myself better in God than in my very self."[10]

It is important to note that for Bonaventure these are not merely static paradigms of the changing phenomenal world. Rather, they are intradivine structures that have as their primary raison d'être the expression of the divine fecundity—the fountain-fulness of the

Father. The very dynamism from which they flow is imparted to them in the Word and flows from them into creation. For when the divinity determines to create—and to create a specific universe—the energy of the act of creation flows from the same wellspring of self-expressiveness that generates the Word and the eternal ideas. Thus the formal structure of the phenomenal world—in all its complexity and intricacy—is the language of God, in a much more profound sense than human language is an expression of the human person. For the intelligible structures of the phenomenal world are external expressions of the very internal reality of the Word as Logos.

This intimate, expressive, linguistic relationship between God and the world establishes the metaphysics of exemplarism whereby all creatures reflect the Word as their eternal exemplar. This leads Bonaventure to call the world a mirror reflecting God, a stained-glass window in which the divine light is reflected in various colors. It is like a statue depicting God and a road leading to God. With technical precision, Bonaventure analyzes how creatures reflect God in varying degrees: as shadow, vestige, image, and similitude. Shadow refers to the generic reflection of God by all creatures; vestige, to the more specific reflection of the Trinity in the power, wisdom, and goodness of all creatures. Image refers to the reflection of God within the consciousness of rational creatures, especially in human memory, intellect, and will; similitude, to the reflection of God in these same faculties reformed by grace.[11]

In this perception of the world, Bonaventure was profoundly influenced by Francis of Assisi. Throughout his writings, he interprets the nature mysticism of Francis in the light of his understanding of the expressive Trinity and the metaphysics of exemplarism. In his biography of Francis, he eloquently describes Francis's mystical experience of creation in terms that simultaneously evoke the experience and suggest the Trinitarian-exemplaristic ontology that he spells out more technically in his philosophical-theological works:

> Aroused by all things to the love of God,
> he [Francis] *rejoiced in all* the works of the Lord's hands[12]
> and from these joy-producing manifestations
> he rose to their life-giving
> principle and cause.

> In beautiful things
> he saw Beauty itself
> and through his *vestiges* imprinted on creation
> *he followed his Beloved* everywhere,[13]
> making from all things a ladder
> by which he could climb up
> and embrace him *who is utterly desirable*.[14]
> With a feeling of unprecedented devotion
> he savored
> in each and every creature —
> as in so many rivulets —
> that Goodness
> which is their fountain-source.
> And he perceived a heavenly harmony
> in the consonance of powers and activities
> God has given them,
> and like the prophet David
> sweetly exhorted them to praise the Lord.[15]

The final sentence refers to Francis's own expression of his mystical experience of nature in *The Canticle of Brother Sun*, composed in 1225 about a year and a half before his death.[16] In the canticle, he praises God in and through creatures: the sun, moon, stars, earth, air, fire, and water. The following is the central verse of the canticle, which treats the sun as part of God's expressive language of creation, for it "bears the signification of you, Most High One."

> Praised be you, my Lord, with all your creatures,
> Especially Sir Brother Sun,
> Who is the day and through whom you give us light.
> And he is beautiful and radiant with great splendor,
> And bears the signification of you, Most High One.[17]

The entire canticle is permeated by the conception that creatures are the language of God in their very being and as such express God. This expression contains within it an implicit praise of God. Hence in the last verse, Francis calls on all creatures to bring this divine expressive language to its full term by praising God in return:

> Praise and bless my Lord and give him thanks
> And serve him with great humility.[18]

The Book of Creation

When treating the Trinity, Bonaventure uses terms drawn from the sphere of language, such as "expression," "speaking," and "Word." When dealing with God's expression in creation, he draws terms from the visual sphere, such as "light" and "mirror," and artistic forms of expression, such a "image" and "statue." However, it would be completely consonant with his vision, and in the spirit of Francis, to speak of the world as the expressive language of God — his poem, canticle, and hymn. In this perspective, then, one could look on creatures as God's nouns; their energy, his verbs; their interrelation, his prepositions and conjunctions. Their complex patterns reveal his grammar and logic; their organic unfolding in space and time, his rhetoric. There is a basis for this linguistic imagery in Bonaventure's use of the theme of the book. In key passages he applies the notion of the book both to creation and to the Word in the Trinity, frequently citing the text from Scripture that speaks of "the book written within and without" (Apoc. 5:1; Ezek. 2:9). He applies "the book written within" to the Word in the Trinity and "the book written without" to creation.[19]

In the second article of the first of the *Disputed Questions on the Mystery of the Trinity*, he speaks of a threefold book: the book of creation, the book of Scripture, and the book of life:

> ... there is a threefold testimony by which we are led, obliged, and elevated to believe it [the mystery of the Trinity]. ... This threefold testimony is the concern of a threefold book; namely, the book of creation, the book of Scripture, and the book of life. ... The book of creation, which I call the first book because it appeals to our senses, offers a twofold witness. ... Every creature is either a mere vestige of God — as is corporeal nature — or an image of God, as is the intellectual creature.[20]

Although the book of creation gives testimony of the Trinity, human beings have been hindered by sin from reading this book accurately. In one passage, Bonaventure says that creation has become a foreign language to us: "Like an unlettered layman who holds a book but has no interest in it, so are we; for this scripture has become Greek to us, a barbarian language and Hebrew, and completely unknown in its source."[21] Hence it was necessary for God to give us another book — the book of Scripture. Bonaventure says:

But when the sins of man had weakened his sight, then that mirror was made dark and obscure, and the ear of our inner understanding was hardened against hearing that testimony. For this reason, divine providence saw fit to provide the testimony of another book; namely, that of the book of Scripture which was written in accord with the divine revelation.[22]

Bonaventure turns finally to the book of life, a term that refers to the Word in the Trinity. The book of life is the source and meaning of the other two books, for both creation and Scripture have their origin and significance there. This book illumines the minds of human beings to read and understand the book of creation and the book of Scripture. Not only does the Word reveal the meaning of these books by direct illumination of the mind, but by the greatest of all divine expressions—the incarnate Word, Jesus of Nazareth. For Bonaventure the fullest divine expression occurs in the incarnation, which restores the capacity of fallen humanity to perceive the light of eternal Truth. In *The Soul's Journey into God*, he states: "Our soul could not rise completely from these things of sense to see itself and the Eternal Truth in itself unless Truth, assuming human nature in Christ had become a ladder, restoring the first ladder that had been broken in Adam."[23]

Mysticism of Human Language

Bonaventure does not limit his treatment of the mysticism of language to the Word in the Trinity and the divine expression in creation. Rather, he focuses directly on human language itself as a locus and vehicle of mystical experience. Human beings are not only part of the book of creation, but also recipients of its communication. They can read the book of creation and penetrate to its meaning in the book of life, the Logos—Meaning Itself. From another perspective, human beings are like the Trinity, for they, too, have the gift of language and can express themselves in language and artistic creation. Two of Bonaventure's treatises—*The Soul's Journey into God* and *On Retracing the Arts to Theology*—examine the mysticism of language. The first deals primarily with the contemplative reading of the book of creation as God's communication, and the second with sharing in the dynamic expressionism of the Trinity.

In chapter 3 of *The Soul's Journey into God*, Bonaventure explores the soul as image of the Trinity. The soul is an image because the Trinity is imprinted in the depths of its memory, understanding, and will as Eternity, Truth, and Goodness. It is in his treatment of the reflection of God as Truth in the intellect that we encounter his mysticism of language.

He proceeds through the method of *reductio*—that is, beginning with a finite form or structure and "leading it back" to its divine ground. "The function of the intellective faculty," he says, "consists in understanding the meaning of terms, propositions, and influences." He proceeds: "Now, the intellect grasps the meaning of terms when it comprehends in a definition what a thing is. But definitions are constructed by using more universal terms; and these are defined by more universal terms until we come to the most universal." This leads Bonaventure to absolute being, for "unless we know what being per se is, we cannot know the definition of any particular substance." He then proceeds through a dialectic of being as perfect and imperfect. Our knowledge of imperfect being implies that we know absolute Being:

> Since privations and defects can in no way be known except through something positive, our intellect does not come to the point of understanding any created being by a full analysis unless it is aided by a knowledge of the Being which is most perfect, most actual, most complete and absolute, which is unqualified and Eternal Being, in which are the principles of all things in their purity.[24]

This passage reveals the essence of Bonaventure's epistemology, which he develops extensively throughout his writings. With Augustine he holds that we have an immediate and direct awareness of God, imprinted by God in our souls. This is a subliminal nonconceptual awareness, a direct intuition of the divinity, which can be brought to self-consciousness by the technique of *reductio* and to luminous consciousness in mystical ecstasy. This epistemological structure of human knowledge provides the basis for a mysticism of gnosis or knowledge that seeks God as absolute Truth in the ground of the intellect. This epistemology presupposes the metaphysics of exemplarism, as presented above. The Word or Logos in the Trinity is the absolute ground of the stability and objectivity of truth, which our minds have access to. The truth, then, of our conceptual processes and our linguistic expression does not depend exclusively on our changing subjective minds but is grounded in the unchanging objectivity of absolute Truth. It is important to point out that this is not a mysticism of the divine abyss, of the Godhead above God, but of the determinate pole of the divinity: the divine Logos as the ground and the light of truth. This Logos, to be sure, is not the whole of the divinity, for it emerges out of the Father, the abyss and fecundity of the divinity, as its perfect expression. Our words, then, can be true because they are grounded in that eternal Word, who is the ultimate true Word who perfectly expresses the Father.[25]

These aspects of Logos mysticism are further highlighted in Bonaventure's treatment of propositions and inferences: "The intellect can be said truly to comprehend the meaning of propositions when it knows with certitude that they are true." When the intellect knows with certitude, it knows a truth as unchangeable: "But since the mind itself is changeable, it can see such a truth shining forth unchangingly only by means of some light which shines in an absolutely unchangeable way; and it is impossible for this light to be a changeable creature." At this point Bonaventure turns to the eternal Logos as the unchangeable ground of truth: "Therefore our intellect knows in that Light *which enlightens every man coming into this world*, which is *the true Light* and the Word who *was in the beginning with God*" (Jn. 1:9, 1).[26]

In a similar way, "our intellect truly grasps the meaning of an inference when it sees that the conclusion follows necessarily from the premises." Such necessary inferences can be seen both in necessary and in contingent terms. For example, in the inference that if a man is running, he is moving, the connection is necessarily true whether such a man exists or not. The necessity does not come from the man's existence, which is contingent, but "from its exemplarity in the Eternal Art, according to which things are mutually oriented and related to one another because they are represented in the Eternal Art." By "Eternal Art" Bonaventure means the Word of Logos as the expression of the Father. When the Father expresses himself in the Logos, he expresses not only all the divine ideas, but also their interrelationship. "From this," Bonaventure says, "it is obvious that our intellect is joined to Eternal Truth itself since it can grasp no truth with certitude if it is not taught by this Truth."[27]

He develops this approach further in the fourth of the *Disputed Questions on Christ's Knowledge*. There he asks whether whatever we know with certitude is known in the eternal reason (*in ratione aeterna*). He answers in the affirmative: "For certain intellectual knowledge even in this life, it is required that we attain in some way the eternal reason, as the regulating and motive reason, but not in all its clarity, but along with our own created reason and as in a glass darkly." In our everyday knowledge, we experience the divine light of Truth, but it is bound up with our own created light of knowing (*propria ratio creata*) and the abstract concepts and impressions drawn from the sense world (*rerum similitudines abstractas a phantasmate*), which constitute so much of our language. Bonaventure says that the eternal reason or Logos is "contuited" (*contuita*), known along with many other elements.[28] "Contuition" is a fundamental concept for Bonaventure and touches the heart of his Franciscan experience and specifically his mysticism of language. It means that we see God along with creation and our conceptual and linguistic patterns. This does not mean that all our knowledge is derived from sense data; he says quite explicitly that "the soul knows God and itself and what is in itself without the aid of our exterior senses."[29] This innate awareness of God can be awakened by the exercise of contuition through the technique of contemplative *reductio*, and it can be brought to ecstatic awareness by divine grace.

Image of Expressive Trinity

For Bonaventure, the soul contemplates the Trinity not only *through* the mirror of language, but also *in* the mirror of its own expressive use of language. The soul is the image of the Trinity in its faculties of memory, understanding, and will, each of which provides a path to the divinity. For example, memory—taken here in the Platonic sense—leads one to the divinity as Eternal ground, and hence to the Father; intellect, as we have seen, leads to the Son as Truth; and will leads to the divine Goodness or Love, and hence to the Holy Spirit. But these faculties also lead one to the Trinity in view of their dynamic interrelation. Bonaventure develops this theme in *The Soul's Journey into God*: "From memory intelligence comes forth as its offspring, since we understand when a likeness which is in the memory leaps into the eye of the intellect in the form of a word. From memory and intelligence love is breathed forth as their mutual bond."[30] This means that in our use of language—in our internal thinking and in our external expression—we reflect the dynamic process of the inner Trinitarian life, as described earlier. For Bonaventure—and the mainstream Western Christian theological tradition—we are Trinitarian images precisely in our linguistic activity. In our formulation and expression of words we mirror the inner Trinitarian life.

This perception allows Bonaventure to explore as a reflection of the Trinity the disciplines related to language. Following a medieval convention, he divides rational philosophy into grammar, logic, and rhetoric, which he sees as a mirror of the Trinity. For "grammar . . . makes men able to express themselves," and thus reflects the expressive power of the Father; "logic . . . makes them skilled in arguing," and thus reflects the Son as Logos, the ground of intelligibility; "rhetoric . . . makes them capable of persuading and moving others," and thus reflects the Holy Spirit as goodness, under the aspect of usefulness.[31]

In his treatise *On Retracing the Arts to Theology*, Bonaventure deals more in detail with the division of rational philosophy into grammar, logic, and rhetoric; and he analyzes speech (*sermo*) from several points of view.[32] When dealing with speech from the standpoint of the speaker, he makes an explicit connection with the eternal Word and with the incarnate Word. He notes that all speech signifies a mental concept. The inner concept is the word of the mind and the mind's offspring that is known to the person who conceives it. This mental word is then expressed in a sensible form—a word that can be heard by a listener. We find the same type of expressiveness in the eternal Word, who is conceived by the Father and who then takes on flesh to be known in sensible form:

> Practically the same procedure is seen in the begetting of the Eternal Word, because the Father conceived him, begetting him from all eternity. . . . But that he might be known by man who is endowed with senses, he assumed the nature of flesh, and "the Word was made flesh and dwelt amongst us," and yet he remained "in the bosom of the Father."[33] (Jn. 1:14, 18)

This opens up a further dimension of Bonaventure's mysticism of language—a dimension of creative action. Like the divinity itself, humans are linguistic beings who have as a primary orientation the capacity to express themselves in language. This capacity is derived from the Trinity, mirrors the Trinity, and participates in the Trinitarian dynamism. The contemplative, the mystic, then, can bring to consciousness this ontological link between his or her linguistic activity and the eternal, creative, dynamic linguistic expressive life of the Trinity.

Can we rightly call this approach of Bonaventure a mysticism of language? Is it sufficiently experiential to qualify as mysticism? Is it not merely a philosophical and theological rational speculative system? First, it falls in the type of intellectual or *logos* mysticism and not affective mysticism of the type, for example, of Bernard of Clairvaux. Nor is it a mysticism of the boundless abyss or undifferentiated divinity, which Eckhart calls the desert of the Godhead. It rather contacts the determinate aspect of the divinity as Truth. Although it moves through finite form, it does not proceed by reasoning in rational categories but through the special intuition that Bonaventure called "contuition." It is true that Bonaventure presents this contuition as a contemplative path and not as an ecstatic experience. But there is solid reason to include such an intuitive contemplative consciousness within the sphere of mysticism. If we were to limit mystical experience to ecstasy, then much traditional material could not be included, such as the experience propounded by Eckhart, who did not place a high value on rapture or ecstasy. Besides, within Bonaventure's system, his mysticism of language could be experienced in ecstasy. It is true that his treatise *The Soul's Journey into God* presents six stages of contemplation that are then superseded by the seventh stage of ecstasy. The journey begins in sense knowledge, and proceeds to the soul, then to God, and finally to ecstasy. The third stage contains as an essential element the mysticism of language. From a psychological point of view, however, it is possible to see all seven stages as moments in a dynamic process that culminates in ecstasy. Thus one can move from any stage of the linguistic process to ecstasy, either in a prolonged contemplative process or in an instantaneous flash: from sense knowledge of spoken words, to the intellectual concepts behind the words, to the Truth expressed in these concepts, to an ecstatic experience of the divine ground of all language.

Significance of Mysticism of Language

What is the significance of Bonaventure's mysticism of language? It is first and foremost a major statement of a spiritual, mystical path in and through language, within an explicitly developed metaphysical system whose chief component is the Christian doctrine of the Trinity. Whatever its intrinsic merit, it does not stand alone. It is part of the mainstream Platonic and Neoplatonic tradition that flowed into Christianity. In the East it flowed through the apologists, the Alexandrian school of Clement and Origen, the Cappadocians, and the Pseudo-Dionysius. In the West it flowed through Augustine, Boethius, and the Pseudo-Dionysius, whose works had been translated into Latin. It continued through the eleventh and twelfth centuries in Anselm, Hugh, and Richard of St. Victor. In the thirteenth century, it entered the early Franciscan school of Alexander of Hales, whose pupil Bonaventure was a major formulator of Christian Neoplatonism in the high Middle Ages. Although superseded in the universities by the newly rediscovered Aristotelianism, it surfaced again in the Rhineland mystics and flowed in various strands through the subsequent centuries. Throughout its long history in Christianity, this Neoplatonism provided, more than any other system of thought, the ontological framework for Christian spirituality and mysticism. Its significance was by no means limited to Christianity, for it played a major role in the spirituality of the classical Greco-Roman world as well as Judaism and Islam. In its influence on the mysticism of Western culture, this tradition is without a rival.

Although pervasive in the history of Western spirituality, this tradition is not monolithic but has taken many forms with diverse emphasis. Bonaventure's version, for example, is much more explicitly Christian than that of the Pseudo-Dionysius, since it makes central to its structure the doctrines of the Trinity and the Incarnation, and even assimilates into its system devotion to the humanity of Christ, which had been recently evoked by Francis of Assisi. On the other hand, Bonaventure's system as a whole and his mysticism of language are based on classical metaphysical principles of Platonism and Neoplatonism, such as the doctrine of ideas, the emanation of *Nous* or Intelligence from the One, the ontological grounding of the ideas in the Intelligence, and the participation of the phenomenal world in these ideas through exemplarism.

Within the history of spirituality, Neoplatonism has been the source of elements that have become classic—for example, the three stages of the spiritual life: purgation, illumination, and union, as well as the two ways of the spiritual journey: the *via affirmativa*, or kataphatic way, by ascending the ladder of creatures, and the *via negativa*, or apophatic way, by systematically negating creatures. In the spirit of Francis of Assisi's love of creatures, Bonaventure developed the *via affirmativa*. In fact, his system is one of the most thoroughgoing examples of the *via affirmativa* in the history of Christian mysticism. It is this that accounts for his developing a mysticism of language. He does not eliminate the *via negativa*, however, for he places it at the pinnacle of his ascent, as the seventh stage of *The Soul's Journey into God*, where he guides the reader to leave behind all sense impressions and intellectual activity, passing over ecstatically into the fire of divine love. Although he becomes apophatic at the summit of the journey, he is kataphatic at each stage along the way, using the gaze of intellectual vision to penetrate by contuition to the divine Logos as the ground of all intelligible forms in the phenomenal world. Thus Bonaventure's mysticism of language has an important place in the typological study of mysticism. For in the present spiritual and academic climate, which has favored the apophatic way and looked on *logos* as an obstacle to mystical experience, he can underscore the validity of the *via affirmativa* and the legitimacy of a mysticism that proceeds through *logos* to the Logos ground. This last point is of paramount importance at the present time, when the great religious traditions are converging and the academic community is attempting to take into account the entire spectrum of religious experience. There is reason to believe that Logos mysticism is the distinctive form of the mysticism of Western culture, which will come to light only in an encounter with the mystical traditions of the East. In this context, Bonaventure's mysticism of language can bring this major type of mysticism to the fore for the enrichment of both contemporary spirituality and the academic study of mysticism.

Bonaventure's mysticism of language raises specific questions related to the academic study of mysticism. What is the role of language in mysticism? Is it merely an inadequate means for a mystic to express an ineffable experience? Is it an external force like other dimensions of culture shaping the mystical experience but not entering into the experience itself? Bonaventure's Neoplatonic mysticism offers the ontological possibility for a much closer link between language and mystical experience—at least those mystical experiences of the Logos type. For words, forms, concepts, and symbols have emanated from the Logos and bear the imprint of the Logos and hence can draw the mystic back with a magnetic pull into the Exemplar from which they flowed. This ontology-epistemology can account for the widespread use of words, chants, and symbols in evoking mystical experience, and it can be extended into the interpretation of cultural factors in the study of mysticism. At the present time, the academic community faces a major task in the study of religion: to assimilate the new disciplines that have developed in the West, especially psychology, sociology, and anthropology. In so doing, contemporary scholars must be cautious not to distort the data they are studying by filtering it through their own philosophical presuppositions.

For example, if a scholar were to study the relation of language to mystical experience with Neo-Kantian presuppositions, he or she would not be able to grasp the essence of Bonaventure's Neoplatonic mysticism of language. For there would be no place within a contemporary scholar's system for seeing a mysticism based on the Logos as the objective ground of truth or of the forms of language participating in the divine Logos itself. Instead, the forms of language would be seen as subjective categories shaping and expressing mystical experience but not entering into its content. The same could be the case in social and cultural patterns and forces. One could view these social and cultural patterns not merely as the product of finite collective subjectivity, but, according to Bonaventure's exemplarism, as forms ontologically grounded in the Logos. Hence one could see how a religious tradition as a social and cultural force could evoke and shape a mystical experience of Logos.

This raises a much deeper issue. The academic study of mysticism calls for the most radical self-criticism on the part of the scholar. Mystical forms of consciousness are the most profound and complex in human history and are deeply embedded in diverse ontological structures as these have been perceived by the mystic and his tradition. Hence effort must be made to take these ontologies into one's studies. This is all the more the case since the academic community is facing the overwhelming task of encompassing the whole of the human religious phenomena—in treating the varieties of mystical experience in the world's religious traditions. The connection between a particular ontology and mystical experience may be much closer than contemporary scholarship is inclined to acknowledge, since mystical experience may often involve simultaneously a revelation of Being. This means that ontological patterns may be not merely abstract interpretations of mystical experience, but structures of reality revealed in the experience. Hence it may be impossible to study mystical experience apart from the ontology in which it is encompassed. This, I would claim, is the case with Bonaventure's mysticism of language.

Notes

1. See George E. Mylonas, *Eleusis and the Eleusinian Mysteries* (Princeton, N.J., 1961); Walter Burkert, *Homo Necans: The Anthropology of Ancient Greek Sacrificial Ritual and Myth*, ed. and trans. Peter Bing (Berkeley, 1983); Burkert, *Greek Religion: Archaic and Classical*, trans. John Ruffan (Cambridge, Mass., 1985), pp. 285-90.

2. *Oxford English Dictionary* (1970), s.v. "mystic" and "mystical."

3. *OED*, s.v. "mysticism."

4. Bonaventure, *Collationes in Hexaemeron*, I, 16; translations of Bonaventure are from the Latin critical text, *Doctoris Seraphi S. Bonaventurae opera omnia* (Quaracchi, 1882-1902), and unless otherwise indicated are my own.

5. Bonaventure, *I Sent.*, d. 2, a. un., q. 2.

6. Bonaventure, *I Sent.*, d. 27, p. 1, a. un., q. 2, ad 3.

7. Bonaventure, *Itinerarium mentis in Deum*, IV, 2; translations of this work are from Ewert H. Cousins, *Bonaventure: The Soul's Journey into God, The Tree of Life, The Life of St. Francis* (New York, 1978).

8. Bonaventure, *Collationes in Hexaemeron*, I, 13.

9. Bonaventure, *Breviloquium*, p. I, c. 8, n. 7.

10. Bonaventure, *Collationes in Hexaemeron*, XII, 9.

11. See Bonaventure, *I Sent.*, d. 3, a. un., q. 2, ad 4; *Itinerarium*, I-IV; and *Collationes in Hexaemeron*, XII.

12. Psalms 91:5.

13. Job 23:11; Song of Songs 5:17.

14. Song of Songs 5:16.

15. Bonaventure, *Legenda maior S. Francisci*, IX, 1; translation is from

Cousins, *Bonaventure*. Although the text does not appear in this fashion in the Latin manuscript tradition, I have set my translation in sense lines in order to highlight the rhetorical structure and the contemplative nature of the passage.

16. Francis composed *Il Cantico di Frate Sole* in medieval Umbrian Italian. For the critical text, see *Opuscula Sancti Patris Francisci Assisiensis*, ed. Caietanus Esser, Bibliotheca Franciscana Ascetica Medii Aevi, vol. 12 (Grottaferrata, 1978).

17. Francis of Assisi, *Il Cantico di Frate Sole*, 11.5-9; translations of this work are my own.

18. Francis, *Cantico*, 11.32-33.

19. Bonaventure, *Itinerarium*, VI, 7; *Collationes in Hexaemeron*, XII.

20. Bonaventure, *Quaestiones disputatae de mysterio Trinitatis*, q. 1, a. 2, concl.; translations of this work are from Zachary Hayes, *Disputed Questions on the Mystery of the Trinity* (St. Bonaventure, N.Y., 1979).

21. Bonaventure, *Collationes in Hexaemeron*, II, 20.

22. Bonaventure, *De Mysterio Trinitatis*, q. 1, a. 2, concl.

23. Bonaventure, *Itinerarium*, IV, 2.

24. Bonaventure, *Itinerarium*, III, 3.

25. On Bonaventure's epistemology, see *Itinerarium*, II-III; *Quaestiones disputatae de scientia Christi*, q. 4; *De mysterio Trinitatis*, q. 1; *Sermo: Christus unus omnium magister*.

26. Bonaventure, *Itinerarium*, III, 3.

27. Bonaventure, *Itinerarium*, III, 3.

28. See Bonaventure, *Quaestiones disputatae de scientia Christi*, q. 4, concl.

29. Bonaventure, *II Sent.*, d. 39, a. 1, q. 2, concl.

30. Bonaventure, *Itinerarium*, III, 5.

31. Bonaventure, *Itinerarium*, III, 6.

32. Bonaventure, *De reductione artium ad theologiam*, 4, 16-18; translation is by Sister Emma Healy, in *Saint Bonaventure's De Reductione Artium Ad Theologiam* (St. Bonaventure, N.Y., 1955).

33. Bonaventure, *De reductione artium ad theologiam*, 4, 16.

Contributors

WILLIAM P. ALSTON. Among William Alston's other works are *Philosophy of Language* (1964), *Epistemic Justification: Essays in the Theory of Knowledge* (1989), and *Divine Nature and Human Language: Essays in Philosophical Theology* (1989). In addition, he has published some seventy articles in philosophy of religion, epistemology, philosophy of language, philosophical psychology, and other areas of philosophy. He is the editor of *Faith and Philosophy: Journal of the Society of Christian Philosophers* and editor of the Cornell Studies in the Philosophy of Religion. He is a past president of the American Philosophical Association (Western Division), the Society for Philosophy and Psychology, and the Society of Christian Philosophers. Among other fellowships he has been a fellow of the Center for Advanced Studies in the Behavioral Sciences at Stanford University, and has held a fellowship from the National Endowment for the Humanities. He has been a member of the faculties of the University of Michigan, the University of California at Los Angeles and at Santa Barbara, Harvard University, Rutgers University, and the University of Illinois at Urbana-Champaign, and is currently professor of philosophy at Syracuse University.

EWERT H. COUSINS. A specialist in early Franciscan mysticism and theology, Ewert Cousins has written *Bonaventure and the Coincidence of Opposites* (1978). He is chief editorial consultant for the sixty-volume series The Classics of Western Spirituality and the translator and editor of the Bonaventure volume in the series *Bonaventure: The Soul's Journey into God, The Tree of Life, The Life of St. Francis* (1978). Involved in the dialogue of world religions, he is a consultant to the Vatican Secretariat for Non-Christians. In contemporary religious thought, he has specialized in Teilhard de Chardin and process theology, editing *Process The-*

ology and *Hope and the Future of Man*. He is the director of the Graduate Program in Spirituality at Fordham University and a visiting professor at Columbia University.

CARL W. ERNST. Among Carl Ernst's publications are *Words of Ecstasy in Sufism* (1984), *Eternal Garden: Mysticism, History, and Politics at a South Asian Sufi Center* (1992), and articles appearing in *History of Religions*, *Islamic Culture*, and the *Encyclopedia of Religion*. He is also the co-editor, with Grace Martin Smith, of *Manifestations of Sainthood in Islam* (forthcoming). He was a Fulbright Islamic Civilization Research Fellow in Pakistan in 1986. Since 1981, he has taught at Pomona College, where he is associate professor and chair of the Department of Religion. Beginning in the fall of 1992, he will be professor of religion at the University of North Carolina.

BERNARD FAURE. Bernard Faure's other publications include *Le Traité de Bodhidharma* (1986), *La Vision immédiate* (1987), *La Volonté d'orthodoxie dans le bouddhisme chinois* (1988), and *Le Bouddhisme Chan en mal d'histoire* (1989). He has also published articles and reviews in journals such as *History of Religions*, *Monumenta Nipponica*, and *Cahiers d'Extrême-Asie*. He taught Asian religions at Cornell University from 1983 to 1987, was a visiting professor at the University of Kyoto in 1988, and is now associate professor in the Department of Religious Studies at Stanford University.

MOSHE IDEL. Moshe Idel is the author of numerous publications on Jewish mysticism, among which the most important are *Kabbalah: New Perspectives* (1988), *The Mystical Experience in Abraham Abulafia* (1988), and *Language, Torah and Hermeneutics in Abraham Abulafia* (1989). He has also edited, with Bernard McGinn, *Mystical Union and Monotheistic Faith, An Ecumenical Dialogue* (1989). He has published several dozen articles in Hebrew, French, and English. He is professor of Jewish mysticism at the Hebrew University, Jerusalem, and has been a visiting professor at Harvard University and the Jewish Theological Seminary of America.

Contributors

STEVEN T. KATZ (editor). In addition to editing this volume, Steven Katz has edited *Mysticism and Philosophical Analysis* (1978) and *Mysticism and Religious Traditions* (1983), and has written *Post-Holocaust Dialogues: Studies in Modern Jewish Thought* (1983), *Historicism, the Holocaust and Zionism* (1992), and the multivolume *Holocaust in Historical Context*, Volume 1 of which will appear in 1992. He is a member of the editorial team of the *Cambridge History of Judaism* and the *History of Nineteenth Century Religious Thought*, and is the editor of the journal *Modern Judaism*. At present, he is professor of Near Eastern studies at Cornell University.

BIMAL KRISHNA MATILAL. Bimal Matilal wrote or edited more than twenty books, including *Moral Dilemmas in the Mahabarata* (1989), *Confrontation of Cultures* (1988), the *Navya-Nya Doctrine of Negation* (1968), *Logic, Language and Reality* (1985), and *Perception* (1986). He edited the *Journal of Indian Philosophy*. Until his death in 1991, he was the Spaulding Professor of Comparative Religion at Oxford University and a fellow of All Souls' College, Oxford.

BERNARD J. MCGINN. Among Bernard McGinn's many published works are *Visions of the End* (1979) and *The Calabrian Abbot: Joachim of Fiore in the History of Western Thought* (1985). He is also the translator of two volumes of Eckhart's work that have appeared in the Classics of Western Spirituality Series, the co-editor of the volumes on Christian spirituality in the *Encyclopedia of World Spirituality*, and the co-editor, with Moshe Idel, of *Mystical Union and Monotheistic Faith, An Ecumenical Dialogue* (1989). In 1978 and 1979 he was the Andrew V. Tackes Visiting Professor at Notre Dame and is now professor of historical theology at the University of Chicago.

STEPHEN H. PHILLIPS. Stephen Phillips is associate professor of philosophy at the University of Texas at Austin. A sanskritist as well as a philosopher, he has published several articles on classical Indian views, and others principally in the philosophy of religion. He is the author of *Aurobindo's Philosophy of Brahman* (1986), in which he scrutinizes the metaphysics of the modern Indian philosophic mystic Aurobindo Ghose, and the co-editor, with Robert Kane, of *Hartshorne, Process Philosophy and Theology* (1989).

NINIAN SMART. Ninian Smart is the author of numerous publications, among which the most important are *Reasons and Faiths* (1958), *Philosophers and Religious Truth* (1964), *Doctrine and Argument in Indian Philosophy* (1964), *The Religious Experience of Mankind* (1976), *The Concept of Worship* (1972), and *The Phenomenon of Religion* (1973). He has also published several dozen articles and reviews in such leading philosophical and religious journals as *Mind, Philosophical Quarterly, Religion, Religious Studies*, and *Philosophy*. In 1979 and 1980, he gave the Gifford Lectures. He was professor of theology at the University of Birmingham from 1961 to 1967 and then became the first professor and chairman of the Department of Religious Studies at the University of Lancaster, England, a post he held from 1967 to 1975. He has also been a visiting professor at Yale University, Harvard University, Princeton University, the University of Wisconsin, and Benares Hindu University. At present, he is the J. F. Rowney Professor of Comparative Religions at the University of California at Santa Barbara.